To Gloria & Gordon Co

Paul H. Poberezny

EAA-I

4-12-99

AS TOLD TO CHUCK PARNALL AND BONNIE POBEREZNY

POBEREZNY
The Story Begins....

As told to
Bonnie Poberezny
and
Chuck Parnall

Illustrations by Bill Blake

Red One Publishing, LLC Oshkosh, Wisconsin

POBEREZNY
The Story Begins....

Published by: Red One Publishing, LLC
P. O. Box 3031
Oshkosh, WI 54903-3031

Library of Congress : 96-92890

ISBN: 0-9655654-0-8 (Standard Edition)
0-9655654-1-6 (Limited Edition)

Printed in the United States of America
Times Printing Company, Random Lake, Wisconsin

To our granddaughters, Lesley and Audra...

May you have the courage and dedication to pursue your dreams;

The teachers with the vision to help you find your way;

And love for your fellow man.

"Gonk"

ACKNOWLEDGEMENTS

It is impossible to complete a project of this magnitude without help and support. We are sincerely grateful to the following individuals for their talent, advice and generosity:

It is said that a picture is worth a thousand words. **Bill Blake's** tremendous artistic abilities and friendship brought humor and life to those situations where photos did not exist.

Special thanks go to **Jeff Ethell** for his willingness to share his knowledge and expertise.

Marnee Lott shared the tedious job of proofreading this manuscript. We are grateful for her many long hours; and for providing another perspective.

We sincerely appreciate the efforts and cooperation of **Ken Sweet** and the **Wisconsin Air National Guard,** for allowing us the opportunity to reproduce photos and material from the book, *Wisconsin's Finest—A History of the Wisconsin Air National Guard.*

This is EAA, written by **Duane Cole** in 1972, provided the first printed history of EAA's early years. This long-time friend granted us permission to use short excerpts from his book in order to enhance our own.

Whether we required a fact or a photograph, various forms of help were forthcoming and enthusiastic. We express our special thanks to **Leo Kohn** for sharing his extensive photo files; **Susan Lurvey** of the EAA Aviation Foundation Boeing Aeronautical Library for her research assistance; and the EAA Photo Staff of **Jim Koepnick, Bonnie Bartel** and **Ken Lichtenberg** for their never-ending patience and help.

For the past forty-four years, the friendship of **Ray & Bernice Scholler** has been unwavering. Once again, throughout this effort, they were a constant source of support, guidance, and love.

Contents

FOREWORD

Our beloved Republic will never be out of debt to Paul Poberezny.

With his similarly dedicated wife, Audrey — and now unto a next generation — the Pobereznys have militantly manned the ramparts against those who would fence off the sky.

Even more significantly, Paul's diligent example of self-discipline and creative enterprise makes it feel good to be an American.

Let's all sit at the feet of this man for 350 pages and grow!

Paul Harvey
PAUL HARVEY NEWS

PREFACE

Being given the opportunity to co-author this book is a privilege and an honor. It also allowed me to get to know Paul and Audrey as do few others, compounding my already considerable appreciation of their accomplishments. Having some experience at starting and running an aviation organization myself, I marvel at the tenacity and ability these two special people have displayed for so many years. Most of us will never comprehend how they were able to sustain such a drive, for it was continuous, and we can only hope to capture a brief insight.

While doing my research, a previously unnoticed personality trait of theirs surfaced—the tendency to understate. Getting either of them to recall their past in detail was not always easy. As with many from their generation, they are modest about what were, in comparison, significant personal achievements. They came from families with little material wealth. After growing up through a depression, they quietly accepted their roles during the war years. While they didn't start out to build an international organization, neither did they back away when it headed in that direction and began to consume their lives. In reality, they are ordinary people with extraordinary abilities. They are ideally suited to each other and their chosen life's work.

DOCUMENTATION

Paul is the consummate collector: he has bits and pieces representing most significant events in his and Audrey's lives. Documents, clippings, photographs, actual parts from airplanes; it's all there, and it provided us with the ability to overrule the sometimes fallible human memory. We are confident that the information presented is as accurate as possible, considering it was compiled some forty to ninety years after the fact.

FORMAT

Because so much content came from the spoken word, it was difficult to make the book read like a polished novel. Actually, that wasn't our goal. Instead, we want you to "hear" Paul and Audrey "talk" about events as they recall them today, and to *see* their words in print as they were written many yesterdays ago. That is why everything that Paul said or wrote will be in **"bold type,"** and for Audrey, ***"bold italics."***

Why did we choose this particular format? The answer is: they like it. And so do we. It is special for you too, because rather than just owning their story, you now have a book that reflects their personality—unique. Just as they are!

Chuck Parnall

Before The Story Begins....

"When are you going to write a book?"

This question has been posed to Paul Poberezny many times over the years. As his daughter, I had a tremendous desire to pursue the project. I knew he had many wonderful stories to share, stories that few others had heard. Whether or not it ever became a published book, I hoped to record the history, if only for posterity. At the very least we would have a lasting legacy to share with my daughter, Audra, my brother's daughter, Lesley...and their children after them.

It was not until Chuck Parnall offered to help that I truly thought "The Book" would become a reality. A gifted writer, Chuck voluntarily provided the necessary time and talent to see the project through completion.

As we progressed, two things became increasingly clear. First, it simply was not possible to tell the "whole" story in one book, thus the need for us to end this first volume in 1958. Second, and most important, it is not a story about one person; it is about Paul Howard Poberezny *and* Audrey Louise Ruesch—two people who became one tremendous strength, and by doing so, accomplished great things together.

As you read this book, Paul will continually come to the forefront. This is not necessarily because he is the stronger of the two; it is because Audrey has never chosen to be in the forefront. She has always been Paul's strength, motivator, shoulder, advisor…and partner. With her tremendous wisdom and leadership abilities, she could have chosen her own field and risen to the top. She instead chose to foster and promote the dreams of others so that their stars could shine even brighter. To Dad, Tom, myself, and our children, she has always been our greatest cheerleader, trusted friend, and fairest judge. Like her mother before her, the only reward she wants—or will accept—is the success and happiness of those she loves.

You will come away from this book with a better understanding of Paul Howard Poberezny. You may, however, feel you still do not know enough about Audrey. That is her choice. She has been, and always will be, a very private person.

Is this book a love story? Yes...but not in the traditional sense. Just a short time ago there were some friends visiting our family here in Oshkosh. On the way to dinner, we made the usual stop at Dad's personal hangar. There, we viewed the PT-23 and Fokker Triplane restorations, a "mystery" project yet to be identified, and his "flyers"—the Bonanza, Piper Pacer, and two homebuilts, the Junior Ace and the Cuby.

All our guests had left the building. As I walked out the door, Dad was the only one remaining in the hangar. I instinctively turned to see where he was and saw him reach to turn out the lights. He didn't know anyone was listening as he looked back into the hangar and said out loud…"Good night planes…I love you all!"

And now, the story begins....

Bonnie L. Poberezny

Chapter One

The Making of a Pilot

"Are you ready, Howie?" The nervous, high pitched voice came from inside a small, beige Whippet coupe, its rough-idling motor gently rocking the little car. Tied to its rear bumper was four hundred feet of well-used manila rope. The other end was secured to a crude adaptation of red metal tubing and silver fabric known as a Waco Primary Glider. It was the spring of 1937 and the scene was a little-used hayfield in the small town of Greenfield, Wisconsin, eight miles southwest from the outskirts of Milwaukee.

Perched precariously on a wooden seat located below and just forward of the thirty-six foot, linen-covered wing was a lanky boy of fifteen. His few years belied an already impressive knowledge of aerodynamics and winged structures gained through considerable exposure to model airplane building and flying. The young lad had nurtured a keen interest in aviation ever since he was five years old.

But today would be different. Today was not only a day for the spoken word, it was a day for action. Today, fifteen-year-old Paul Howard

Poberezny was about to take to the air for the very first time! His success depended on a unique combination of raw talent, dogged determination, and natural instinct. There was no instructor and no instruction—just a strong and unwavering belief in his ability…and an unquenchable desire to fly!

"Where does a dream begin? For me it was at the age of five, and my dream was the airplane. Those days, as has each one since, have been memorable to me. Every day of my life I have spoken the word: AIRPLANE."

Paul Howard Poberezny

Too few of us ever reach our goals. Those who do, possess a rare combination of drive and ability. While it is true that fate or circumstance often plays a significant role in creating a milestone, the opposite can occur just as easily. In most cases, the key to success belongs to the individual.

A glance at the inventory of Paul Poberezny's meager beginnings would cause one to quickly discount him from any future starring role in aviation. The son of a poor Russian immigrant worker and a southern lady from Arkansas, he was surrounded by family—and an environment—to which aviation meant little. If the name *Poberezny* was ever to rise to prominence in this field, it would be due to the fires of desire being fanned from within.

A few miles from the hayfield, a diminutive twelve-year-old girl busied herself playing hide-and-seek with several neighborhood friends. Her father appeared on the porch of the tidy, white frame house at 3801 South 56th Street, spotted his daughter and summoned her to lunch with a single, brief command: "Audrey!" The little girl quickly ran home.

Time and circumstance would bring these two people together. The rest they would do themselves.

"I was thrilled by the sight and sound of these flying machines as they chugged by, and I always stopped to count their wings…."

Paul Howard Poberezny

Chapter Two

From The Beginning

Paul's father, Peter Poberezny, was born in 1897 to a working-class family in the Ukraine, the second of three brothers. Shortly after the turn of the century, the older brother immigrated to Canada. In 1908, Peter and his younger brother followed; Peter was barely eleven years old. While his brothers were content to live the rest of their lives in Canada, Peter developed other aspirations. He became a wanderer, a jack of all trades searching for his station in life. Considering he was not yet a teenager when he began his life's journey, his adventures illustrate the differences between his society and ours. Paul continues....

"My dad was an immigrant from the Ukraine, a part of southern Russia. Little is known about his parents or any family history from that period, although I remember hearing my grandfather lost his life as a result of an accident in a quarry, leaving my grandmother with three young sons to raise.

"The oldest, John, left the Ukraine and settled in Windsor, Ontario, Canada. My dad was the middle son, the youngest was Joe; they both soon followed John to Canada. Little is known of the fate of my grandmother who chose to remain in the Ukraine. My dad later heard that many lives were lost during the war and few of the family had survived. It was most fortunate the three sons left when they did!

"At that time, young people in European societies were more involved in the work force. They didn't have the schools and the many diversions we have today. Their work ethic came from having to work hard together in order to survive and make a living. Children shared the workload with their parents on family farms and businesses, or in factories as laborers. I believe this work ethic came to the United States with those who immigrated from Europe before the early nineteen hundreds.

"Our grandmas and grandpas worked very hard to make a better life for their kids, as did our parents. Today we have provided such a wonderful life that there is really no challenge left to the children, other than entertainment. Ask any young person what is important and he or she will probably say, 'I can't wait until I'm sixteen so I can get my driver's license—and my car!'

"But who's going to pay for the car, and how are the kids going to operate it if they don't have any income? Even working at McDonald's or Hardee's isn't going to bring in enough money to pay for all the entertainment they seek. Besides, it is difficult to hire young people to perform such simple things as cutting grass. They either don't want to work or they have no idea how to perform the many tasks we consider to be so simple and so basic.

"This lack of knowledge and discipline means that our parents' respect for quality and craftsmanship may no longer be passed on, and their work ethic could soon disappear. With little training and guidance received during youth, the pride of developing the skills needed to become self sufficient will no longer be important. Certainly, the future will be much different from what we have enjoyed."

Peter Poberezny spent the first two years in his new country working on a farm. For his labor, he earned a grand total of twenty-three dollars! During his third winter in Canada, he went to work for the Hudson Bay Construction Company driving dog teams across the frozen northlands. The next winter he drove again, this time over an eight hundred mile route, covering an average of forty miles per day. In between, he worked freight lines between Manitoba and British Columbia, including one trip on the Great Northern Transport between Vancouver and Portland, Oregon.

In the spring of 1912, four years after arriving in Canada, the nomadic fifteen-year-old crossed into the United States and began to drift west, eventually reaching San Francisco. From there he traveled northeast to Billings, Montana, spending a month or so with a railroad section gang.

Continuing his eastward journey, he worked the fall harvest in Larimore, North Dakota, earning the princely sum of sixty-four dollars—more than twice the income gained after two years on the Canadian farm! Sadly, he was relieved of his fortune a few days later in Grand Forks, North Dakota, where he was robbed.

Peter worked in St. Paul, Minnesota, for a short time, then moved on to Savana, Illinois, where he signed with the Burlington railroad section. After that, it was off to Chicago and then south to Quincy, Illinois, where he found work as a moulder for the Excelsior Stone Foundry. While in Quincy, he played for a local baseball team, and that fall enjoyed a successful try-out with the semi-pro Missouri League. This meant moves to Hannibal, Missouri, and, after a few months, Houston, Texas. Quickly tiring of life in the dugout, Peter returned to Hannibal where, on July 5, 1916, he enlisted in the United States Army; he was eighteen years old.

Peter at the Excelsior Stone Foundry

Machine Gun Troop - 7th Cavalry

Not caring that civilian life had already provided plenty of travel opportunities, the US Army added more of its own, this time with a southern twist. Peter was assigned to the machine gun troops of the Seventh Cavalry in Casas Grandes, Mexico, under General Pershing. In February 1917, he was transferred to Columbus, New Mexico, and from there to El Paso, Texas, for a six-month stint with the border patrol. After the United States entered World War I in 1918, Peter was the first person to join the newly reorganized 305th Cavalry. He was appointed regimental saddler and put in charge of the equipment school. Five months later he

was transferred again, although this time not to his liking. A series of moves resulted, mostly at Peter's request, before he secured a favorable position in March 1919 as a Marshall at the Fort Leavenworth prison in Kansas. He later transferred to the nearby prison farm colony where they raised food for the inmates. A year later he became its manager.

The following passage is taken from the *History of Leavenworth County*, published in 1921 by the Historical Publishing Company of Topeka, Kansas:

> *"Mr. Poberezny is a member of the Railway Brotherhood. He is a good dairyman and manages the farm well; he is also very industrious. He made a good record as a soldier and has many friends throughout the country."*

The threads of Peter's early life of travel and adventure would someday weave a similar fate for his male offspring—both of them! But in the meantime....

Peter's thoughts turned to finding a wife. There had been many opportunities to socialize with the opposite sex, but they generally favored short term relationships. It was up to the print media to provide the desired, long-term solution, as Paul explains....

Young Jetta with her mother, Sarah Jane Patterson

"My dad and mom met by correspondence established through a publication listing pictures and addresses of ladies with whom lonely soldiers could correspond. A serviceman always looked forward to letters from friends and home, and Dad was no exception!

"My mother, Jetta Dowdy, was born in Statesville, North Carolina, on July 31, 1898. She was the fourth of thirteen children, including three sets of twins. Her dad, John C. Dowdy, was a contractor and architect involved in the designing of schools and other public buildings. Her mother, my grandmother, was Sarah Jane Patterson. Mother attended grade school in Statesville until the family moved to Jonesboro, Arkansas. There she completed grade school and high school, and later would meet my dad.

She always claimed it was her sister, Hortense, who sent her picture to the magazine. Anyway, it was through this writing relationship that a marriage was eventually struck."

On July 6, 1920, the "mail order" marriage between Peter Poberezny and Jetta (Jettie) Dowdy of Jonesboro, Arkansas, took place. It would last until death separated them more than half a century later.

Jettie Dowdy

On September 14, 1921, fourteen months after they married, the young couple was blessed with the first of their three children, a son they named Paul Howard Poberezny. Although we know him today as "Paul," during his youth he was called "Howard."

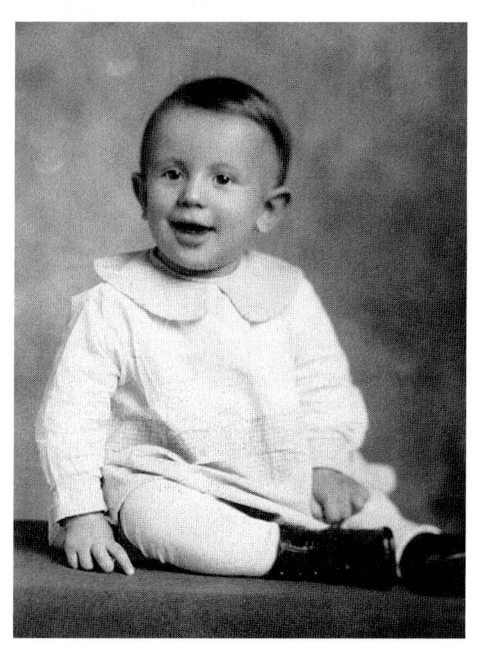

Paul "Howard" Poberezny

Apparently Peter's nomadic appetite was not yet satisfied because he decided to leave the prison farm in Kansas. But until he could find work, Jettie and her newborn son did what so many others have done over the years—they moved in with her parents....

"Dad finally found work in Milwaukee with the Bucyrus Erie Company that made cranes and other heavy equipment. My mother arrived soon after Dad found an apartment on the south side of Milwaukee in the Ukrainian and Polish area...a natural combination since both languages are very similar. Being a southern lady, Mom was bewildered to be placed in an environment where people dressed and talked so differently. Although she never did learn the language, she certainly became accustomed to hearing broken English from my dad! Later in my life when I was among my father and his friends, I would often slip into the same broken English they were speaking. I don't know why I did it; I suppose

to make me feel more like those I was talking with. I still catch myself doing it to this day."

When this job ended, the family briefly chased employment to Winnipeg, Manitoba, Canada; but soon returned to Milwaukee. Initially forced to perform odd jobs, Peter finally found steady work as a laborer with the construction company, Wenzel and Hennoch, building sewers and water mains for the growing city.

The first Poberezny home was quite small, consisting only of a kitchen, a bedroom, and a small living room that also served as Paul's bedroom. A coal stove was used for cooking and provided their only source of heat; water was hand-pumped from a well in the backyard. The family bathroom was an outhouse perched at the rear of the lot....

"My earliest recollection of living in Milwaukee was in what one would call a tarpaper shack. It was one of several built and owned by Mr. Steinmetz and was located on the corner of 95th and Oklahoma in the town of Greenfield. Although quite a ways out in the country, it was still considered to be a southwest suburb of Milwaukee. Today, Oklahoma Avenue is a main road; but back then it was gravel, and the road in front of our house was dirt!

"We were situated between two cemeteries: St. Mathias bordering our back yard and the Jewish Cemetery across the street. Because of this, my dad coined a name that stayed with our street for many years—'Ghost Alley.' "

The daily struggle to survive continued in Ghost Alley. On July 21, 1923, Paul's sister, Martha, was born. Five years later a second son, Norman, completed the family tree.

Paul's first "best friend"....

"Ghost Alley is where I found my first long-lasting friendship with another lad about a year or so older, Eddie Holpher. I had walked up the gravel road to Eddie's more modern home and saw him riding around in circles on the lone piece of concrete in our area. I thought Eddie was rich because he was riding on a very nice looking tricycle. I really envied him and remember his offer to let me ride his old one. We struck a friendship that remained strong until the beginning of World War II—a war that separated many from their friends and loved ones."

Eddie Holpher, Howard and Martha in front of the "tarpaper shack"

The Pobereznys eventually moved next door into a newly constructed and much larger house, also owned by Mr. Steinmetz. The new house contained something that would play a vital role in Paul's developing interest in aviation: a small, wooden garage with a dirt floor and a crudely fashioned chicken coop attached to the rear. The primitive structure eventually became Paul's first airplane workshop.

When Paul's sister was asked about her early life, she said, "We lived in a small home, but to us it was everything. Mom was an excellent cook and made bread, sweet rolls, and all the good things we liked to eat. So many children miss out on 'scratch' cooking today because work involves both parents. We had pets, usually dogs, and we raised chickens in the chicken house in the back yard where we also had a garden."

It sounded so picturesque until she added, "Of course there was the 'privy toilet.' We were not acquainted with Charmin—it was more like old newspapers and catalogs! And even at my young age, I always wondered why the house didn't burn down, as heat from the coal stove had scorched the wallpaper!"

One day, Paul added an unusual creature to their pet inventory....

"A little piglet fell off a passing truck; I chased him down and brought him home where we made a pen in the backyard in which to keep him. We named him 'Elmer' and he was soon the favorite neighborhood pet. Eventually Elmer got too big and a neighbor, Mr. Vikes, was asked to butcher him. We were saddened to lose our friend, but

the need to put food on the table was great…although Martha and I refused to eat any part of him!"

Paul's world was expanding....

"92nd Street, then known as Woodlawn Avenue, ended about a block south at an intersection of Beloit Road known as 'Whiskey Corners,' aptly named because there was a saloon on three of the four corners. One of them, the Eagle's Nest, also housed a grocery store to which I made many trips for Mom. There was a blacksmith's shop situated down the street, along with a few other small shops. Behind Kozmuth's Dance Hall was a small park that served as an attraction for the local residents and farmers who chose it as a place to have picnics or meetings. This area would provide a backdrop for many of my future escapades.

"Oklahoma Avenue wandered westward to National Avenue and 'Dead Man's Curve,' and then another mile or more to that ever wondrous airways beacon and the emergency landing field on Beloit Road. Beloit Road was one of those country roads that wound its way some fifty miles through southwestern Wisconsin to the little town of Beloit. Situated near the Illinois border, it was just north of Rockford, Illinois —another town that would later become very significant in my life!

"It was in this environment, crude by today's standards, that my interest in airplanes began to develop. Our local celebrity was a bachelor and auctioneer named Arthur F. (Patty) Ott. He could often be seen wearing his stove pipe hat and driving his carriage around with a wedding party in the back. Each year Mr. Ott plowed our family garden. It was my job to remove the clods of grass and help smooth out the ground before seeding. Often while doing this chore, I would hear the sound of an airplane approaching. I was thrilled by the sight and the sound of these flying machines as they chugged by, and I always stopped my work to count their wings. Of course in those days, most of the airplanes had two. I had no idea as to their actual size and thought the people who flew them were quite small, perhaps midgets—surely no bigger than a foot high!"

The reason Paul saw so many airplanes was that their house on 95th Street lay close to an airmail route linking the cities of Milwaukee, Madison, Lone Rock, La Crosse and Minneapolis. Compared to today's modern electronic airways, these routes were quite primitive. By day, the air mail pilots navigated with maps and dead reckoning; by night, they followed

light beacons mounted on towers located approximately ten miles apart. It was visual navigation at its peak. The success of each flight depended more on the ability of the pilot to acquire the next beacon or town than on the reliability of his crude instrumentation. In time the sounds coming from the airplanes following this pathway of light gradually changed to a deeper pitch, signaling the introduction of larger engines and airframes. But the biplanes were always up there, constantly feeding Paul's dreams of flight....

"The neighbors began to notice my interest in airplanes and would often say to my dad after he got home from work in the evening, 'That crazy kid, Howard, will someday fly one of those planes!' I was always called 'Howard' and didn't know my first name was Paul until I had to produce a birth certificate when I entered military service at the beginning of World War II."

Other aviation influences found their way into Paul's young life....

"Pulp magazines containing aviation stories about flying aces and their battles, Bill Barnes and his racer (and many others) were all popular reading in the twenties and thirties. Much real and imaginary was written about the heroes of the sky in World War I: getting the Hun in an aerial encounter, or landing behind German lines to rescue a downed flier—the hero always arriving at the airplane just in time. With one swing of the prop, the engine would cough, catch, and, under a hail of rifle fire, the Spad, Sopwith Camel or Nieuport would stagger into the sky with its grateful human cargo. As I sat on the front porch reading this material, my imagination put me into the cockpit with them, silently moving the controls and feeling the response–even though I had never touched, or even been close to, a real airplane."

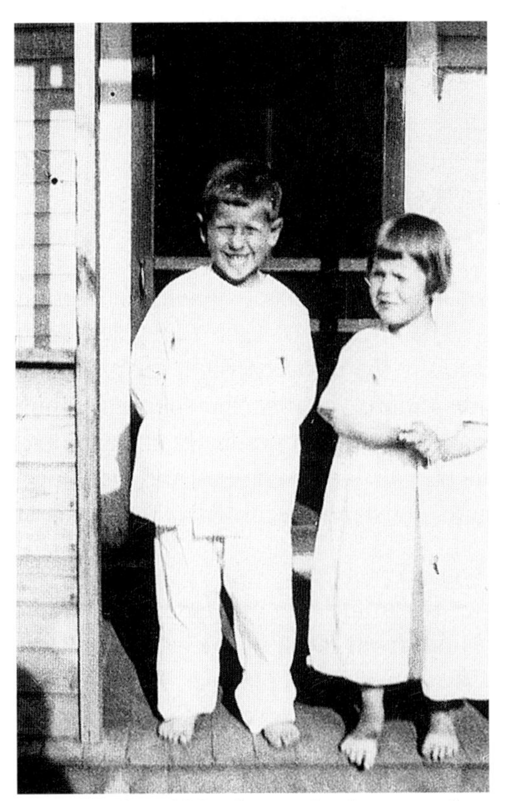

Howard and Martha on the front porch in Ghost Alley.

As the neighborhood grew, there came more families and more children. Warm summer evenings were usually spent on front porches, the adults chatting about the day's events while their offspring played nearby....

"The girls next door, Violet, Rose and June Monta, added to the games we often played, such as kick-the-can, Annie-Annie-over, hide-and-seek, and foot races. It wasn't long before the singing and musical talents of the girls was also heard. Their harmony and guitar playing was enjoyed throughout Ghost Alley by the many folks who appeared each night on the front porches in the waning hours of daylight."

Howard, Martha and Norman Poberezny

But for Paul, it was the sounds of the airplanes passing overhead that kept calling him as they tirelessly chased those silent beacons of light...

Paul and Audrey have the opportunity to meet Mrs. Charles Lindbergh during the EAA Commemorative Tour in 1977.

Chapter Three

Paul's First Hero

The 1920s were good for aviation. The disruption caused by the Great War had faded and most of the world had returned to an upbeat mode. During this period the airplane was becoming more visible, especially in the United States. Because of their isolation from the battlefields of WW I, Americans had not been exposed to the vast numbers of airplanes as had their European counterparts. As a result, whenever an airplane did appear, be it barnstorming from a nearby pasture or performing death defying feats at a scheduled event, it was a major attraction and large numbers of curiosity seekers flocked to see it in action. There was something special, something heroic, about those who dared to challenge the third dimension in their curious flying machines.

On the practical side, speed, altitude, distance and payload records were constantly being broken as airplanes, guided by human hands, pushed beyond all known boundaries. Many of these accomplishments were quickly surpassed. A few were long lasting: one was unforgettable!

Shortly before 8:00 A.M. (eastern) on Friday, May 20, 1927, a tall, handsome man climbed into a little silver monoplane named *Spirit of St. Louis* and took off into a hostile eastern sky. Thirty-three and a half hours later, Charles Augustus Lindbergh touched down on French soil and into the pages of history—the first solo pilot to cross the Atlantic Ocean from New York to Paris. The "Lone Eagle" immediately captured the imagination of the entire world and neither he, nor aviation, would ever be the same again.

The significance of his accomplishment was soon indelibly etched into history. It was a magical moment that guaranteed the future of a fledgling

industry. It meant that reaching destinations throughout the world could be reduced to a matter of days and hours, rather than weeks or months. The public was consumed with speculation and excitement, as was a small boy from "Ghost Alley" in Milwaukee, Wisconsin....

"I remember my mother running into the kitchen. She just heard the news from a neighbor who was listening to his crystal set, a radio of years gone by. I was standing on the shelf where Mom stored our few plates, looking for something...I don't remember what. She said, 'Lucky Lindy made it! He landed in Paris—what a thrill!' It was a thrill that has lasted my lifetime. His inspiration not only touched me, but so many other young men and women who also made their careers in aviation. It would last for many years, even until this day, for those who knew his remarkable story. We owe a great deal to the men and women who, in one way or another, were involved in the building and financing of the Spirit of St. Louis and its flight. In particular, we salute the courage and foresight of one man: Charles Lindbergh. Lindy literally took the country—and most of the world—by storm. It was a historic event, the likes of which there have been so few before or since. And he did it all on his own, without backup systems or legions of support people to help him. It all came down to one man...and against all odds, he won!"

"Later on, while flying the Atlantic many times as a military pilot, I would often look down on the vast ocean below and marvel at how, with crude instrumentation, an unreliable engine and no co-pilot, Lindy's feat was even possible. It gave me a much greater appreciation of his accomplishment; few pilots would ever experience such an achievement! And I never imagined that in 1977 I would have the opportunity to meet Mrs. Lindbergh when EAA commemorated her husband's flight around the United States. But that's another story!"

As a result of Lindbergh's flight, aviation became more attractive to young people. It was so different, so thrilling...and so dangerous! Even the pilots' uniform—leather helmet, goggles, boots and jodhpurs—identified them as being unique and added to their celebrity status. Aviators were heroes to the youth of the day. They dreamt of following in the footsteps of such famous pilots as Eddie Rickenbacker, Billy Bishop and now, Charles Lindbergh—real heroes who had earned their place alongside the imaginary ones in the pulp magazines. These were the dreams that would one day propel Paul Poberezny into his own special niche in aviation.

Chapter 4

School Days, School Days

Paul attended kindergarten at St. Mathias Catholic schoolhouse, an old, two-story wooden building located across from the church, just up the street from his house. The following year he transferred to public school....

"My first year in grade school was at Johnson School. Located about a mile away from our home, it was surrounded by country roads, woods, swamps and farms. We walked to school every day, come rain or snow or whatever the weather might be! It was unheard of to expect buses to pick us up at our doorsteps or to have our parents drive us in their cars. Every morning and afternoon before class, we all lined up on the gravel outside the schoolhouse door, turned, and said the pledge of allegiance to the flag. It was common practice then and gave us great inspiration—I only wish it had the same emphasis today!

"Sometimes we built forts in the woods along the side of the road and hung dead grass snakes in the doorways to scare the other kids away. However, it never worked, because when we returned our places were always torn down. We wished those kids would build their own forts so we could tear *them* down!

"The playground at our school had several swings, teeter-totters and a slide. Nearby was the Keifer farm, with its cows, pigs, chickens

and goats—goats that used to come to the playground and slide down our slide with us during recess!

"There was no school cafeteria, just a room where we ate the lunches our moms had made. They contained mostly bread, butter and jelly sandwiches, and we washed them down with milk from the little quarter-pint jars that came from the large wire cases brought to the school by the milkman.

"We had outside toilets, the same as what most of us experienced at home; of course, they were not heated either. The girls' toilet was on one side of the school, the boys' on the other. If you had to go while you were in class, you raised your hand indicating one finger or two, as in 'V' for Victory. For me it was embarrassing, because everybody knew where you were going—and why!

"There were two grades in each classroom, although the total number of students in each class was much smaller than it is today. I always enjoyed a front row seat because the teachers liked me—so much that I was often asked to stay after school and write *I will not talk* a hundred or more times on the blackboard!

"Many winters, the snow was piled above our heads along the side of the roads. We liked winter and enjoyed making slides, snowmen, and snow angels. When the snow really got deep, we made tunnels and snow forts. During one particularly bad storm, Dad didn't come home for five days; he had to plow snow for the county. Of course the equipment they used wasn't anything like that of today!

"I was never very involved in sports, although I did like to play baseball; I suppose that came from Dad! Unlike him, however, I usually ended up on the second team and out in right field...my mind was always on those airplanes and the little men that flew them."

"Those airplanes" were rapidly evolving from objects of curiosity into serious forms of transportation. New designs were constantly setting speed, endurance and distance records, often on a daily basis. Load carrying capacities were increasing, as was the reliability of their engines; no longer was castor oil spewing from open valves and spraying the pilots in open cockpits. The "flying circus" image was dying and in its place was a brand new era: an era of promise.

Children often dream about their destiny, yet because they are young, their dreams are subject to frequent change. Paul was an exception—his never changed. Before, after, and during school, his thoughts focused more and more on aviation. He dreamt of having his own airplane to free himself from the bonds of earth. But how does a lad of little or no means go about acquiring one? Paul tells us....

"I decided to convert part of our chicken coop into an airplane factory. I don't know if this was the beginning of my dream to build airplanes in the future, or if it was an influence created by reading the many magazines that showed men and women working in airplane factories and building real airplanes that flew. I was about eight years old when I built my first airplane factory. I also remember Dad's anger when he came home and saw what I had done to his chicken coop! It was a crude beginning of what would later in life be the many garages I would convert into airplane shops.

"In those pre-depression days, our family had little—even less later on! I remember scrounging in the dump down the street for some solid coaster wheels with the thin rubber tires. By taking the tire off the rim, I had a pulley that I could then mount with nails; by adding a clothesline, I had a conveyor belt for my crude assembly line.

"From Mr. Kocs' new IGA store, I took the broken orange crates that supplied material to build my crude airplanes. Using a hatchet, I carved the 1/2- or 3/4-inch end boards into the general shape of a fuselage. The side panels were usually 1/4-inch wood, and I cut them into the shapes of wings and tail groups. Nails pounded into the fuselage at the appropriate places became the landing gear. I attached the pieces with wire to the conveyor belt, which was eight or ten feet long, and slowly moved them to the other side of the chicken coop. Over on the little bench, I nailed them together as I listened to the clucking of the chickens laying their eggs. The completed airplanes were then taken to the family garden where I had carved out a little airport in the dirt. I would often be seen running around the yard, or up and down the gravel road in front of the house, holding my airplane and making buzzing sounds as if it had an engine."

But orange-crate airplanes can't fly! Every time Paul heard a real airplane approach, he'd climb to the top of the garage, trying to get closer to that magical machine in the sky. If he wasn't near his garage, he'd scale the

nearest vantage point, which most often was a tree. Like most kids, he became so engrossed in getting to the top that he'd often forget about the need for a proper descent. One day, after jamming his knee between two branches in the old schoolyard tree (bad enough that the janitor had to be summoned to set him free), he began looking for easier ways to return to earth....

"Somewhere I had read or seen something about parachutes. Maybe it was at the State Fair in West Allis where they occasionally had a hot air balloon with a man who jumped out of the little gondola and parachuted to the ground. It wasn't long before I was on the roof of our garage, holding a bed sheet with a clothesline tied to each corner. I jumped—quickly learning my first lesson about gravity...and pain! Fortunately, no broken bones resulted from this knowledge."

It was all part of Paul's favorite educational process: hands-on learning and getting involved!

"Airplanes and people would enter and then leave, only to reappear sometime in the future…."

Chapter Five

The Depression Years

After the stock market "crashed" in 1929, the ensuing economic slowdown quickly became a depression and spread like wildfire throughout the country. Soon there was massive unemployment and bread lines full of desperate workers with fading hopes and shattered dreams. Families wondered from where—and when—their next meal might come. Survival was foremost in the minds of parents and children alike, meaning those little extras that make a child's life so special were often lost in the struggle to exist. Paul recalls this period in his life....

"The late twenties and most of the thirties were trying times for many families throughout the United States. It was a time of the Great Depression and it affected the lives and living standards of so many families, including ours. Mr. Steinmetz would come to our home in his long dark coat and hat, looking for the monthly rent—money that was not there! Dad, as were many other fathers, was out of work. In order to feed his family, he pulled our little coaster four miles into West Allis to pick up goods being distributed to needy families. The term used for our situation was that you were 'on the county.' He brought home brown paper bags with the contents stamped on the outside in purple letters: dried beans, dried peas, apricots, prunes, flour, and other basics of life. Mom used the bags for our school lunches, but we made sure they were turned inside out so those whose dads were still working wouldn't see that purple stamp. We weren't proud that our dad did not have a job and that we were on relief. Dad wasn't proud either; it bothered him a great deal to not be earning a living for his family.

"Our pigs provided not only pork chops, salted hams, and the material to make sausage, but also the lard that, with a little salt, became our butter. Ma was an excellent southern cook, but since she was now surrounded by Russian, Polish and Ukrainian families, she used her talent to make many good 'old country' dinners. Khalopchi (pronounced 'Halupki'), Kapushta and Borscht were some of our favorites, as were her ever-popular bread and sweet rolls.

"Ma's cooking was always in demand. All the neighborhood kids liked her treats—especially her pies! For years, she operated a very profitable hamburger stand at the State Fair in West Allis, where she and her friends sold all the wonderful foods Mom would prepare. We may not have had much during those times, but thanks to Ma, we certainly ate well."

Paul's crude orange-crate airplanes soon gave way to more sophisticated and accurate facsimiles....

"As I grew older, model airplanes were the next step. I'd go to the picnics at Pleasant Valley Park and collect empty bottles from the Manhattan Soda Water Company, turning them into Mr. Kocs' store for a rebate of two cents. A young neighbor buddy of mine, Harold Paasch, was also interested in model airplanes. Although not as avid a builder, he shared my enthusiasm and was often a partner in retrieving soda water bottles. At the time, ten or twenty cents bought a lot of model airplane glue, 1/16- and 1/8-inch balsa stringers and 1/16-inch sheets of balsa wood. The smell of glue would again become familiar to me in later years while covering and doping the many real airplanes I was to design and build.

"The closest model shop, which was actually in a hardware store, was at the corner of Greenfield and National Avenues, a five mile walk each way. It was exciting for me to wander through the rows of hardware, tools, and plumbing fixtures, and then end up at the west wall by the little section with the model airplane kits and supplies. Those same five miles seemed much longer on the way home, as I wanted to get back and start building.

"When I was ten or eleven years old, I converted part of our attic into a model airplane shop. It measured approximately twenty by thirty feet, so I was able to have all my pulp magazines, balsa, glue, and stick pins in one area. As was typical of old homes, our attic had a low ceiling; I had to stand on the steps with my model workshop on the floor. Even during those hot summer days when the temperature was ninety or a hundred degrees, it is where I could be found, building

balsa models of Little Dippers, Curtiss Falcons and Howard Racers. My favorite place to fly my Little Dipper, a Comet design, was to climb out on the front porch, wind the rubber band, and watch it fly—often times into a tree!"

It's been said that life is a series of cycles…that history often repeats itself. Paul's life is filled with such phenomenon. Airplanes and people would enter and then leave, only to reappear some time in the future....

"In the sixth grade I bought a model kit of the Curtiss Robin with a 24-inch wingspan and spent many hours building it in my attic airplane shop. When it was completed, I took it to school to show Mrs. Schebel, my third and fourth grade teacher. As she was then my favorite teacher, I told her I had built the airplane for her to see. I recall vividly its yellow wings and red fuselage—the same colors as the one in EAA's Pioneer Airport hangar today. Mrs. Schebel said she really liked the model and appreciated my bringing it to show her."

When a person is highly motivated toward a specific direction or purpose, he or she will actively search for ways to satisfy that interest: the end will usually justify the means. Combine this with the mischievous nature of youth....

"I would often go to the nearby swamp and climb a tree during recess. As my weight crept upwards, the branch would bend, causing me to fall into the water. Was it done on purpose? Though I wouldn't admit it to my teacher, Mrs. Leone (or to my mother), it certainly was, for it meant that I had to go home where I could work on my model airplanes!

"One day I ended up with just my bottom-side in the water. I trudged back to my seat where beneath me dripped a large pool of water. I was getting impatient as I waited for Mrs. Leone to notice—I wanted to get back to my model airplane shop! But it never happened. As she told me later, school was very important, and she had long ago caught on to my tricks. On more than a few occasions my palms remembered her ruler."

Children find ways to enjoy life, regardless of their circumstance. Fertile imaginations easily overcome a shortage of material possessions. Still, it's always more fun to share life's experiences with others your own age....

"During one's early years, there are young folks around one's own age who will always be remembered—Billy Ratzmann was one of them. He lived two houses down and across the street from our house. While older than the rest of us, he wasn't the bully type. Instead, he was the kind of fellow we all looked up to—two years make a big difference in one's early life! Some time ago, Billy and his wife, Betty, moved to Oshkosh. Until Billy's passing, they both served many thousands of hours as Docents at the EAA Air Museum.

"Billy, Eddie Holpher, Harold Paasch and I, along with Al Gromacki, Kenny Larson, the Dropp Brothers and Billy Ring, would often be seen playing baseball in the nearby field. When it was time to eat, Dad's calling, 'Howard!' could be heard for blocks. I would quickly drop my bat and head straight for home."

After years of ignoring their existence, "girls" suddenly attain new status in the minds of young boys. Instead of being held as "the untouchables," they become "the desirables!" From this point onward, impressing them is considered acceptable behavior....

"It was during this era that George Raft, a movie star of by-gone years, was so popular. Al Gromacki tried to copy his image by slicking his hair back with perfumy, oily material. Quite a few of us were then attracted to Marian Kienzle, a dark-haired, good-looking girl who was

two or three years older than myself. She lived in a nice home about half a mile away…a popular place to walk by at night. We hoped that we would either get a glimpse of her, or that she was outside and would talk to us.

"One night catastrophe struck! We were planning to see Marian, only this time I was going to make my hair slick and oily like Al's. I didn't have any hair tonic or oily substance, but I thought a little of our pig's lard would do the job. Soon my hair was looking just as slick as his, and we headed out. A short time later Al began to razz me, saying I was turning gray. I guess I was—the lard had begun to turn white! Al got to see Marian alone that night…years later, he and Marian were married."

Because there was little or no money for entertainment, families created their own. When they did go out, it was generally a family outing....

"Pleasant Valley Park, earlier named Shooting Park when it contained a skeet shooting area, was located in a wooded area out in the country and was a popular place for picnics on the weekends. Model T, Model A, Essex, Hupmobile and other automobiles could be seen trailing dust down the gravel roads as they headed for the picnic grounds. The moms, dads, and kids played games for a while. Then the parents would drink beer and dance to Heinie and his Grenadiers, a well-known local German band that played polkas and waltzes. While the parents danced, the kids often ran between them and slid on the slick hardwood floor. The sides of the hall were raised and other kids could be seen sitting along the rails, watching and having fun.

"In addition to the many picnic tables spread out under the large groves of trees, there was a small midway consisting of four or five buildings where ice cream and soda was sold and some carnival type games could be played. At the end of this area was the Rathskellar, a long building that sometimes emitted loud noises. It was here the famous Milwaukee beer was sold. Little did I know that this building would one day serve as a work shop for the repairing of a Waco glider.

"To us kids out in the country, visiting the park was something we all looked forward to each summer weekend; it was an important part of our life…as one might say today, it was 'where the action is!' It was not uncommon for airplanes to fly over local picnic areas and drop leaflets and Eisenglass Caps—a bill-like cap that slid over one's head, much like one would see in the old days on a bank teller. Adults *and* kids scurried to find as many as they could."

Aviation is not cheap: never has been; never will be. Even at Paul's level of participation there wasn't enough money to satisfy all his needs. That meant only one thing....

"One of my first real jobs was rolling sod and carrying it over to the truck on my shoulder. The job lasted several months, but quickly terminated when a big grass snake slithered out of the sod and down my shoulder, falling to the ground. Another more seasonal job I held was picking radishes, corn, and raspberries at the local truck farms where wages were fifty to seventy-five cents a day. Of course there were always the empty bottles!

"Another time, being a bit short on both bottles and cash, Harold Paasch and I decided we ought to have a chicken sale. Off we went with several Rhode Island Reds from his parents' farm, holding them upside down by their legs while they cackled loudly and flapped their wings wildly. We went to the neighbors and offered the hens for sale for whatever they would like to pay, dreaming about another Comet model airplane kit or some balsa and glue. But we soon learned that young boys don't go around selling other people's chickens. Our would-be customers soon had us hightailing it back to the Paasch farm with those same hens tucked under our arms that were to have been our quick fortune."

His career as a chicken retailer thus cut short, Paul took to dealing in inanimate objects. He figured they could be sold without the fear of being caught. He was right, at least for a short while....

"In my youth, the junk collector, or 'rag man' as we called him, was a common sight. He visited each neighborhood on a wagon pulled by a horse, collecting almost anything: used clothing, rags to be baled, or just plain junk. He'd call out, 'Ah rags! Ah rags!' usually with a heavy accent, and people would run to him with their meager used material, trying to convert it into a few pennies. One day, I sold two of Dad's used tires for little or nothing and headed off to the hardware store for more model supplies. The verbal thrashing I got when Dad came home and found out I had sold his hard-earned tires was long remembered!

"Another unsuccessful venture again involved myself and Harold. We crept into the woods behind the Catholic church, cut down some Christmas trees, and sold them. When we were found out, which always seemed to be the case, both Dad and Father Priese were quite angry at us...another verbal thrashing!"

It was inevitable that basic balsa gliders and rubber-band powered models would soon give way to the next level of challenge: powered flight. But adding power meant additional cost, and our young aviator's financial status was already suffering from withdrawal symptoms....

"I heard about a gas model airplane contest to be held at Curtiss Wright Airport. I bought a kit and asked Mom to loan me the money for a Cyclone Model D model airplane motor. Somehow I convinced her I could pay her back from the prize money being offered to the winner. I joined the NAA Model Airplane Academy and finished building the airplane.

My free flight model...before it crashed!

It was a free-flight version, unlike the more popular radio controlled models of today, and I took it down to Pleasant Valley Park to get some flying experience. The first few flights went fairly well—one did not! For whatever reason, the airplane went into a steep spiral and I sadly watched it disintegrate several hundred feet in front of me.

"Though to me this was a major catastrophe, I kept building models. Crash after crash, rebuild after rebuild, I learned more about aerodynamics and construction techniques. While scouring the books, I also discovered that model building was much the same in design and construction as the real thing."

With a growing background of experience gained through trial and error, Paul was primed for further adventures in aviation. One of them would not be long in coming—he would soon meet face to face with the real thing!

Chapter Six

At Last, a Real Airplane

When the dreams of youth come face to face with reality, one of two things can occur: lasting motivation or extreme disappointment. For Paul, it was the former....

"One foggy, dreary day in early spring, I was returning from an afternoon at the movies in West Allis. It was about 8:00 P.M. when I dragged myself through the door to our home. I was tired, but when Mom told me a real airplane had landed down by Pleasant Valley Park that afternoon, I quickly headed down our gravel road and across the field to the park. A real airplane, she had said. I was scared—I had never been up close to one before. Cautiously I walked along the edge of the woods…no sign of it there. I quickly ran across the field on the south side of the park. Where could it be? At any moment I expected it to jump out at me.

"Suddenly, in the dimming light I saw a shadow. There it was! A huge monster standing so very high, its two big wings spread out from the tall fuselage. I didn't approach it right away; I just walked around and around, wishing it was still daylight. Eventually I began to lose my fear and ventured closer. Finally I touched the wing. Oh, what a thrill! A real airplane! Little did I realize at the time that my life's work would not only touch airplanes, but people as well.

"I didn't want this wonderful airplane to get away from me, so I quickly ran home, grabbed a blanket, and returned. It was still there! I crawled under the wing, wrapped myself up in the blanket, and lay there all night in the mist and the rain...looking up at the under side and imagining that someday I would be a pilot. I tried not to fall asleep; I kept thinking about my dream to fly, and to design and build airplanes—and that someday they would all come true!

"Morning came too soon, although it gave me a better opportunity to inspect the airplane. I cautiously climbed up on the wing and looked into the cockpit. The first thing I saw was something I had read about so many times in the past: the joy stick, or control stick as it is more commonly called today. But in those days, it was the rudder bar and joy stick that operated the controls. Possibly it got it's name because of the pleasure it could bring a pilot during flight...of course with proper use!

"I finally scurried home to get ready for school. Though I would much rather have stayed with my beautiful airplane, it was off to Johnson School. All day I worried that it would not be there when the last bell rang. After what seemed to be the longest day ever, the bell finally rang and I headed straight for Pleasant Valley Park...the airplane was gone! Filled with disappointment, I went home. Mom told me that when the weather got better that afternoon, she heard the sound of the engine. Standing on the front porch, she watched the airplane take off and head south.

"And to me...into eternity. I often wondered what kind of biplane it was. It wasn't a Jenny, but it did have a water-cooled engine, probably an OX-5. Who was the pilot? Nobody knew. We heard he was forced down because of the bad weather and fog—things I was to learn much more about later in my flying life."

Fate had intervened on our behalf. By failing to recognize the identity of his first airplane encounter, Paul developed an affinity for all airplanes with two wings. His affection would later expand to include any airplane, a trait that makes him unique among aviators!

"Paul's dad must have dreaded coming home at night!"

Chapter Seven

An Angel He Was Not

Paul Howard Poberezny was considered by most to be a normal child. Although he held an unusual passion for aviation (and spent a large percentage of his waking hours pursuing it), he still found time to orchestrate and instigate the familiar youthful pastime of being downright mischievous.

Halloween has traditionally been a thinly veiled excuse for prankish behavior. Running true-to-form, Paul and his friends, Eddie Holpher, Harold Paasch, Billy Ring and Billy Ratzman, used the occasion to pursue their favorite annual prank, that of overturning outhouses along Ghost Alley. One year, the boys disturbed a very unhappy tenant....

"We once pushed over an outhouse with Mr. Higgins, a local railroad employee, inside. Understandably he was very mad and it took him many years to forget the incident—if he ever did!"

On occasion "the boys" headed out on a nighttime watermelon hunt—they always seemed to taste better as the spoils of dishonest labor....

"When we were out stealing watermelons, the farmers would sometimes hear us and fire a shotgun blast into the air—it was a good warning for us to get going! As we were running, we hoped the second shot, which was often filled with rock salt, wouldn't catch up with our behinds! I'm sure that today someone would have them arrested for protecting what was theirs...but we certainly got the message!"

Another nighttime prank included placing an assortment of boards and pumpkins on the road, then concealing them with corn stalks. After setting the scene, our perpetrators would hide behind a tree to watch in glee as the "victims" approached in their cars. One night, they picked the wrong car....

"...the squad car stopped and began shining its spotlight around the area—this time we were really scared. We scattered and ran to our homes, staying there until well into the next day and thinking that all the police in the county would be looking for us."

One cool, fall day Paul decided to give Mother Nature a helping hand....

"We used coal for cooking and to heat our home in the winter. The coal truck came through our neighborhood every so often to drop coal off to those who needed it. We kept ours in a pile near the garage. One day I took some coal oil, which we used for our lamps, and lit the coal pile...hoping it would warm the area. My dad was pretty upset with me when he returned from work."

Children often display a cruel sense of humor—especially when dealing with other family members. As part of an ongoing harassment program aimed at his sister, Paul coined the endearing term, *Four-Spot.* The nickname was designed to constantly remind Martha of the four beauty marks on her left cheek. Another of Paul's tricks was to lock his sister in her bedroom. If she tried to escape out the window, he would dump cold water on her from his vantage point on the roof!

Later on in high school, he continued with such minor misdeeds as removing the hinge-pins from cupboard doors in the lab. When a victim went to open the door, it would fall noisily to the floor. Paul was usually the first to laugh, thus sealing his guilt. Yes, he was a normal child in most ways!

Because of this mischievous streak, discipline played a prominent role throughout Paul's childhood. In those days, it was acceptable for parents to employ a reasonable degree of physical punishment without fear of violating the child's "human rights," or inviting outside concern. In order to instill much-needed discipline and responsibility, the family was a self-governing unit, in this case headed by a dominant male figure....

"Dad had a very loud and strong voice with a heavy Russian accent that could be heard echoing all over the neighborhood. All he would have to do was yell 'Howard!' which meant 'come home!' Whenever I was in trouble, he used his voice, hand, and thumb to direct the punishment, which was usually given at the famous family rocking chair. He'd whistle; his hand would flash, with the thumb pointing to the rocking chair; and he'd say, 'rocking chair!' I'd have to sit in it for a period of time, from half an hour to an hour, sometimes two! When Mom passed by, I would quietly whisper to her, 'Please ask Dad if I can get out of this chair.' Sometimes she would; sometimes she wouldn't, depending on what I didn't do or should have done. I guess that old-fashioned European discipline had a great deal to do with my upbringing.

"I believe fear is something everyone has—fear of losing a privilege, fear of losing money, or even fear of losing respect. One of the most common fears is to see flashing blue and red lights approaching from behind while driving an automobile. If one is truthful, it is fear that raises the right foot off the accelerator—even though you may be obeying the law at the time. As the police car drives by heading to another call, one realizes that fear is also respect. In this case, respect for the law."

While Milwaukee winters are often long and harsh, the summers can be hot and humid. This was all the reason our adventurous lad needed to start a backyard construction project one summer....

"The backyard of our small frame home contained a number of smaller trees, one large willow, a small garage, chicken coop, pigpen, and coal pile. Not very far from the edge of the cemetery sat the family outhouse. We also had space for a garden and the old hand pump, from which our water was drawn for cooking, drinking, and the Saturday night bath in the metal laundry tub.

"One hot summer, Eddie Holpher and I decided we needed a swimming pool! Knowing that water would be a problem, we felt the pool should be located in the backyard of our house, not too far from the well. Along with several other neighborhood boys, we found some shovels and started digging. After digging all day, we eventually created a hole about two feet deep and maybe eight by twelve feet across. With the aid of an old rain gutter to serve as a trough, we all took turns at the pump handle in an attempt to fill our pool. We pumped and pumped, but no matter how fast we worked, the water disappeared into the ground.

"We briefly got the water level up to five or six inches, but realized we were creating a muddy pond, not a swimming pool. We did get in and splash and romp around a bit until Dad got home—then all heck broke loose! It must have been at least ten o'clock that evening before we finished refilling the hole!"

Paul's dad must have dreaded coming home at night—maybe that's why he worked such long hours! It was better to leave the home front to Jettie; these things didn't seem to bother her as much.

As a youth enters the teen years, he or she begins to embrace, if only because of peer pressure, a wider variety of interests. In addition to pursuing aviation and pulling pranks, Paul also enjoyed going to the movies (or going to a show, as it was called). This simple act is something we take for granted today, but during Paul's youth it was an exciting and eagerly anticipated privilege.

Although there were no multi-screen movie complexes with digital surround-sound stereo and other special effects, just being able to watch stories unfold through a flickering, black and white, 16 mm film with a synchronized sound track, was a captivating experience for a generation whose audio-visual exposure centered around radios, telephones and faded photographs in the family album.

The movie theaters themselves were quite different too. Most likely they were housed in ornate buildings with elaborately sculptured balconies and large, dusty stages bracketed by long, dark, velvet curtains…and one screen! Even though the movies were shown only in black and white, the motion and the sound made the silver screens come alive for Paul's generation....

"Many times we walked the three or four miles to West Allis to see a movie at one of the theaters, or showhouses, as we called them. Occasionally, Dad cranked up our Model A and drove us, but most of the time we walked. We often sat through the same movie two or three times. Arriving at around 1:00 P.M. with our few nickels for the show and some popcorn or candy, it was an all-day adventure, and we often didn't get home until eight or nine o'clock at night.

"I couldn't wait for the newsreels, Movietone, Pathé and others, to show the national and world activities. I didn't realize that much of the news was over a month old, although it didn't really matter to me. I was just interested in seeing airplanes—any airplanes—and those black and white newsreels helped bring the world of aviation a little bit closer. Of course, I also enjoyed airplane movies such as *Lilac Time* and *Dawn Patrol*; they were my favorites and my first priority. My second choice was cowboy shows, and Ken Maynard was my cowboy hero."

"...one of the few times I was disappointed in a fellow airman."
Paul Poberezny

Chapter Eight

More Flying Machines... One Letdown

Paul loved everything about aviation. It wasn't just things with wings and propellers that attracted his interest; he also made crude kites using wooden cross pieces covered with newspaper. Many pieces of string in various lengths and sizes were knotted together so that his kite might fly higher than the others....

"I flew them all year round, whenever there was a good wind. In the winter, on those rainy, icy days, my kite would slowly descend to the ground under a coat of ice. It was a lesson I learned early in my flying career while looking out on the leading edge of the wings of the many airplanes I flew and often seeing that same phenomenon of ice building up and reducing the performance of the airfoil."

Sailing shares many aerodynamic principles and theories with flight. Maybe this explains why so many pilots enjoy equally the challenge of working an airfoil (sail) of a boat and manipulating the airfoil (wing) of an airplane....

"Being adventuresome, and always wanting to try something different, I once built a wind-driven iceboat. After a sleet storm, one would see me sliding down the ice-covered roads, driven by the wind on my crude machine made of two-by-fours, an old sheet, and ice skates for runners. Sometimes I dragged it down to the pond by the park, cleared off some snow, and skimmed across the ice for a short distance."

Paul's focus always returned to airplanes because they required pilots to fly them; anything else was a short-lived adventure. To him, a flying machine must have the capacity for sustained and controllable flight before one could fully appreciate the experience. Yet the same question remained unanswered: how to accomplish it?

As he approached his mid teens, the physical boundaries of Paul's world began to expand. He found himself in search of a place that had real flying machines....

"Milwaukee County Airport, now known as General Mitchell Field, was the only airport I really knew anything about, and that was from reading about it in the newspapers we sometimes had. I longed to go there and see real airplanes, but as it was some nine or ten miles from home, it was too far for a youngster to stray!

"I was fourteen when I was finally given the opportunity. With instructions to be home before dark, Mom packed a lunch and sent me off at daybreak. Never had I been so far away from home by myself. I walked for a while, rested and ate part of my lunch, and then walked some more. By the time I arrived at the airport, my lunch was gone; but I quickly forgot about food! Standing at the fence next to the old, white, wooden terminal building and gazing at the biplanes and Ford Tri-Motors, was a thrill I shall never forget. I wanted to reach out and touch all of them, but the attendant, Mr. Hart, said rules prohibited young lads from doing so.

"There was always a lot of action at the airport—at least there was for me! Midwest Airways had their old wooden hangar next to a more modern one made of stone that housed Westphal Airways, a dealer in Waco airplanes. On many future trips, I recall peering in the windows of the old Midwest hangar and the shop operated by the Knaup Brothers, who later became good friends of mine. What a joy to see the Buhl Pups, Fleets, Monocoupes, Ryans; and the OX-5 aircraft of the era: the Travel Airs, Curtiss Robins and American Eagles. Often times sitting on the grass nearby would be an Army plane, a Curtiss Hawk

or Falcon; one time I even saw a Keystone bomber, which was a huge biplane of the era.

"My passion for collecting aircraft parts started out behind the Midwest hangar where I found a piece of airplane fabric. I carried it home and kept it in my room, marveling that this material covered with airplane dope and painted red had actually flown. I don't recall from what type of airplane it came, but it was a treasured piece that added inspiration to my wanting to be a pilot."

Paul enjoyed frequent trips to the Milwaukee County Airport over the next few years. At first he used the most basic mode of transportation—his feet! Later he obtained a battered old bicycle that, as long as the tires held air, trimmed his travel time considerably. This allowed him more time to be around airplanes and meet those who flew and maintained them. Unlike today, when most airports are sequestered like dangerous animals and aviation is promoted primarily through books, films and video games, it was still accessible to kids like Paul who stubbornly pursued their interest....

"The first air race I went to was at Milwaukee County Airport. At last I saw the Howard *Pete* and *Mike* racers I had read about so much in the model airplane books. They were each flown at different times by the famous pilot, Benny Howard.

Howard "Mike" Racer

Howard "Pete" Racer

"There was also a new Cessna racer flown by Johnny Livingston. It was a yellow and orange mid wing airplane with retractable landing gear, which was quite unusual for the period. To us kids, it didn't look

right when the gear was hidden; we thought the wheels and landing gear should always be visible in order for it to be a real airplane. During the race, which used the airway beacon and the Catholic church steeple as pylons, Johnny had to pull up and make a forced landing when an oil line broke. The airplane was covered with oil and the engine was smoking when he landed—what a hero he was to me that day!"

CR-2 Cessna Racer

"Another time, the famous race pilot, Roscoe Turner, flew over Pleasant Valley Park in a Lockheed Air Express. It had a parasol wing mounted on the same type of airplane Wiley Post made famous as the *Winnie Mae*. Roscoe then flew back to land at Milwaukee and returned in an open, four-door Ford V8 with the top down. He was ushered to the stage of the outdoor bandstand in his uniform—the familiar breeches, shiny boots and waxed mustache. As Roscoe was one of my many idols, I climbed a nearby tree to get a better view. He had his lion cub with him, which had become a hallmark of his career. Until he got too big, 'Gilmore' often flew with Roscoe on his trips throughout the country."

Roscoe Turner, "Gilmore" and friend

Heroes are made, not born. Charles Lindbergh, Roscoe Turner, Johnny Livingston, Jimmy Doolittle, Amelia Earhart, Billy Mitchell, Steve Wittman, Bobbi Trout, Steve Wittman, Benny Howard, Louise Thaden, "Pancho" Barnes, and many others were bonafide aviation heroes of the time. They expanded the frontiers of aviation by flying into the unknown ...at no small risk to themselves!

Paul simply must experience the thrill of flight! But how could he overcome the high cost of flying? He and his friends would be frail old men before they cashed in enough empty soda bottles to pay for one brief airplane ride! There must be a faster way to get into the air....

"While looking through the window of the Westphal hangar one day, a gentleman by the name of Red Berg came outside and greeted me. He was an electrician at Allis Chalmers and owned the Curtiss Robin with the bright red fuselage and yellow wings that was in the hangar. He told me that if I would polish his airplane, he'd give me a ride. How thrilled I was! My arms were soon busy applying and wiping off the wax. It wasn't an easy task, but after several trips to the airport the project was completed, and I was all set for the thrill of my lifetime—my first airplane ride!

EAA's Curtiss Robin...reunited again!

"Sadly, it would not be in that Curtiss Robin. Mr. Berg reneged on his promise and asked me to leave the hangar. What a disappointment—one I have never forgotten to this day. I don't know why he changed his mind; he never told me.

“This particular airplane changed hands several times since then, and eventually was placed in the custody of the EAA Air Museum. After all those years, I finally had the opportunity—not to ride as a passenger, but to fly the airplane myself! When I did, it brought back a flood of memories—including one of the few times I have ever been disappointed by a fellow airman!”

It would not be the last time this airplane played a part in Paul’s life!

Chapter Nine

Mr. Homer F. Tangney

The education system in the thirties was considerably different from the bureaucracy it has become today. At least at visible levels, there was more apparent interest in the student as an individual *and* in providing a climate in which to learn. Schools were filled with respect and discipline—both now very much out of style! Paul adds....

"Though I didn't realize it at the time, I now understand how important teachers are in the development of our young men and women. I was not the best student, but because our schooling was so much different in those days, teachers were able to take the time to develop other interests their students might have—even when they were outside the school curriculum. Teachers were not held accountable by as many rules and regulations or the fear of being publicly scorned for doing their job. We students respected them as adults holding a position of authority, and they always dressed to a high standard, even on their meager salaries.

"In today's society, teachers are considered by many to be 'babysitters.' Because they are restricted from using good old-fashioned discipline, they often work in constant fear for their own well being—even their lives! There is something very wrong with such a system. I have often told teacher groups, 'You are the most important individual in a

young person's life. Do not look down on yourselves; you put lasting memories into your students' minds. They may not remember the names of some of their relatives, but they can always remember those teachers who made a difference in their lives. I know; I was helped by many of my wonderful teachers!'

"I have great respect for education and have tried in my own way to develop programs that assist young people; Project Schoolflight is but one example. The talents needed to build an airplane are numerous: welding, woodworking, reading drawings, using drafting equipment, performing sheet metal and engine work, and learning new systems such as hydraulics. However, of greatest importance is to develop a respect for quality. Aviation is known for its high standards; through programs like Project Schoolflight, we try to instill the same high standards of aviation into the character of the students. Whether or not they become involved in aviation is not important, nor is it our goal. What *does* matter is that they become better at *whatever* they choose to do, be it a doctor, carpenter, mechanic...or just a good citizen. America *can* become a better place through aviation."

Paul's Eighth Grade Graduation picture
(Paul - top row, center)

In the fall of 1936, Paul was assigned to West Milwaukee High School along with students from an expanded area that included Muskego, St. Martins and Hales Corners. It was a tremendous social change....

"After barely graduating from the rural Johnson School, going to a big city high school was a hustling and bustling experience for me. I didn't know if I was going to like it; it seemed so complex and so busy. Algebra, Ancient History, Chemistry, Science and English were subjects for which I cared little. I did enjoy Mechanical Drawing, as it was the only class that offered the opportunity of trying my hand at designing aircraft!"

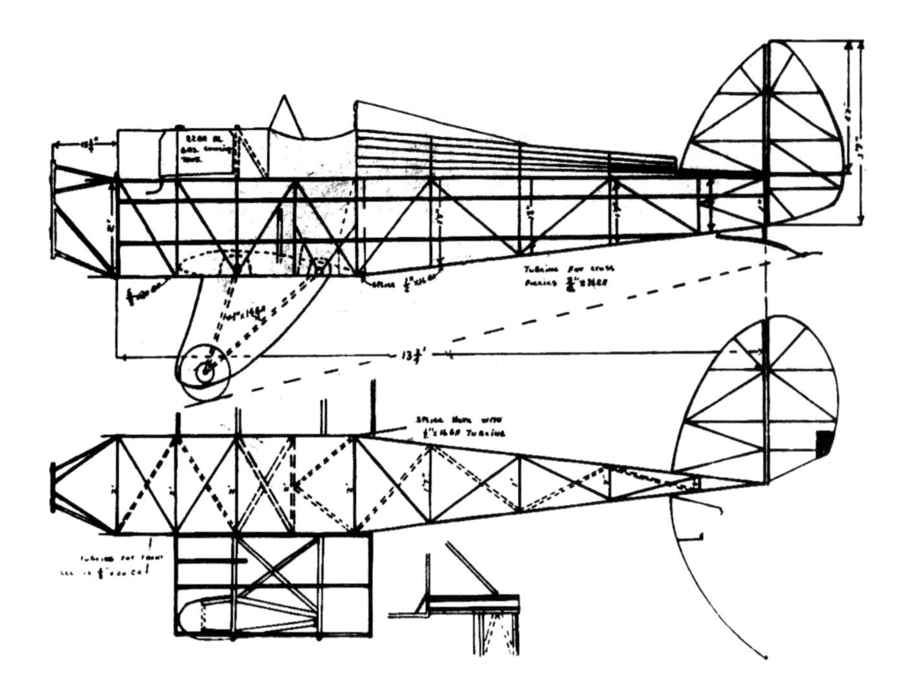

Paul's first airplane design - a 1936 Mechanical Drawing assignment

Most of us recall someone from our past who became a major factor in helping us form our future. Because of the captive nature of the school system, it is often a teacher who fulfills this pivotal role....

"Once I learned there was a model airplane club in high school, my interest brightened. It was called 'Wings' and was supervised by my Ancient History teacher, Mr. Homer F. Tangney—a man who would truly change my life! After school, I attended the weekly club get-togethers. Another member of the club who would become very important to me in later years (during the formation of EAA) was a fellow student by the name of Val Brugger.

"Mr. Tangney had a sincere interest in aviation, having been a member of a glider club in Milwaukee. A year earlier, he encouraged the Industrial Arts teacher to build a primary glider as part of his

woodworking class. The teacher had agreed and the project was underway. It had an all-wood fuselage, wood wing ribs, wings, and tail group. This year, one of my tasks was to help bring the glider out of the boiler room and into the woodwork shop where we accomplished additional work on it during the period. Thanks to Mr. Tangney's suggestion, I also began to enjoy Industrial Arts classes.

Homer F. Tangney

"Mr. Tangney was a bachelor, a short, pleasant, stocky man who lived up the street from the school. He knew of my interest in model airplanes from the Wings Club and began to notice that I was often drawing sketches of airplanes during his Ancient History classes. One day after school, he called me in and asked if I would be interested in a battered, slightly damaged, Waco Primary Glider. I couldn't hide my enthusiasm; however, I didn't have the money to buy even a damaged one. Mr. Tangney said he felt that my interest in aviation was sincere and that he would give me the machine if I agreed to complete it. He also said that he would pay for all the spruce, fabric, aviation dope, and other materials needed for its restoration!"

Little did Mr. Tangney realize that his offer would change the course of history! As one looks back on Paul's sometimes erratic and often difficult journey, this one innocent act of faith by a caring and perceptive high school history teacher must be considered *the* major turning point in Paul's life....

"While walking home after school that day, I had my first visions that I really was going to be a pilot. This wonderful gift from Mr. Tangney would serve to change my life from this day on. Looking back, it is difficult for me to believe that I could have been so fortunate. As a result of his kindness, this recognition of my interest by a teacher, I have attempted to carry on the faith he had in me to others who also love aviation."

It is impossible to appreciate how such a simple action could spark a career that would touch millions of people throughout the world. If every child (or at least, a lot more of them) had someone take a similar interest in their lives, where would we be today? It wouldn't have to be a teacher; it could be anyone who cares enough to make a difference. Our world would be a much better place if there were more people like Mr. Homer F. Tangney, the Ancient History teacher at West Milwaukee High School.

Okay "Howie," it's time to stop dreaming and get to work. This wasn't a poorly constructed reject from somebody's failed project; it was a factory-built unit from the Waco Airplane Company of Troy, Ohio. When the glider was damaged, the club decided to dispose of it rather than repair it. For lack of a better solution, they allowed one of their members (Mr. Tangney) to take it home. Its future became Paul's challenge....

"But where was I to work on and rebuild this monster with its thirty-six foot wing span? The only answer was the family garage. I figured that if Dad left his car outside, and Ma moved her washing machine over, then I could rearrange the tools, salted pork, meats and hams that were hung and stored in the garage, and have my first airplane shop. Dad didn't put up much of a fuss and so, along with Eddie Holpher and Mr. Tangney, I took the glider from his garage, put it on a trailer, and trucked it to my home. Another day was spent making wooden horses and hanging the steel tube fuselage and tail group, which didn't need recovering. How proud I was to have an airplane so near to me, even if it was a glider. I don't know if Mr. Tangney ever realized it or not, but his gift contributed a great deal to my lack of enthusiasm for schoolwork—and for my absence on a great number of days!"

What a wonderful break for our budding pilot-to-be! Just when there appeared to be little hope, the door to a future in aviation suddenly flew wide open and all his self-imposed limitations vanished. The challenge was gratefully accepted....

"My transportation problems had eased somewhat and I could get around quicker to purchase supplies. I had friends with automobiles, and my first steady job working part-time at the local DX filling station, making twenty cents an hour. I could now chip in for gasoline to get to the airport to buy dope (aviation!) or any other supplies needed in the repair of the glider. On my frequent trips to Milwaukee County and Curtiss-Wright airports, I continued to bring back pieces of airplanes...there always seemed to be old wrecks lying around! With the permission (and sometimes without) of whomever owned the junk that was laying beside the hangars, I began to accumulate what could be called my first attempt at creating an air museum. Broken wing ribs, an old bent wheel from a crashed Travel Air in which both the pilot and passenger lost their lives, fabric from a Great Lakes that was involved in another fatal accident, old airplane tires, broken propellers, and other parts were all nailed to the walls of the garage that was now converted to an airplane workshop.

"Many hours were spent working on the glider. Its wood wing had been heavily battered during the earlier landing, so it was necessary to take all the fabric off in order to make repairs to a number of broken ribs. The new fabric, unbleached muslin, was purchased at Penney's and installed...another learning process! The fuselage was then painted red, while the wings and tail group were done in silver; it was almost ready to fly! Eddie Holpher was helping me with the final assembly when we discovered we were missing some of the clevis pins for the turnbuckles. This time, nails bent over would do!

Howie and his glider - ready to fly!

"The glider didn't have a regular landing gear, just a hickory skid along the bottom of the fuselage, with small skids on the bottom of each wing, near the tip. We pulled it down to Pleasant Valley Park and positioned it across from the baseball diamond, heading into the wind. Eddie had a little four-cylinder Whippet coupe that we were going to use to launch it. Mr. Tangney had given me approximately 400 feet of rope that had been used at the glider club. We backed Eddie's car into position in front of the glider. One end of the rope was tied to the bumper of the car, the other to the release hook on the glider. We tried the release several times: a pull on the cable between my legs and the rope would let go. Eddie then eased the Whippet forward until the rope was taut, awaiting my signal to proceed.

"I had long been reading books on how to fly, establishing in my mind the positions of the control stick, rudder bar, and ailerons—and what would be the result of their movements. I felt I was ready for my

first flight! With several farm and neighborhood kids looking on, I gave Eddie the signal, and he gave it the gas. The Whippet's wheels began spinning in the grass as he tried to build up speed. I'll never forget the fresh smell of the grass and the clear, clean spring air as we bumped along the open field.

"My right wing was dragging and the glider attempted to turn right. I pushed the rudder bar and moved the stick to the left to raise the wing and maintain a straight line behind the tow car. It leveled, but before I could react the left wing went down and began riding on its skid. The glider now started to veer in that direction. I quickly brought the stick back to neutral and, at the same time, pulled back. In an instant I was in a new world! I looked down on the top of Eddie's car, thinking I was a hundred or more feet in the air, although I was probably no more than fifteen or twenty! I pulled the rope release; the rope dropped out of sight and the glider settled heavily to the ground. It was then I learned to keep the nose down when the rope was released!

...in a new world!

"I felt exhilaration beyond belief. We towed the glider back and made over a dozen flights that day, each time going a bit higher until I eventually reached an altitude of approximately 100 feet. I would cut the glider loose and glide straight ahead over Eddie's car to a bouncy landing on the not-too-smooth field. The controls felt sloppy at low speeds, but became more responsive once it began to fly. It would start to fly at about 25 mph and land into the wind at less than 20 (mph).

"Later in my career, having instinctively learned to put the nose down when the rope was released (a situation similar to losing engine power in an airplane), I escaped injury on several occasions when my engine failed immediately after takeoff."

That spring day in 1937, fifteen-year-old Paul Howard Poberezny became a pilot!

Ryan Brougham - Paul's first powered airplane ride

Chapter Ten

More Influences...More Firsts!

The ability to acquire a reliable source of spending money has been an elusive goal for generations of young people. Being no different, Paul was constantly in search of more funds to buy model airplane kits, aircraft supplies and aviation magazines. There was always another job to be found, but he already had one that demanded too much of his spare time…time he would much rather be spending on his aviation interests. He began devising schemes to make some of that "easy money," thus avoiding the more painful option of physical labor....

"Even at an early age, Eddie Holpher was quite an accomplished accordionist. During our freshman and sophomore years, he was often asked to play his accordion at the local dances held in Kozmuth's Hall. Eddie once asked me if I knew how to play drums. Of course I didn't, but he said he could teach me if we could find a drum and one of those wire brush drumsticks that gave it a swishing sound, and another regular one. We didn't have money to purchase a real drum, but we did locate an old player piano with something that looked like one inside. Soon I was holding this 'thing' between my knees, trying to follow

Eddie Holpher

Eddie on his accordion. It was quite a challenge, but it seemed that I just didn't have the proper rhythm…my venture into the entertainment business quickly slipped away."

Without skipping a beat, no doubt! Even though Paul wasn't quite ready to hit the road as a traveling musician, at least he was looking at all his options. But until he could develop more marketable skills....

"I had been working part-time at the DX Filling Station on the corner of Oklahoma Avenue and 92nd Street, the same spot where years earlier I met Eddie and his tricycle. Gas was 15 cents a gallon and came from two pumps, regular and high test; we also had one grease rack where we greased the many automobiles. I got to wear my oil-spattered coveralls and a filling station cap with the DX insignia on the bill. At the same time, my friend Al Gromacki was working at the A & P store on 76th & Greenfield. Knowing I always needed extra money, Al asked the store manager, Mr. Vanderboom, if he might consider using me to help stock shelves in the evenings, and bag and carry out groceries for the customers on Saturdays. He said 'yes,' and I had a second part-time job."

Al Gromacki

Hard at work at the DX Station

Sandwiched in between school, failed entrepreneurial attempts, and many hours stocking shelves and pumping gas, was the fun part—working on and flying the Waco glider. Every time Paul got airborne, which was quite often, he gained valuable experience. His flying skills were being honed by a method that is becoming increasingly rare in this age of computer assisted design: trial and error. Soon he was making as many controlled landings as takeoffs. And because the flights took place in the local area, they began to attract crowds of local folks, many of whom knew the young pilot....

Paul (with helmet and goggles) stands proudly before his Waco Primary Glider

"In the audience one day, was a gentleman by the name of Victor Hansen. Victor worked for the Milwaukee Journal and lived in a beautiful home some four or five blocks away. He often came over with his son to watch and, on occasion, launch me into the air behind his beautiful 1935 Ford V8 sedan. One day he asked if I would like to go up in an airplane with a motor on it. I didn't hesitate to say 'yes.' He drove me, along with his wife, Virginia, and son, Junior, to the Milwaukee County Airport where he purchased a ticket for me to ride with Mr. Jim Knaup of Midwest Airways. My first powered airplane ride was in the right seat of a 1928 Ryan Brougham, an airplane built by the Ryan Company and similar to the design of the Spirit of St. Louis.

In the air again—what a thrill!

"I will never forget the thrill of hearing the engine start and seeing the blue smoke come out of the exhaust stacks! As we taxied out for takeoff, I marveled at there not being a tow vehicle present. Then there was an increase in noise from the engine, a short, bumpy takeoff roll, and soon...the joy of sustained flight at what were to me such high altitudes. To look out the side window and watch the right wheel and landing gear move along the backdrop of the City of Milwaukee was a sight I shall never forget. It was a most memorable day."

As he continued to forge his way along the fringes of aviation, Paul was influenced by a growing number of people. One of them was George Hardie. George was already well known as an excellent aircraft modeler and a respected source of aviation history. Paul paid frequent visits to the two-story home, talking, asking questions and borrowing copies of airplane books and magazines to read. George recalls meeting the younger Poberezny: "I was several years older than Paul and was involved with building model airplanes and following the historical aspect of aviation. Paul was in the same high school class as my younger brother and sister, which is how I first got to know him. He had an interest in model airplanes and would sometimes come over to my house for information and guidance. As he mainly had an interest in flying and I didn't want to become a pilot, our visits eventually ceased." They would meet again at the 1953 Milwaukee Air Pageant.

Airplanes were not the only form of transportation that earned a permanent place in Paul's life; he also developed a lifelong interest in motorcycles. Maybe it was because they too are considered to be inherently dangerous (mostly by those who know little or nothing about them!). Maybe it was because motorcycles, like airplanes, are another unique form of transportation. Most likely it was because he had one on permanent loan: free transportation....

"Motorcycles have always intrigued me—a mechanical device powered by a small engine that I usually viewed as something to be removed and put onto an airplane. I acquired an old Henderson motorcycle from a friend, Eugene Van Gemert. Actually, he let me use it indefinitely! Its engine held a special meaning for me, as Ed Heath had powered a number of his little parasol airplanes with converted Henderson four-cylinder, air-cooled engines. Our neighbors would remember Howard and the 'Smoker,' as they called it, coming down the gravel roads of Ghost Alley. It got its nickname because I caused it to produce a thick, white smoke by putting a mixture of kerosene, oil

and gasoline into one of the tanks, regular gasoline into the other. After the engine was started and heated up on the regular gas, I would change to the mixture. Although it didn't run as smooth, it left a nice trail of white smoke up and down the road. My justification to the complaints Mom received from our neighbors was that I was just trying to kill the mosquitoes!"

"It was along about 1938 when I heard about the Milwaukee Light Plane Club that was meeting in a barn-like, two-story building in an alley off 3rd and Burleigh. Here was a place where men were building real airplanes as a hobby. It didn't take me long to go down there and meet these older gentlemen…at least they seemed older in comparison to my age, although they were probably only in their twenties! Irv Miller, who later was to have great influence on the forming of EAA, Al Luft and several others, were doing such wonderful things there. There was an upstairs loft and an alley that contained homebuilts and other aircraft under construction. I remember a Waco 10 being hoisted up to the second floor to be completely restored. There were Heath Parasols and other individual designs there too, such as Irv Miller's 'Belly-Flopper'—a machine in which you laid prone to fly it. It was to be powered by two 40 horsepower Continental engines, but it would not be completed until after World War II.

"To stand and watch, or sometimes be allowed to help, added to my growing enthusiasm for aviation. I learned a great deal by listening to and watching these gentlemen at work. Al Luft gave me an old Heath Parasol fuselage, tail group, and wings that I immediately trucked home to my garage. With my limited experience I didn't work on it very much, but it did add to a collection that brought many neighborhood boys to visit my garage museum. Later, I had the privilege of flying several Parasols powered by a variety of engines."

If it wasn't airplanes or motorcycles influencing him, it was people. Real heroes were in good supply, and Paul had his share....

"Two gentlemen influenced me a great deal in my early years. Of course, the first was Charles Lindbergh and his famous New York to Paris solo flight in 1927. His affect on aviation and those of us who follow it can never be completely documented. The other was a man who became known as Douglas 'Wrong Way' Corrigan. While Lindbergh's exploits are quite well-known throughout the world, Corrigan's adventure is much less so.

"I remember being intrigued by a newspaper story telling about a Curtiss Robin flown by a Mr. Corrigan from California. The article stated that he was denied permission to fly across the Atlantic to Ireland (his motivation to attempt this voyage likely came from having worked as a welder on the original *Spirit of St. Louis* in 1927). To prove that his airplane was capable, he had already flown the 165 horsepower, Wright J6-5 powered Robin (with extra fuel tanks) across the United States to New York, much the same as Lindbergh had done years earlier. I couldn't understand why our government denied his request as I felt his feat, even then, would bring great recognition to our country. But the denial held fast, and so Mr. Corrigan loaded his airplane with fuel and took off heading back to his home state of California.

"Nothing was heard from him for hours and hours. The press wondered in print while the radio commentators wondered out loud. Nobody had seen him flying across the mountains, plains or valleys of our fine country. Then came the wireless reports from Ireland: Doug Corrigan had landed in their country! He had flown *east*, instead of west! His compass must have been off and he got lost...!

"At the same time, the famous Howard Hughes concluded an around-the-world flight in his beautiful, twin-engine Lockheed Electra, complete with all the latest navigation equipment. But it was Doug Corrigan, a simple and dedicated man, who took the country by storm while Howard Hughes' flight took a back seat. I kept the newspaper clippings of Corrigan's flight, hoping that someday I, too, would make a long, cross-country flight in a Curtiss Robin."

It wouldn't be too many more years before Paul *would* routinely make such flights, albeit under completely different circumstances. Later, another combination of events would eventually lead Paul to a meeting with Douglas Corrigan and his famous Curtiss Robin.

The next person to make a lasting impression was a fellow named Ben White. Ben's full-time job was working as a milkman. He chose that occupation because it allowed him plenty of daylight hours in which to pursue his real pleasure. You see, Ben White was also a pilot....

"One day I walked to the Milwaukee airport and was browsing around the old hangars on the east side when I heard a different sound. It was an engine, all right, but it didn't have the familiar pitch of an OX-5, with it's smooth, muffled, rhythmic noise. Nor was it the sound of a radial engine—it was more of a sharp bark. I ran toward

the sound. As I rounded the end of the hangar, I was presented with one of the most beautiful sights I had ever seen!

"There sat a small, sleek, cream-colored race plane, its low wing and red stripe down the side making it look like one of the Howard racers that were then so well-known to us young model airplane builders. It had an inverted four-cylinder, air-cooled engine. Each cylinder had its own short exhaust pipe which gave it that special sound. I stood there watching the pilot in the cockpit while another man, his mechanic I thought, tinkered in the engine compartment. I later learned that he was Hans Krumsreiter, a Milwaukee detective and also a pilot.

"I stood in the propeller blast behind the airplane and felt specks of oil being thrown on my face. I had read many articles in the old pulp aviation magazines about oil being thrown back from the engines of the World War I airplanes and I felt proud and privileged to have oil from an airplane touch me. What I didn't know was that my white T-shirt was also becoming speckled with oil. Later Mom asked me what happened to it; I firmly told her that it was airplane oil and I never wanted it washed off!

Ben White and "Ozzie"

"After the pilot shut down the engine and got out of the cockpit, I noted he had bib overalls on, the striped kind that milkmen wore. Sure enough, on the front it said 'Luick,' which was the name of a major

Milwaukee dairy at the time. He noticed me staring, so he walked over and introduced himself. He said his name was Ben White, and then asked my name and where I lived. He told me that he and Hans built the airplane from their own plans in a little garage near 53rd and Wisconsin Avenue. They named it *Ozzie.* He said he was a milkman because it allowed him so much free time in which to build and fly airplanes after delivering the milk. I later discovered that Ben came from Waupaca, where he had learned to fly in an OX-5 powered American Eagle."

Ben understandably failed to suspect the degree to which he was about to become involved in Paul's quest for aviation knowledge. Maybe that's because Paul didn't know himself. Anyway, Paul soon coaxed Ben into storing *Ozzie* in his garage. Ben agreed because the engine, a product of the Tank Brothers in Milwaukee, never did run to his satisfaction. Each time he flew the airplane, he was afraid he might damage it; he and Hans went along with storing it in a safe place for the time being—without the engine, of course!

Paul and "Ozzie"

Ozzie held the honor of being the first complete airplane in Paul's "museum." Paul spent hours sitting in its silent cockpit, flying around make-believe pylons with famous racing heroes like Steve Wittman, Roscoe Turner, Johnny Livingston, Benny Howard and Art Chester. Even more important, the little racer became the catalyst that helped develop another of Paul's endearing attributes—his unique ability to communicate with others....

"I was asked by Mr. Tangney to give a presentation on behalf of our high school model airplane club. Eddie Holpher and Glae Rogers helped me get *Ozzie* to the school and assemble it on the stage. As it didn't have an engine, we installed a dummy cowling. I was very proud to see it sitting on the stage, but I was also a bit fearful at the thought of giving my first public lecture about airplanes...I guess one

calls it 'stage fright.' However, I gave my talk to the students and even answered a few questions; they seemed to be quite interested. After nervously retreating from the stage, I was followed by a fellow student giving a piano recital—one of many we listened to during our high school years. That student was Walter Liberace!"

We already know that Paul was no musician! But had he been so inclined, there certainly was a fine example to follow in young Liberace!

The little Waco glider flew on a regular basis. Paul eventually tired of pulling it around on its skid, so he designed and installed a landing gear system. This was significant because it proved that anything—even a factory design—could be improved upon. As expected, most of the parts were scrounged. Ben White donated the wheels, and the local blacksmith welded up the framework; Paul installed it with Eddie Holpher's help. The new landing gear worked well and was a significant improvement to the machine's ground handling. Now it operated like a real airplane, instead of a sled!

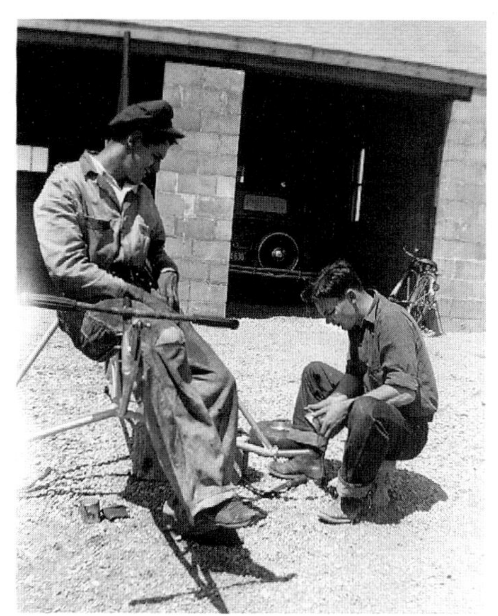

Paul and Eddie designing a landing gear for the glider

No longer a sled!

Looking to further expand the utility of the glider, Paul decided to add night gliding to his repertoire. He correctly assumed the need to see where to land once he got airborne. As the field had no lights, and there was no electrical system in the glider, Paul decided to carry a portable system—his flashlight! It was another idea that didn't work out; the experiment failed miserably and the night flying program ended after one scary flight!

Eddie Holpher flew Paul's glider one time. Paul felt he owed Eddie that much, since Eddie had probably logged as much time towing the glider as Paul had flying it! But the replacement pilot didn't possess the same piloting skills. The glider got airborne all right, but then entered a 90 degree climbing arc and crashed into the trees at the edge of the field. Eddie was shaken up but not hurt...other than his pride. The wrecked glider was dragged over to Rathskeller Hall where it underwent major surgery. However, its flying days were over and it soon joined the other lifeless artifacts in the garage; Paul was making the transition to powered flight....

"There was no doubt Ben White was my idol. He was instructing in a 1935 Porterfield 35-70, a tandem seat, high wing monoplane, powered by a LeBlond 70 horsepower, five-cylinder radial engine. Ben invited me to join the Milwaukee Flight Club, which had four members at the time. The fee was three hundred dollars. It sure took a lot of pumping gas at the filling station and stocking shelves at the A & P store to come forth with that much money.

"By the time I had the necessary amount, the Porterfield had been relocated to Waukesha Airport because the loose cinders on the runways at Milwaukee had badly nicked its propeller. At Waukesha, the runways were grass and the atmosphere more 'homey.' A Stinson Tri-Motor filled the east end of the big WPA-built hangar. There were Waco 10s and American Eagles with OX-5 engines, Waco Straightwings and Curtiss Robins, including one with a powerful 220 horsepower, J-5 engine. Quite a few homebuilt airplanes were also based there...a wonderful variety of airplanes to influence this enthusiastic young man!

"I remember my first flight with Ben; it was November 15, 1938. Ben was in the front seat and I in the rear, wondering how to land this airplane when I couldn't see ahead! Although it was a bit under-powered, it was a beautiful flying machine, and I have fond memories of my first powered flight as a student."

Paul continued his flying lessons, borrowing his dad's car or begging rides from his friends to get to the airport. He flew whenever he saved up

enough money: sometimes five or six times a month, sometimes not at all. He flew his first cross-country flight on Christmas Day 1938, but didn't fly at all in February or March of the next year. In April he began flying again; in May the Porterfield moved back to Milwaukee County Airport. Apparently, the club members preferred to have it closer to home, in spite of the potential for propeller damage. The problem of aircraft accessibility (or lack of it) continues to haunt aviation to this day....

"Milwaukee County Airport had one east-west concrete runway; the others were covered with cinders. I performed many approaches and landings on those cinder runways during the final periods of instruction prior to my going solo."

The first solo flight is both a challenge and a victory. The challenge comes from successfully acquiring all the aviation knowledge and skills necessary to survive a flight without the helping hands of an instructor on board. If the flight is a success, which most of them are, then victory appears as one's mastery of the third dimension. If not, well, there's always sailing....

Paul and the Milwaukee Flight Club Porterfield

"The big day finally came. I made several good landings with Ben and was taxiing back for another takeoff when he suddenly jumped out of the cockpit and said, 'It's now all up to you!' I'll never forget the thrill (and the bit of a scary feeling) as I ran up the engine, checked the mags, and turned the airplane so I could see the base leg and final approach. Both were clear of other airplanes, so I swung around into the wind and opened up the throttle. I was amazed at how quickly the airplane got airborne, as it was the same old 70 horsepower engine

chugging along out front. But the load now being lightened by approximately 175 pounds seemed to add much to its power. All three of my solo landings were satisfactory and I taxied back after a memorable twenty-five minute flight. I was so proud when I later went home to tell Mom and Dad that I was now a 'real' pilot, even though I had already made hundreds of flights in my glider. It was May 13, 1939, and I was seventeen years old."

Not bad for a lad who was forced to delay his lessons due to a lack of money! Paul soloed with less than eleven hours of dual instruction and in less than six month's time, including the two month pause for his financial R and R....

"I continued flying from Milwaukee County Airport and on June 13, experienced my first engine failure and forced landing. I can't remember if it was a Friday, but I was solo and had no problem with the landing. The next week, our family left to visit our grandparents (Mom's parents) in Jonesboro, Arkansas. While there, I checked out in a Stinson SM-8 powered by a Wright J-5 engine. When we returned to Milwaukee, I continued flying the Porterfield and soon enjoyed my first flights in a LeBlond powered Monoprep and an American Eagle with an OXX-6 engine, the one with a dual ignition system. Later that year I flew my first Waco, a Straightwing powered by an OX-5. Little did I know that I would soon become very familiar with the flying characteristics of the OX-5 powered American Eagle biplane."

The joys of aviation must always be tempered by the stark reality of the danger that can suddenly—and unexpectedly—become an unwanted partner. Nothing is without risk—certainly nothing that involves operating machinery. It wasn't long before Paul witnessed the dark side of aviation....

"Tragedy struck our club. One Sunday afternoon I was driving to Milwaukee to fly the airplane. As I neared the airport I noticed a number of automobiles parked up ahead. As I got closer, I saw the tail and aft fuselage section of our Porterfield lying in the creek running west of the airport. I parked the car and ran to the sight of the accident—the battered and lifeless body of my good friend, Ed Sutton, lay amidst the wreckage. I'll never forget that sight as long as I live, although I have seen many others since. According to witnesses, Ed had taken off from one of the cinder runways to the southeast and made his turn to downwind. On downwind the engine was heard to be misfiring. As he turned onto base leg, the airplane stalled and spun in. I still have the control stick from that airplane in my Mini-Museum at Oshkosh."

Milwaukee Student Flier Dies in Plane Crash

—Journal Staff P

EDWARD J. SUTTON (inset), student flier, was killed Sun when his plane, the wreckage of which is shown, crashed side the Milwaukee county airport. Story on page 1, Part I.

Fortunately, this graphic tragedy didn't dampen Paul's enthusiasm for flying.

Ben White had recently purchased a new Piper Cub with a 40 horsepower, Continental engine. Unlike most Cubs, this one came from the factory dressed in shiny black paint, highlighted by bright lemon-yellow stripes running down both sides of the fuselage. Paul began to fly it on local and cross-country flights, adding to his flying time and improving his navigation skills. The latter didn't mean dialing in a radio frequency and following an electronically activated pointer to a destination; it meant learning how to translate the visual panorama unfolding beneath the wings into features depicted on the crude maps he carried in the cockpit. Rare was the civilian airplane that sported a two-way radio, never mind a navigation system. Just maps and good old dead reckoning....

"I made a number of cross-country flights in the Piper Cub. I remember one long flight to Adams, Wisconsin, a distance of some hundred miles or so, and having to let down through an overcast that was several thousand feet thick before I could see the ground. Sometimes I wonder how we and many others of that era ever did it."

Or lived to tell about it!

That fall, Ben moved his operation to Curtiss-Wright Airport in Milwaukee. He also upgraded the engine of his black Cub to produce 65 horsepower. Whether this caused the first wild seed to be planted in our young aviator, we'll never know; but it did signal a subtle change in Paul's solo flying habits....

"Wow—what power! The new engine added to my enjoyment of this wonderful machine. I remember it was the time of the Homecoming football game at West Milwaukee High and I had skipped school (again!)...I just wasn't too interested in football and football stars with their fancy sweaters and numbers. Instead, I went out to the airport, got in the Cub and headed for the playing field. According to many of the kids, teachers—and the principal—I was down pretty close to the goal posts and certainly made my appearance well known. Mr. Barkley, the principal, later had me in for another talk. Fortunately, the CAA never found out!"

The black Cub was registered as NC23254. Thirty-seven years later, Paul built the very first replica J-3 Cuby using plans given to him as a Christmas gift by his wife, Audrey. It wasn't a kit; it was a "plans-built" airplane, and Paul built it "from scratch," as he did so many others. His replica Cuby carries the same registration number and the same black paint scheme with bright lemon-yellow stripes as the Cub he flew back in the late 1930s, except this one has a 90 horsepower engine!

Paul's homebuilt Cuby, NC23254, as it appears today ...a mirror image of the past!

Paul puts his Cuby to good use. It has become a medium through which he shares his enthusiasm for aviation by flying Young Eagles (and others) whenever he can. He recently loaned the aircraft and its use to EAA; many hours were flown by staff and volunteer pilots as they introduced a significant number of Young Eagles to the thrill of flight while demonstrating the aircraft to Pioneer Airport visitors.

Some airplanes end up in museums; some spend all their lives in the air!

"Look Mom, girls can fly too!

Chapter Eleven

Audrey

"If you really want to know my first impression of Howard Poberezny, I guess it could be said that I was not impressed with him at all! He had no outstanding characteristics that would make me notice him. While I took school very seriously, his mind was always elsewhere. While I took pride in my appearance, he apparently did not. I really don't know why I eventually became attracted to him...I think maybe it was because of his persistence."

Audrey Louise Poberezny (nee Ruesch)

A year earlier, in September 1938, a pretty and petite young girl of thirteen made her freshman debut at West Milwaukee High. Her name was Audrey Louise Ruesch, and she had just graduated from

Hillcrest Public School. While she was looking forward to her new environment, another student, a junior named Paul (Howard) Poberezny, entered the school year with a much different attitude, one of disinterest and resignation. He was far more interested in aviation and his rapidly approaching seventeenth birthday than he was in becoming a junior in high school. Nothing had changed on his priority list.

The shy freshman girl and the overconfident pilot soon crossed paths, although nothing much happened between them that first year. For her, it was just another encounter with a junior. But for Paul, it was a lot more....

"At West Milwaukee, one was usually not lost in a maze of students. This is why I soon began to notice Audrey, she a freshman and I a junior. I would observe her coming to school, always extremely neatly dressed and with such a baby face. She would get off the streetcar and walk down the sidewalk to the west entrance of the school. I usually waited around to get a glimpse of her before going into class."

West Milwaukee High School

Audrey recalls the situation from her slightly different perspective....

"I certainly wasn't looking for anybody. He (Howard) was there, but so were a lot of other boys. I went through my whole freshman year without really knowing him."

Paul (Howard) couldn't get Audrey out of his mind; it was a case of love at first sight. He didn't seem to worry about her initial lack of reciprocal feelings. Already known for his tenacity, he had no doubt his dream girl would someday share his life....

"It seemed that I knew her before we ever spoke. It was apparent to me and to everyone else that she was the best dressed girl in school. I soon found out where she lived and that she was the only child of Thomas and Lillian Ruesch."

Here we have all the ingredients for a classic love story—the girl "almost" next door…he with those funny, inexplicable feelings; she doesn't even know he exists! When they finally do meet, they first develop a friendship; romance, courtship and marriage would follow in proper order. Eventually they would achieve the most elusive of all plateaus, that of sharing their lives together. Theirs is a story of friendship, love and trust…a story that has become increasingly rare in our age of fast foods and quick relationships. Today, Paul and Audrey have been married for almost fifty-three years. They are an inseparable team; they are the first family of sport aviation. This is how they became an "item"....

Audrey was the only child of Thomas Nicholas and Lillian Ellen Ruesch. They had met at Heiden's Dance Hall in Milwaukee where Tom often played the concertina. Since both were raised in farm families of German descent, they shared a similar ancestry and work ethic…it wasn't long before they were married!

Tom Ruesch was a handsome man of average build. He came from a family of four that included his parents and an older sister. A hard-working and capable worker, he always gave his vocation an honest return for its wages. As a family man, he was a good provider and a good father—strict, yet fair.

Baby Audrey with her daddy

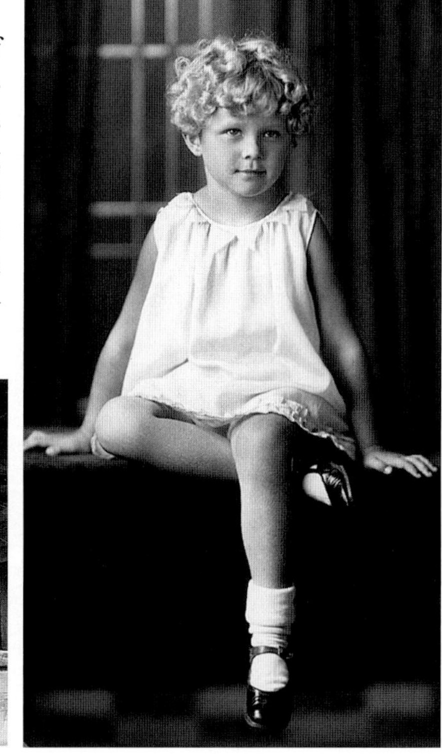

Audrey

The time Tom cherished most was when he was at home with his family. There, he could indulge in a variety of creative pursuits that included reading, fashioning articles out of wood and playing his favorite musical instruments, the concertina and the violin.

Lillian Ruesch, nee Eilbrecht, was one of twelve children—ten girls! Her traditional family upbringing meant that she would learn all the home-making skills such as baking, cooking, sewing, etc. While there may have been a few territorial arguments with her sisters early on, their wardrobes would later provide an unexpected windfall. Lillian was a good wife and mother, and she provided the perfect complement to her husband, Tom. They too were a team.

Tom and his beloved daughter

Audrey Louise was born on January 24, 1925. The Rueschs were proud of their new daughter and dedicated their lives to ensure that she was afforded every possible opportunity within their modest capabilities. Audrey talks about her family's early years....

"Before he married Mom, my dad lived at home with his parents. He built and then operated a gas station and auto repair business on part of the homestead land he had purchased from his parents. When he and Mom got married, his parents' house was remodeled to provide separate living quarters for both families. I vividly remember being bathed in a tub in the huge kitchen near the wood stove where it was always warm.

The Ruesch Family

"Some time later, new living quarters were built for us next to Dad's business and we now had a home of our own. After a few rough years of trying to make ends meet (people were not too good about paying their bills and Dad just couldn't say 'no'), we traded the property to a man who turned it into a bar. He seemed to do much better. We ended up with a house at 3801

South 56th and Forest Home Avenue, and Dad went to work at the Allis-Chalmers Manufacturing Company. Life was much better for us after that."

The move to the modest white frame house on South 56th Street took place when Audrey was six years old. It is critical to our story, because by living at that address, Audrey would eventually attend the same high school as Paul. Later on, this house would host the beginnings of the EAA era. But for now, it was simply the Ruesch family's new home.

Throughout her childhood, Audrey gradually developed a distinctive personality, one that allowed her to confidently pursue a most challenging life. At an early age she learned to accept and adapt to a variety of situations....

Audrey and the boys!

"For a long time, there were only two other girls my age in our neighborhood. As is often the case with three, one is left out. Sometimes it was me, but I didn't let it bother me! I wasn't afraid of being alone or having to look after myself. I'd go climb trees or play ball with the neighborhood boys; they were always around. If they weren't, I'd find my cat and dress her up again.

"That darned cat sure was a neat pet. I'd put all sorts of clothes on her, place her in my baby carriage and push her around the neighborhood. She wouldn't move the whole time; she'd just lie there like a stuffed animal—even when it was a hundred degrees outside! When I took my afternoon nap, I'd take her with me. She would lie quietly, waiting until I was asleep. Then she'd take off and do whatever cats do when they're not being dressed up by little girls! Somehow, she could tell if I was awake or asleep, because I never did see her leave and she was always there when I awoke."

Audrey's cat...undressed!

"Mother and I would often walk the two and a half miles each way to the Catholic cemetery and tend to the graves where Gramma and Grampa Ruesch were buried. While we were there, we usually saw the Catholic Priest, Father Gormley. He always said that I should come and keep house for him; for doing so, he would give me a nickel a day and some ice cream! I'll never forget him because he was such a kind person."

Audrey was learning how to cope with most any situation. It might have been the beginning of an independent streak, or simply a desire to be more self-sufficient. Whatever the basis, these qualities eventually blended into what could be termed her "quiet determination." Audrey Louise would always be her own person, with her own set of rules and her own methods of survival.

Tom Ruesch enjoyed working with his hands. He created furniture and other household items out of pieces of wood fashioned on a small lathe in the workshop he had built in the garage. At other times, he'd tuck a violin under his chin or place a concertina between his hands and play music for hours. Occasionally he moved to the front porch where he entertained the neighbors as well as his own family. It was said that Tom Ruesch had the unique ability to put hand and mind together for his own enjoyment, as well as for others. Audrey adds....

"Dad was very talented. Having had his own automobile repair shop for years, he was mechanically inclined and could fix or make just about anything. He also was an avid reader and a talented musician. I admired him a lot."

Audrey and her mom

Meanwhile, her mother took advantage of the fact that the nearby legion of sisters regularly discarded a considerable amount of good, used clothing. She carefully selected from the items and skillfully remade them to fit her daughter's slim frame. By the time Audrey entered high school, she had a well-deserved reputation for always being well-dressed in public....

"Mom's talents and ambition centered around us. She was a good homemaker, an excellent cook, and a talented seamstress who could make something beautiful out of almost nothing."

To this day, Audrey has faithfully maintained a quality public image. To her, a person's appearance *does* count. Not only can it make for a lasting first impression, but in her case, it also reflects the strong inner person and deep sense of self-confidence and personal pride.

For the Ruesch family, life continued on a pleasant and happy course. Audrey loved her parents and was very close to them....

"We often played music or cards together at home. If we went out, which wasn't often, it was always together, as we didn't have money for baby sitters. But mostly we provided our own entertainment. We didn't have much, but we were always very happy together. I learned that 'love' is much more important than having a lot of things."

Audrey began to pick up on her father's musical ability, except she chose the piano to express her talents. They often played together while her mother served as critic and audience. Unlike her dad's solo presentations on the front porch, their duets were a private experience…something the family kept to themselves. This special time together served to strengthen the bond between them—a bond that would too soon be partially severed by the fragility of life and the unfairness of death!

There was no doubt Paul had been smitten by this diminutive girl with the baby face, the quick wit, and the seemingly endless wardrobe! Yet in spite of his growing attraction, it was some time before he translated his feelings into action. Nothing much happened between them during their first year together at school—except maybe in Paul's mind! But the next year....

"How I exactly 'broke the ice' in talking with Audrey, I don't recall. However, we finally did talk and our friendship began to grow. We talked a lot in school and yet for a long period of time did not date. We passed notes or put them in each other's locker through the little ventilation holes."

There are undoubtedly as many variations to courting as there are couples. When Paul finally gathered up his nerve to visit Audrey at her home, he came face-to-face with a brand new challenge—her parents! He would never forget his first (and only) meeting with Audrey's father....

"When I was able to borrow Dad's car or ride the old Henderson motorcycle, I would drive by Audrey's house, hoping to get a glimpse of her. One evening, I finally gathered up enough courage to visit her at home and I drove past her house several times on my motorcycle.

Audrey and her protective dad!

Finally I stopped, got off, and went up to the door. I was nervous…no, I was really scared—I had never even pushed a doorbell before! Where we lived, the doors were always open; we never locked them. Our neighbors would either knock and walk in, or just walk in without knocking.

"I rang the doorbell. The door finally opened and there was Audrey's dad. He asked me what I wanted. I asked if Audrey was home. He said, 'She went to bed. You come back when you're dry behind the ears!' "

So much for making a good first impression! Historically, a girl's father has always been a tough hurdle, possibly more so in those days! Audrey recalls the incident....

"Actually, I wasn't in bed. I was lying on the couch in the living room, which in our bungalow style home was off to one side and just out of sight of the front door. When the doorbell rang, my dad went to answer it. I heard Howard ask for me and my father's reply. I was embarrassed to go to school the next day, but I soon put the incident out of my mind. Nothing was ever said of it or of Howard again."

Was Tom Ruesch unjust for dismissing Paul in such a brusque manner? Probably not! He had a well-defined set of values and standards and Paul obviously failed to meet them. Even in today's more liberal society, many parents would agree with Tom's swift character assessment and response. When you think of it, here was a seventeen-year-old ruffian who had been cruising up and down the neighborhood on a noisy old motorcycle trying, as he put it, "to gather up enough courage." Now he was standing at the front door, in less than quality attire, asking to see this good man's cherished fourteen-year-old daughter—his only child!

The typical family structure at that time was quite different in that it was unusual to find both parents away at work; at least one of them was always nearby. And because families spent more time together, parents were more involved in their children's daily activities, as Audrey recalls....

"Dad was a very strict but loving father whom I loved and respected very much. Yet even though he was firm, he never laid a hand on me. My mother would give me a swat every now and then, but not him—he never touched me! He did make threats, though. He'd say, 'Look out kid, if I come in there...!' That's all he ever had to say or do. I was so worried about what might happen when he said it, that I never tried to find out. Of course, I can't imagine I was ever that bad anyway!"

Did her family's brand of discipline work? Apparently so. For example, Audrey was allowed to ice-skate every winter evening at Jackson Park as long as she caught the nine o'clock bus home. Her father waited at the bus stop to walk her the two blocks to their home. Even though there was no acceptable excuse for missing the bus, none was ever needed....

...off to Jackson Park

"Things really were different then. I remember as a kid that my mother was fairly strict too. If I came home crying, after being pushed into a rose bush or something, and told her that 'so-and-so' pushed me, first she'd tend to my wounds and then ask, 'And what did you do?' It was never accepted that the deed was done without some blame on my part too!"

Paul adds another observation....

"You also had respect for your neighbors. If they called your parents to tell them you were doing something wrong (as they often had cause to do in those days) then you got it! So many wonderful people today take the side of their kid because they don't have time to know what he or she is doing."

If rules are vague and arbitrarily enforced, the system tends to break down!

When Audrey was barely fifteen years old, her father suddenly died from a heart attack. It was the first real tragedy of her young life....

"Our world came tumbling down on March 26, 1940, when my dad passed away from a massive heart attack. He was forty-two years old and had no previous signs that anything was wrong with him. His death was totally unexpected and we were devastated."

Under this photo, Audrey had written "That Daddy of Mine!"

Tom Ruesch left behind a strong belief in the importance of the family environment and an appreciation of personal discipline. With this legacy, along with the close relationship she maintained with her mother, Audrey developed her own unwavering personal disciplines and family values. Throughout her life, she used them to maintain her dignity and sense of purpose. Looking back, we can see why this young lady was a perfect match for our slightly rough-around-the-edges and often floundering, aviator-dreamer.

Paul remembers the sad occasion....

"I was never able to talk to Mr. Ruesch again, as he passed away from a fatal heart attack not long after our first meeting. His death was a great blow to both Audrey and her mother, and I am sure the feelings and the decisions that had to be made at the time were very, very difficult. It was now only the two of them, although her mother still had a number of sisters, two brothers and both parents living in the area. I remember thinking maybe someday I would marry Audrey and take care of them both...such is the thinking of a young man in love!"

With her father gone, the music also died. It was something special they had enjoyed doing together. But now that she couldn't share it with him, Audrey didn't want to continue....

"I just wasn't interested in playing the piano anymore, not without Dad. I didn't play it again; Mom sold it and that was the end of it. She also decided to rent our house. We moved in with one of her sisters and her family until we could find an apartment. I returned to school, saddened by my loss, while Mom took a job with the Wisconsin Telephone Company. I later imagined how well my dad and Howard might have worked together, what with Howard's interest in building airplanes and Dad's talent of working with wood."

On the porch of her Aunt's Apartment

Audrey and her mother moved into an apartment at 30th and West Pierce. While only a short walk to National Avenue and a brief ride on the street car to school, it was six miles from where Paul lived. But even that failed to alter his determination to continue seeing her!

Love, courting, and the automobile! The automobile was really not invented as a form of transportation: it was created so teenagers could court in private! Because it offered a form of mobile independence, the automobile probably did more to promote budding young romances than any other invention of the early twentieth century—including the darkened movie theaters of West Allis! Of course, in the late thirties and early forties, the high cost and low numbers of these four-wheel laboratories served to hold their use in check....

"During my time at high school, automobiles were scarce. After learning to drive our tan, 1934 Ford V8 sedan with wire wheels, I relied on Dad's good will to let me drive it on occasion. I felt, as did many young men, the thrill of being behind the wheel—learning how to shift and experiencing that wonderful feeling of an expanding world. Sometimes I would create excuses so I could drive. One that worked best was to pour out the remaining bit of milk when no one was looking. I knew I'd soon hear, 'Howard, go get some milk!' Off I'd go to the Bewitz Store at 92nd and National, about two miles away.

"Many of us also had the opportunity to drive the Ford Model T with its three foot pedals, the center one being used for backing up. We learned how to crank-start the engine—and to never place our thumb around the handle in the event of a kick-back!"

Paul's father hadn't enjoyed the luxury of borrowing an automobile while he was courting Jettie, so he was understandably hesitant to allow his eldest son the use of his family's only means of transportation. One day in the not too distant future, his fears would be realized. But for now....

Ready for a big date with Howard!

"I had gotten my driver's license at the age of seventeen and Dad began letting me use the car more often. I must say I still feared him, as he was a very firm man. Often times I would ask Mom to ask him if I could use the car. Most of my use would be to drive to work at the A & P store or go to the airport; later it would be to date Audrey. When we began dating, we often went to nearby West Allis to see a movie. The old Grace Theater was only two blocks from where she lived. Many times when I was not able to use Dad's car, I walked the six miles to take Audrey to the show—and the much longer six miles back! As a good three miles were in the country, I always looked over my shoulder, hoping someone would stop and pick me up. I was too bashful to put my thumb out."

Going to the movies with Paul proved to be a financial setback for Audrey, who has always looked much younger than her years. She explains....

"Until I dated Howard, I could get into the movies for children's prices. When I began going with him, he had to pay full price for both of us. I didn't like that too much, even if it was his money, because after that I always had to pay full price too! Howard was pretty nice when we

went out—except that he always wanted to talk about airplanes! Of course, there wasn't much else to do except go to the movies or to the A & W for a hamburger. We talked a lot about other things...but mostly I listened to his airplane stories!"

What joys a simple pleasure like eating a hamburger can bring to the dating environment! Paul discusses their eating habits....

"In addition to the movies, I would take Audrey out to the airport or over to the county fairgrounds to visit the A & W. We'd sit and talk and savor their delicious hamburgers with raw onions and a big scoop of butter melted over the choice beef. After washing it down with their famous root beer, it was usually time to take her home...Mrs. Ruesch was always concerned about her daughter's timely arrival."

Unlike today, when we often have as many garages attached to our houses as we do bedrooms, a family was then considered fortunate to have one garage and one car—especially a working family still recovering from the depression. It was not unusual for that one automobile to serve many masters. But too many masters can sometimes spoil the automobile....

"One evening I was stocking shelves at the A & P when my close friend and buddy, Eddie Holpher (the one with the Whippet automobile) asked if he could use Dad's car. I had borrowed it myself to go to work. It was a four door, gun-metal gray, 1938 Chevrolet sedan—the first new car Dad had ever owned! I agreed to let Eddie borrow it, although I don't remember why he wanted to use our car rather than his own. Eddie promised to be back at nine o'clock so I could take the car home. After work, I went outside and waited in front of the store. A quarter after nine came and passed, then nine-thirty and nine forty-five. Finally, a West Allis squad car pulled up; leaning out the rear window was my friend Eddie, saying, 'Howie, I wrecked your dad's car!'

"More than a little fear rushed through my body as I got into the squad car. We drove to 92nd and Greenfield where, sure enough, Eddie had wrecked our car. He said he had to swerve to avoid an oncoming car and went off the road—right through a small refreshment stand! There sat Dad's brand new car with pieces of lumber on the roof and scattered all around it.

"Dad was then a foreman at Wenzel & Hennoch, a major sewer construction company in the Milwaukee area whose plant was located

Audrey, Howard and the ill-fated '38 Chevrolet

less than a mile from the accident. Since Dad was working the second shift, the police took me there. He was talking with several of his men when I came over, but he stopped and proudly introduced me to his fellow workers as a young airplane pilot. It was then I told him the sad news.

"I was on foot for almost a year! When I had some extra change, Eddie would gladly drop me off at the A & P store or the airport for my 10 or 15 cents gas money. I didn't get any free rides from Eddie, and yet Dad never received any repayment from the Holpher family for the repairs that had to come out of our family's meager funds."

While Paul may have been forced to walk or hitch rides in pursuit of his other interests, when it came to courting Audrey there was little change. She felt his "grounding" really didn't affect their relationship at all; Paul's dad liked her and would usually let his son have the car for their dates. Sometimes he was able to borrow a car from his friend, Glae Rogers.

Before we leave our courting couple, there is one item we should address. The reason for doing so now, is that the subject will surface throughout the story in one form or another. What we are referring to, is their vastly different standards of dress! Audrey was continually being complimented on her attire, while Paul…well, let's be kind and say his dress reflected the fact that he spent all his money on aviation! To be fair, he came from a poor family; to be critical, he could have done better! Audrey adds....

"No, I certainly wasn't impressed with his dress! What upset me most was that Howard would dress poorly at school. I didn't mind him looking like he did while he was working on his airplanes, but I didn't think it was proper at school or in public. Today, he chooses his daily work clothes; other than that, I select his wardrobe. Even when he travels alone, I always pack for him. If he was left to do it on his own, there would be no telling what sort of costume he'd show up in!"

Paul dismisses his shortcoming....

“At the time I didn’t know that Audrey wasn’t too impressed with my dress. I guess it could have been improved, as I often wore mis-matched colors with my green tweed pants that had both a belt and suspenders.”

One could say that Paul preferred redundant systems—a natural thought for any pilot! Besides, is it not true that opposites attract?

Audrey’s influence is showing!

The owner of this Aeronca C-3 ran out of gas and landed in a field near the DX Station. Howie gladly cleaned and fueled the airplane for the owner, who then took off from the road in front of the station.

Chapter Twelve

Audrey's First Flight... Paul's First Airplane

By 1940, the war in Europe was well underway, providing American newspapers, radio and newsreels with a growing source of information about this latest failure of man to live together. The fast-paced aerial activity shown in the movie newsreels added more fuel to Paul's burning desire for flight. If there was a way he could stay in the air on a continuous basis, he'd do it—even if it wasn't always legal. However, if nobody asks....

"Most of the pilots at Racine, including Mr. Carlisle Godski, operator of the airport, thought I held a Private license. I had passed my Student license off as a Private and no one had ever asked to see it. I soon got a checkout in their new Piper Cub Coupe, a beautiful two-place, side-by-side machine. My idea was to give Audrey her first 'high class' airplane ride."

It is important for a young pilot to demonstrate his special skills to his favorite girl, but it is less effective to do so in a tandem seating arrangement. That's why Paul decided to check out in the side-by-side Cub Coupe. Audrey soon got her first taste of "that vast ocean of air" Paul repeatedly refers to....

"I borrowed Dad's Chevrolet and drove Audrey to Horlick Airport, a small, grass strip located about five miles west of Racine. On September 18, 1940, Audrey had her first airplane ride—an hour and a half flight in a Cub Coupe. We flew up to Muskego Lake, some twenty-five miles to the northwest. It was a place we had often driven for entertainment as they had roller coasters, merry-go-rounds and other amusements. As we circled around the area, I was very proud, although I still felt a bit awkward flying from the left side with my left hand on the stick and my right hand on the throttle. I thought all airplanes were supposed to be flown with the right hand on the stick.

My first airplane ride

"I doubt that Audrey will ever forget the dives and pull-ups—especially the time I pulled the nose up a little too far! The airplane 'whipstalled,' the nose dropped sharply, and up we went against the seat belts—it felt like going over the top of a roller coaster with your eyes closed! I must admit that I, too, was surprised...and discovered another learning experience in the business and pleasures of flying!"

Audrey's comments on her first flight were more succinct....

"I didn't care for that one maneuver, but otherwise it was fun! Flying really never bothered me; I took to it quite well and went for many flights with Howard. Later on, he took his dad and me for a ride in a Waco with a 220 horsepower Wright engine. We were in the front cockpit and Howard was in back. I don't think Grampa felt very comfortable in an open-cockpit airplane.

He certainly wasn't fond of turning. Every time the airplane banked he grabbed my hand...I'm sure he was relieved when it was over."

Europe was being devastated by the powerful war machine that emerged from the ashes of a depression-ravaged Germany. Although the United States was not yet directly involved in the war, the subject was included in most conversations. Rumors and half-truths circulated freely, each adding to the speculation that world war was imminent. If, or rather *when* it occurred, there would be a need for many young men and women to fulfill its horrible destiny. From a distance, innocent teenagers living within the safe confines of their homes and families might mistakenly think war is a glorious affair, or that it is something gallantly fought for honor and right. The present is so easily infected with the ideals of the past....

"While visiting at the Racine airport I met another fine gentleman, a pilot by the name of Ray Crowley. We called him 'Owly' or 'Owly Crowley.' He and I struck up a good friendship and soon began to discuss the many rumors then running through the airports of America, stating there was a need for pilots to fight against Germany. Canada, being tied closely with England, had become a training ground for Commonwealth pilots—the cry had now gone out for volunteers from the United States. Eddie Holpher, who only had a few hours in the air, Owly Crowley and myself decided we should go to Canada and join the war effort.

"Owly" Crowley

"I was in my senior year at high school that October morning in 1940 when the three of us boarded a Greyhound Bus for Detroit and Windsor with only a few dollars in our pockets. I hadn't even told my parents; I just left them a note. I did tell Audrey and Mr. Tangney of my plans, and he had written me a nice letter of recommendation. We took the bus through the tunnel at Windsor and nervously went through Canadian Customs on the other side. The agent must have seen a number of our types come through because he immediately

pointed us in the direction of the recruiting office a few blocks away. We were told there was a chance you could lose your citizenship by joining the Royal Canadian Air Force and serving another country in war time. At the time, we didn't think much about it.

To The Royal Canadian Air Force

Milwaukee, Wis.
1463 So. 52nd St.
Oct. 14, 1940

To Whom It May Concern;

This is to certify that I am personally acquainted with Paul Howard Poberezny, and that I have the highest regard for him as a young man of honesty and truthfulness. And also as a young man very much interested in aviation.

When I first met him as a freshmen in the high school in which I teach, he was very much interested in model planes. Since then he has progressed to the flying of gliders and for the last two years to power flying. At present he holds a Private Pilot's License and has nearly one hundred hours to his credit.

I know that he is very much interested in flying and intends to make that his life's work and that he is the kind of young man that will make good in the flying end of aviation.

I knew Mr. Poberezny for five years and I am very glad to recommend him and I am willing at any time to answer inquiry concerning him.

Respectfully,

Homer Gangney

"We stayed in a little hotel while we were questioned as to our suitability. Owly was rejected because of color blindness, Eddie because his log book didn't show enough time; they returned home with what little money they had left. However, I was accepted and remained behind, all alone in another country. I soon began to get lonesome for Audrey and to think that I might not ever see her again. After a short while I, too, returned home. I decided to go back to school and work at building up my flying time for the future when my country would join the war."

Although it was not Paul's time to serve in the military, he never abandoned his idea of doing so. From now on he would focus on developing his flying skills. So while his peers were trying to scare up money to buy a car, Paul had a much different goal. Automobiles were of interest to him only as a means of getting to and from the airport and Audrey's place. True, he had spent time tinkering with his friend's old Henderson motorcycle, but it was just something to get around on. Aviation was his main interest, and

he wanted an airplane. Besides, is there a better way to get flying experience than in one of your own? The problem would be deciding which one, and who would pay for it....

"I have always loved biplanes. To me a biplane is a more natural design for an airplane. Was I influenced by the World War I airplanes I read about in the pulp magazines, or was it because the Wright brothers' airplane had two wings? For whatever reason, as a young lad, whenever biplanes flew over I always felt a special warmth and love for them—they seemed to be the *real* flying machines.

Paul and the Crites' J-5 Straightwing Waco

"Back in the mid-thirties, an Army pilot would often land at Curtiss-Wright Airport to visit his folks in Wauwatosa. He'd fly over our neighborhood in a Curtiss Falcon or Hawk, probably coming up from Chanute Field, near Rantoul, Illinois. While Eddie Holpher or Billy Ratzmann and I were daydreaming in the fields next to Pleasant Valley Park, we marveled at the machine as it sped by over our heads. The lower wing was shorter than the top, and it had a distinctive, sharp bark coming from the straight exhaust stacks on the Curtiss Conqueror engine. We were sure it was a good 'stunt' plane."

Curtiss Falcon

Even though most of Paul's aviation "firsts" involved monoplanes, he's always had an affinity for airplanes with two wings. It should then come as no surprise that he would choose a biplane as his first flying machine....

"During my trips to Waukesha County Airport, I always noticed one biplane in particular—it was an American Eagle. There were two versions made with the OX-5 engine: a short-nose and a long-nose. (I later learned that the American Eagle factory in Kansas City discovered the short–nose Eagle was tail heavy. To improve its center of gravity, approximately one foot was added to the engine mount.) This Eagle had the long nose and was owned by Dale Crites and his twin brother, Dean, operators of Waukesha Airport and the Spring City Flying Service. The two brothers were well known and regarded as experts in the flying business.

"I continued working at the DX filling station and stocking shelves at the A & P store in order to earn money to support my flying activities. As I was still building model aircraft, I often purchased supplies from a rather large and successful model shop operated by Laverne Garmon. Laverne was an aviation enthusiast who had some flying time in a Cub. I expressed my enthusiasm about the American Eagle to him and stated that the purchase price was $250. He said he was interested in sharing its ownership with me, so I went home to ask Dad if he would loan me $125 to purchase my half. I promised to pay him back from my future earnings. (It was many years before I learned that Dad had gone to the bank and borrowed the money, which was a lot back in 1940. At the time, his salary was around $19 a week, and with that he supported Mom and three children.) But the papers were signed in November 1940 and the airplane was ours. I was a nineteen-year-old senior in high school—the only one with an airplane!

Paul's first airplane - an American Eagle

...it was huge!

"As I sat in the cockpit and looked it over, everything looked so big...no, it was huge! Standing on the wing walk in a slight bend, your head would touch the upper wing—it was a monster! My checkout was given by Dale Crites, who was well known for the volume of his voice while instructing. He would sit in the front seat during his instructional flights. When he wanted to say something in the air, he'd pull the throttle back, turn around, and yell his instructions over the rear windshield to the student in the back seat.

"My first challenge was how to taxi such a big airplane. It was larger than a Stearman, but had no brakes and a tail skid—the use of which has become a lost art today. We taxied out to the east end of the sod runway. Stick forward, full rudder, and a blast to the tail...being careful to determine the radius of the turn and the speed at which one taxied. There was no need to check the mag, as it only had one. Water temperature: normal. Oil pressure: normal. After a look over one's shoulder for other airplanes, apply the throttle. The rpms rose to 800, 1000, 1100, 1200, 1300 and, barely, 1400. After a short run we were airborne. What a thrill!

"The airplane had a rudder bar and a joy stick, both familiar controls from my glider days. Water temperature was controlled by a lever in the cockpit that opened and closed shutters mounted in front of the radiator. The trim tab for the horizontal stabilizer was a large lever on the left side of the cockpit that could be moved back and forth to adjust for nose-up or down trim. In level flight and with the correct propeller, an OX-5 develops 90 horsepower at 1425 rpm. My engine must have been a little tired because it would barely do 1400 rpm, and 20 or 25 rpm more on an OX-5 engine makes a lot of difference! Of course, it doesn't compare to the whirling propellers of today and their much higher revolutions."

Paul's partner - Laverne Garmon

Paul's partner in the Eagle had an enthusiastic attitude, but little flying experience. Manipulating a large biplane with a tail skid, no brakes, and a cranky OX-5 engine, is quite a handful for an experienced aviator, never mind a novice. Yet in spite of Laverne's limited flying background, Paul checked him out in the aircraft. He flew it successfully—for a while....

"Verne certainly was an avid aviation enthusiast and a real fine gentleman. His biggest disappointment came while landing on a small strip over on 124th and Cleveland Avenue. He hit a big boulder that was unseen in the tall grass and badly damaged the landing gear. Though they weren't making the airplanes any more, we sent five dollars to the company in Kansas City to buy a new left landing gear 'V.' It was a lot of work, but we got the airplane jacked up and the new gear installed. Our next task was to get rid of the boulder. When dynamite didn't budge it, we decided to move the airplane. By then, Laverne wanted out of our deal, so I borrowed more money from Dad and the Eagle was all mine!"

Maybe he should have said, "*...and the Eagle was all Dad's!*"

Having one's very own airplane at your beck and call opens up many new horizons: travel, meeting new people, developing your skills as a pilot and a mechanic, and more. Each is part of the unique learning curve that accompanies airplane ownership....

Pilot - and Owner!

"Little did anyone know that the Eagle would be my college education: it gave me opportunities to meet people through forced landings; it provided experience in the maintenance of the engine and airframe; and it helped further develop my piloting skills. The Eagle took me to many places within fifty to sixty miles of Waukesha, which were then great distances for us fledgling pilots and the unreliable engines!

"Slim Schobert, a 6'6" friend, owned an American Eaglet, which is a two-place, tandem, parasol-type airplane manufactured by the same company that built my Eagle. His was powered by a 45 horsepower, three-cylinder, air-cooled Zekely engine. It was always a sight to see Slim get into his little Eaglet and sit there, looking like a giant grasshopper. Another acquaintance, Bud Perry, had purchased Freddie Mattson's short-nose Eagle, and the three of us would often team up to do a little barnstorming. We'd fly over such Wisconsin towns as Burlington, Waterford and Muskego, circle around while 'gunning' our engines, and then land in a farmer's field. Most farmers were proud to have a flying machine land in their fields—but not so today! People came out and we earned gas money by taking them for a ride for fifty cents or a dollar, sometimes a five-gallon can of tractor gas. Even though I was not licensed to carry passengers, I had fun and received a great deal of education."

"Slim" Schobert

American Eaglet

Flying and maintaining an airplane is only part of the package. Unlike earth-bound vehicles such as automobiles, boats and motorcycles, an airplane requires a dedicated environment from which to operate. The skies may be vast empty spaces open to all who accept the challenge of flight, but when it comes time to land, a pilot must be more selective....

"I always envisioned that someday I would have my own airport. There was a big field not too far from our house owned by Patty Ott, the local auctioneer who plowed our garden each year. While his field wasn't the smoothest one around, it was only about a half mile away from our house. It would afford me the opportunity to walk or ride over on my bike and to haul gas from the nearby filling station where I worked. I visited Mr. Ott to see if we could work out a deal.

"He was an older gentleman who lived alone in a house that certainly needed the touch of a housekeeper. He agreed to let me use his pasture if I would provide him with several buckets of coal from Dad's meager coal pile, and a quart or two of Mom's canned pickles or peaches. He also asked that a wider shoe be put on the tail skid so it would not dig up his alsac alfalfa.

"The field was located in the area of 96th and Morgan Avenue, across from a tavern with a picnic ground called Zainer's Grove. How proud I was when some of my buddies from Waukesha Airport flew over and we'd have three or four airplanes parked in front of the tavern and picnic area. This always meant a few more passengers to haul so more fuel and parts could be purchased.

"I was now going quite steady with Audrey, so it was not uncommon for me to land on her grampa's farm out on Colby Road. I remember the first time I did so. As I proudly parked the airplane, he said to the family, 'Stay back, it might kick!' I guess he compared it to one of his horses. Many times I left the airplane on his farm, snuggled up next to the fence leading from the barn to the pasture."

Preparing for another flight

Audrey would occasionally spend Sunday afternoons driving with Paul to the local airports, content to watch as he flew or tinkered with an airplane. When she couldn't go with him, he would often strike out alone in the Eagle....

"I often flew down to Racine in my Eagle, as there seemed to be a lot more activity there on weekends. It was typical of small airports of the day: several old hangars surrounded by a wide, flat field. You'd see Monocoupes, Wacos, Fleets, and one time, an old Standard biplane. I always felt proud to sideslip in over the fence and put the Eagle down in a three-point attitude. After a short roll, I'd blast the tail around and taxi up to the fence by the auto parking lot."

Now that Paul was becoming quite skilled at guiding his airplane around the skies, the importance of presenting a proper image began to materialize. Those years he spent reading about heroic pilots and their exciting adventures had left their mark; he realized that his basic uniform of dirty bib overalls and greasy shirts needed a little help. A Roscoe Turner he was not, but one has to start somewhere....

"There were always spectators at Racine, sitting in their cars and admiring (or so I thought) the pilots and their airplanes. I figured it would be a nice touch to have a cigar stuck in my mouth! I'd seen a lot of other pilots do it and, although I didn't care for the smoke, it seemed like the thing for me to do too! One Sunday afternoon I left Patty Ott's field and headed out on the twenty mile trip to Racine. I landed, taxied up to the fence, and very proudly got out with a cigar stuffed in my mouth. Surprise! Standing there were Mom, Dad and a couple of their friends. Just by chance, they had taken a Sunday drive to the Racine airport. I gulped, and out of my mouth came the cigar. Dad never said anything...I guess it was another step towards manhood."

The longer a person operates a mechanical device, the more likely it is to require maintenance. Early airplane engines were not always noted for their durability and that, along with the relative inexperience of our youthful operator, soon dictated the need for a major overhaul of the Eagle's weary powerplant....

"My OX-5 engine was getting tired; the valve guides were worn and sloppy, as were the rocker arms. I needed a new engine and I began saving my meager dollars toward that day. I learned about one in excellent condition up in Larsen, Wisconsin, not too far northwest of Oshkosh. I called one of the Larsen Brothers who owned the OX-5 airplanes and parts. He said he had an engine that he'd let go for ten dollars—how much would it be worth today? I borrowed Dad's car and drove up there pulling a trailer; we loaded the engine and I brought it home.

Final stages of the engine change.

"Eddie Holpher, who was also very mechanically inclined, said he'd help me with my first engine change. The airplane stood behind Patty Ott's house and we had no hoists and no way to get the old engine off the airframe. Then we found one. By rolling the airplane over to a nearby ditch and dropping the wheels into it, we brought the engine down to a reasonable height. With the help of some neighborhood kids, it was soon off. We were careful not to take too much apart.

"With old and new engines side-by-side, we matched those parts we had taken off to where they had to go back on. I took the expansion tank home, cleaned it, and painted it bright red. The engine mount was then cleaned and repainted silver. Once again using local kids, we installed the new engine and put everything back together."

The true test of a mechanic's faith in the work he or she performed on your equipment is to ask that person to go with you on the first test flight! However if you serve as both pilot and mechanic, then you have automatically accepted the dual role. You have no one else to turn to, and no one else to blame....

"Next came the test hop, which happened to be on a day I hadn't gone to school! We did some run-ups and found the engine performed quite well: it actually had a few more rpm than the old one! I taxied over to the northeast corner of Patty Ott's field, swung around into the wind and opened the throttle. The few extra revolutions gave a feeling of increased power and after a short run we were airborne. I circled the field for fifteen minutes, waving to Eddie and the neighbors to let them know all was going well—but I knew where I was going next!

"I turned northeast and followed Beloit Road toward my school, some five miles away. It was late afternoon; the dismissal bell would soon ring and I was hoping Audrey would come out of school and see the big biplane circling overhead. After two turns, the engine sudden-

ly began to misfire and lose power. What a predicament...I had to land quickly! About a block away was an empty field next to the old Chain Belt Company. I swung around, glided in for my landing, and rolled to a stop, all the while wondering what went wrong. I didn't want to go into the school but I knew Eddie would be wondering where I was...I must get to a telephone.

"As I got out of the cockpit, lo and behold, along comes a police motorcycle with a sidecar, driven by a short gentleman in the uniform of the day—puttees around his legs, blouse, gunbelt, and the familiar hat with a bill on it. It was none other than Mr. Uebelacker who, besides his duties as a West Milwaukee Police Officer, served as our truant officer. I was already quite familiar with him from earlier times, as well as having listened to him play the clarinet in Billy Buech's Polka Band. It was apparent to him that I was in the wrong place at the wrong time, and I couldn't disagree!

"He queried me about my situation. I told him what had happened and that I had to get in touch with Eddie and tell him to bring some tools so we could make any needed repairs. He agreed, saying he would wait and guard the airplane, as people were now beginning to arrive. I went into the school to use the telephone just as the dismissal bell rang. I know I was not a pretty sight with my greasy bib overalls, greasy hands, and still wearing my helmet; when I spotted Audrey, I could see by the look on her face that she was not too impressed either!"

An accurate observation! Audrey comments on the incident....

"At the time I'm sure I didn't realize what skills it took to land the airplane in that small field. But even though I was not thrilled at Howard's appearance as he walked toward me, I admit I was feeling a bit proud of him!"

Paul might have felt proud too, had he not a sick airplane to worry about....

"I made my call to Zainer's Grove and asked them to tell Eddie I had landed in the Chain Belt field by the high school and that he should meet me there with the tools. Then I returned to the Eagle. As he didn't know what to do with my airplane, Mr. Uebelacker took me to the West Milwaukee Police Station in his sidecar. He and the Police Chief decided that in the interest of safety, the wings should be removed and the airplane hauled away. They didn't think that it would be safe to take off and fly over the houses in the area. I certainly did not go along with their idea, but at the time, I felt kind of helpless and did not object.

"By the time we got back to the airplane, a lot of people were there, including Audrey, many of my classmates, and even some teachers. I thought I might try the engine one more time—sort of a 'ground check' to satisfy Mr. Uebelacker! With stones placed in front of the wheels, I climbed up to the cockpit to crack the throttle and turn on the switch, and then jumped down to give the prop a swing. To my surprise, it fired right off!

"I listened to the engine: there was no misfiring. I kicked the stones away from the wheels and jumped into the cockpit without saying a word to anyone, hoping they would believe I was just going to check the engine out. I must admit to feeling a bit like a hero, sitting in the open cockpit with all my friends and buddies standing around and staring in amazement—the only kid in school flying!

Coming in for a landing.

"I ran the engine up a bit and the airplane started to move. I pushed full rudder, full stick forward, blasted the tail around, opened the throttle, and was soon away—there was no need to dismantle the Eagle now! I circled the field one time, waved, and then headed southwest out Beloit Road...all the time wondering what could have gone wrong. Was it carburetor ice, water in the fuel, or possibly bad spark plugs? As I neared Patty Ott's field, it happened again! The engine began misfiring and losing power, and the airplane started losing altitude. Fortunately, I was close enough to make the field without difficulty.

"Eddie was still there and hadn't gotten my message; he was worried and was wondering what had happened to me. I told him the story and we decided to take a closer look. Off came the cowl. A quick look at the single Berling magneto told the story. There was water around the area where the spark plug wires went into the magneto, shorting it out. But where did the water come from? We started the engine. With Eddie in the cockpit, I climbed up on the wing. Standing on the front flying wire fitting, I immediately saw our problem—a small hole beside the water temperature bulb fitting on the expansion

tank. From it, water was squirting back onto the magneto. I guess my soldering job had not been the best. We made the necessary repairs and went home...I dreaded having to go to school the next day!

"Sure enough, the next morning was similar to so many others I had experienced before, reporting to Mr. Schwei, the detention officer, and Mr. Uebelacker. As expected, they did their duty. Yet when I think back, they did it with compassion. Maybe, just maybe, they knew this was the beginning of an aviation education!"

One of the teachers at West Milwaukee High during this period was Sylvia Becker (later Becker-Shimon). She remembered Paul's aerial intrusion....

> While there must be many pages of stories (about Paul) that could be written, one in particular stands out in my mind. It occurred on the day the students were urged to choose and dress like characters (real or imaginary) from literature or history. They would then go to the stadium where the best would be picked and given some sort of reward. Of course, 'Howie' was absent that day.
>
> That afternoon we were compelled to watch a rare sight over the grandstand—someone was flying an orange 'crate' around and it threw everyone into a state of fear! When the so-called plane landed, Homer Tangney took the young man into the office where he was lectured, no doubt, by Mr. Barkley (principal). Homer was fond of Howie so he would not find a means to punish him. At any rate, whatever punishment was meted out, it was for most of us, a big joke. I often wonder about adorable Audrey and how she is doing. What a delight she was! But that Howie...he was different!

By now Paul had flown quite a variety of different aircraft, including the Porterfield, Piper Cub and Cub Coupe, Waco 10, Stinson SM-8, Funk E, Monoprep, American Eaglet and, of course, his American Eagle. It was time for another new adventure!

Audrey preparing for flight in an OX-5 Waco

Chapter Thirteen

Paul's First Homebuilt Flight... And Busted!

To a young lad full of the joy of flight, having to deal with a government agency was not only foreign, but potentially confrontational. Paul was flying with a Solo license, which was one level higher than Student. It meant he had successfully demonstrated landings and takeoffs to a CAA Inspector and passed a short verbal discussion on how to navigate with a sectional map. Solo pilots were not permitted to carry passengers and were limited to flying within 100 miles of their home airport.

After Solo came Private, Limited Commercial, Commercial, and Air Transport. Each was further broken down into categories for both single (S) or multi-engine (M), with increasingly higher numbers being assigned to the more complicated airplanes. The Solo license was discontinued before the war and the numbered categories later changed to a horsepower rating system....

"The pre-war CAA pilot license structure was more than a little complicated. For some reason, aviation was attracting regulatory interest far in excess of any other mode of transportation. Cars, boats, even motorcycles, have never been subjected to the same degree of bureaucratic interest as have airplanes. The question is, why? Understandably, when an airplane is used as a means of public transportation, safety must be a major concern and government should get involved as it does with other forms. But for private aviation, which compares with owning an automobile or a boat (except there is another dimension added), why is it we have so much regulation and manpower assigned to its operation?

"Being forced to have mechanics with two separate ratings thoroughly inspect an airplane every year seems to be more than a little overkill. And for those who fly (drive) an airplane, to have to undergo a physical examination and a proficiency check at least every two years (at considerable personal expense), places more burden on aviation than would ever be accepted by automobile owners. The irony is that we accept being in an earth-bound vehicle at closing speeds well over 100 mph, separated by maybe five or six feet from a head-on collision with a driver who could be talking on a portable telephone, putting on makeup, watching TV—or is drunk! But let an airplane go one minute over its annual inspection, or a pilot fly with an expired medical, and you have a field day for attorneys."

"Once I acquired my American Eagle, I flew it mostly from local fields such as Patty Ott's, Audrey's grampa's, and a field at 124th & West Cleveland Avenue. After I began to feel more comfortable with the airplane, I ventured further away from home, soon landing at other fields and airports. I was flying in and out of Waukesha Airport quite a bit when I met a gentleman by the name of Ben Turna. Ben was six or seven years older and owned a very nice OX-5 powered Waco 10. He let me fly it many times and I was impressed with its appearance and performance—it was a lot classier than some of the other biplanes of that period. Ben lived with his parents in Wind Lake, Wisconsin, a small community surrounded by several beautiful lakes, located fifteen to twenty miles southwest of Milwaukee. His parents operated a small tavern there.

"Ben had just purchased a homebuilt airplane built by the Munson Brothers. The airplane was complete but hadn't flown. As he didn't have much flying experience, Ben asked if I would test hop it. To me, an airplane was an airplane and I readily agreed. It was stored at Ben's place in a nearby building he used as his airplane workshop, so I drove out to look at it. The *Munson Special* was a two-place, open cockpit parasol wing machine with a 90 horsepower, five-cylinder, air-cooled Warner swinging a cut-down, steel Hamilton propeller. There was no shock absorbing system on the landing gear and the wheels were solid aluminum, having come off a midget race car. To get ready for this big event, I spent $1.98 on a new shirt and pants from Penney's. Khaki seemed to be the appropriate color for this test pilot-to-be!

"The task of assembling the airplane began. The tail group had already been installed, so it was now just a matter of hanging the wings. As they were getting ready to do so, they discovered the bolts to the pylon-type center section were missing. It was down to Ben's shop

for some rod. They threaded both ends, put a nut on one, and hammered it over. In a matter of thirty minutes, four wing-bolts were made. Of course it was crude and certainly not up to today's standards.

"Ben decided they would tow the airplane the two blocks from his shop to a field just north of Turna Tavern, across the street from a public picnic ground. Billy Ratzmann drove me out to the site in his dad's Model T Ford...I can still hear the banging and chugging of that famous automobile. It was early afternoon before the airplane was ready and a large crowd had gathered from the picnic area, including local farmers and some folks just driving by. We ran the engine and it sounded good. I must admit to feeling quite proud sitting in this unproved airplane—a real honest-to-goodness test pilot who had no idea what was about to happen to him next!

Ben Turna and the "Munson Special"
Paul's first homebuilt...and first test flight!

"After several ground runs and a couple of trips to the filling station for auto gas, we were ready. The narrow airstrip was approximately 1500 feet long. Getting one of the old biplanes in wouldn't be much of a problem but it would turn out to be more than a challenge for the *Munson Special*! As the airplane had no brakes, the magneto check before takeoff was limited. I opened the throttle and began to bounce heavily across the rough field. As we lurched into the air, the nose wanted to keep climbing. I pushed forward on the stick, while at the same time grabbing the lever on the left side of the cockpit to adjust the horizontal stabilizer trim. I quickly found that as I pushed the trim lever forward, which should have been the proper movement, the airplane wanted to climb even more. With some concern, I reversed direction and was able to trim the aircraft to my satisfaction. Apparently the trim system was designed exactly opposite to what I had been used to. However, I caught it, made my adjustments, and began a slow, circling climb over the airstrip.

"The engine ran very well and I continued circling for fifteen or twenty minutes, watching the people on the ground wave their handkerchiefs and hats. Everything seemed to be fine, so I decided to make my approach for landing. As I swung around into the wind to land, I began to realize the field was a lot shorter than what I felt was needed for this airplane. With no brakes, a safe landing may not be possible. What to do? I thought of Audrey's grampa's field and headed east for the Eilbrecht farm, knowing it was Sunday and that Audrey and her mom would probably be there visiting her grandparents. I circled the farm, and the folks in the front yard waved; but Grampa Eilbrecht's farm was not suitable for the *Munson Special* either. What to do next? Should I dare cross 'no-mans land'—the civil airways—where unlicensed airplanes were not permitted to fly?

"With all the commotion that had been stirred up in our area about homemade and unlicensed airplanes, I was very apprehensive about crossing this imaginary line. But I had to go somewhere before I ran out of gas and ideas, so I headed for Brown Deer Airport on the north side of Milwaukee, feeling that everyone in the world was looking at me. It was a typical busy Sunday afternoon and a large number of airplanes were there. Bob Huggins, another skillful pilot, was the Chief Flight Instructor at the airport.

"I circled, found a break in the traffic, landed and taxied up near the fence where the automobiles and spectators were parked. It was not long before the airport manager was next to the airplane, telling me I had to leave. He said that Milwaukee County had an ordinance stating there could be no flying of homemade airplanes. He also said that if the Sheriff should happen to come by, my airplane would be impounded and I would be arrested. It sounds much like it does today, with all the many FAA restrictions and enforcement actions. He said he would give me a prop, but that I should leave as soon as possible.

"Back in the cockpit, the engine started easily. I taxied out and took off, feeling apprehensive and wondering where I would go next. Should I go back across the airways and find a field closer to Wind Lake? I was sure everyone was wondering where I had gone, and that Ben was concerned about his airplane. As I continued my climb, I thought of the West Bend Airport, as I had been there several times. Having no map, I flew west until I recognized the familiar road running from Milwaukee to West Bend. From there I turned north and headed for the airport just east of the town. It was getting late. As I circled the airport, I observed only a few parked airplanes, no cars in the parking lot, and no signs of any movement around the hangar.

"I turned into the wind, touched down, and rolled to a stop well short of the river that runs along the south side of the airport. I taxied back, found a spot and tied the airplane down. Nobody was around, so I walked three miles into town, stopping at the first open filling station. I had no money, but the owner helped me place a collect call to Turna's tavern. I told Ben's dad what had happened and asked him to tell Ben I was leaving the airplane at West Bend and hitchhiking home. He said he would tell him. I'm sure Ben was relieved at hearing his airplane was safe and still in one piece.

"I thanked the gentleman at the filling station for his assistance and for the soda pop he gave me, and walked toward home, hoping to get some rides. It was almost midnight before I got there…with a few short rides it had taken me four and a half hours! Mom and Dad were still up as they had been very worried; they hadn't heard from me all day and knew I was going to fly this homemade airplane.

"The *Munson Special* sat at the West Bend airport for about a week. I wanted to move it to Waukesha, but I knew the CAA Inspector drove by that airport every day on his way to work. While I was still afraid of getting caught, I thought that if I got up real early in the morning and had Eddie and Billy drive me to West Bend, I could sneak the airplane into Waukesha. By taking the propeller off and making the airplane appear unairworthy, the inspector might think somebody just brought it out to run it up and taxi it at a later time.

"We left before daybreak, arriving just as the sun was coming up over the horizon. After pouring five gallons of DX auto gas into the fuel tank, Eddie turned the propeller and the engine roared to life. After a short warm-up, I told them I'd see them at Waukesha Airport, taxied out, opened the throttle and was soon gone. The cockpit seemed a bit windy, even though I had my helmet on (I still didn't have the money to buy goggles). Flying along in the smooth air, I was overcome with the beauty and freshness of the morning and the vivid greens of the fields passing below. As I flew by Holy Hill, a tall peak on which is constructed a monastery, I waved to the monks and they waved back. It was a feeling of freedom I will never forget...the cool, clear, morning air and the visibility for miles and miles.

"I circled Waukesha airport and quickly landed. No one was around, so I parked up against the fence amongst Freddie Mattson's short-nose Eagle, Jimmy Miles' OX-5 Swallow, several Waco 10s and a long-nose Eagle we called *Anteater.* The airplane got its name because the nose had been lengthened considerably to provide proper weight and balance for the light, five-cylinder, air-cooled Kinner engine that

was now installed. I had tied some tools to the front seat; while I waited for my buddies, I took the propeller off and laid it between the wheels, under the belly. They soon arrived and we all headed back to Ghost Alley.

"The airplane sat there for several weeks. During my many visits, no one ever mentioned anything about it. I still wanted to fly the *Munson Special* from Patty Ott's field: it was so close to my home and out of the way. Besides, after penetrating the airways twice, I was confident I would not be caught by the dreadful CAA...another early morning departure was planned.

"After the fifteen mile drive to Waukesha, the propeller went back on; Eddie swung the prop and I took off, headed for Patty Ott's. My American Eagle had balloon tires and shock chords, which made landing in farmer's fields much easier on the landing gear—and the pilot! It was quite a different case with the *Munson Special*, as it had no shock struts. The high pressure tires on those midget race car wheels made for a very bumpy landing. The *Munson Special* and its pilot felt every jolt! After landing, I decided to taxi the airplane home and park it in the vacant lot across the street. This entailed some fancy footwork and blasting of the throttle to taxi the seven blocks up the gravel road to Ghost Alley. I was followed by a number of neighborhood kids and adults, wondering what that crazy Poberezny lad was going to do next.

The "Munson Special" parked at Waukesha.

"Less than a week later, as I was getting ready for school, there was a knock on the front door. I went to answer it, but upon looking out the window, saw an automobile that made chills run up and down my back. It was a gray 1940 Plymouth Coupe and I knew exactly who owned it—Mr. Al Goddard, the CAA Inspector! I didn't have to wonder why he was there! My mother went to the door and I have to admit I was plenty scared. I heard him ask if I was there. Mom said I was getting ready for school and could she help. He explained that he had seen a homemade airplane at Waukesha airport on his way to work.

Since he also used Oklahoma Avenue, he noticed the same airplane was now sitting here among the houses and he was kind of wondering how it got here. Sensing he wasn't about to get any more information, he thanked Mom and left. Instead of getting into his car, he walked across the street and hung a red tag on the *Munson*'s ignition switch, grounding the aircraft."

He was kind of wondering how it got there! A simple thought indeed, yet possibly one not so innocently left behind to tighten the knot of fear that was growing like a cancer in Paul's stomach. Just like it's not good to fool with Mother Nature, it's nearly impossible for a young "wet-behind-the-ears" pilot to fool the clever watchdogs of the mighty federal government *all* the time! Paul's plan was full of holes and he finally got caught! The subject of this apparently innocuous visit would one day cause him to leap from the frying pan into the fire....

"Owly Crowley and I were always doing a little barnstorming. Several times I loaned him my Eagle so he could cover a couple of fairs in the Elkhorn and Burlington areas. He had a private license and could legally carry passengers; I had my student license and could not. I must admit, however, to working a few local fields in order to raise money for fuel and oil, the two major items needed to keep the old Eagle going!

"As I hadn't heard anything from the CAA or Mr. Goddard for some months, I felt that my flying a homemade airplane in the civil airways had been forgotten. Maybe the war clouds on the horizon had busied those at CAA so they didn't have time to worry about homemade planes. I was wrong! A letter eventually came addressed to me from Mr. Goddard, stating he would like to talk to me about some alleged incidents relative to my flying, and could I stop in at the CAA Office at Milwaukee County Airport to discuss the matter with him within five days? Real fear now swept through my body! It was worse than sitting in a dentist's chair!

"I borrowed Dad's car and arrived at the old wooden CAA building on the north side of Milwaukee airport. The building was no bigger than a large house and served as the CAA office as well as the airline terminal. The familiar secretary we knew only as Hazel was there as she was for many, many years, working first for the CAA, and later, the FAA. A fine lady, she told me to sit down; that Mr. Goddard would be available soon. After about an hour that seemed like days, I was invited in to discuss the matter of my flying with Mr. Goddard. He said I might as well tell him the whole story and he'd see what he could

do to help me. (I would recall this moment each time I heard the term, 'We're from the FAA and we're here to help you!' It's a phrase well known among aviation people these days!)

"I began my story about test-flying the *Munson Special*: crossing the civil airways enroute to Brown Deer, West Bend and Waukesha airports and ending up in the vacant lot across the street from our house. I felt some relief at having it removed from my conscience. It was then Mr. Goddard told me that wasn't what he wanted to talk to me about—it was my flying the Eagle and carrying passengers on a certain weekend in Burlington that had been brought to his attention! I suddenly realized I had told him something I shouldn't have! He had not even asked about the *Munson Special*! His concern about the passenger flying incident could easily be answered, for it was Owly Crowley with his private license who had been flying my Eagle, not I. I explained this to Mr. Goddard, but his attention was now on the other matter: flying an unlicensed homemade airplane in a civil airway!"

CIVIL AERONAUTICS BOARD
WASHINGTON

December 5, 1941

REGISTERED

Mr. Howard Poberezny
Route 11, Box 129
West Allis, Wisconsin

Dear Sir:

On December 5, 1941, the Civil Aeronautics Board revoked student pilot certificate No. 194438 held by you.

A certified copy of the Board's order is enclosed herein.

For your information, section 20.311 of the Civil Air Regulations provides:

"No person whose pilot certificate has been revoked shall apply for or be issued a pilot certificate of any grade or rating for a period of one year after the revocation, except as the order of revocation may otherwise provide."

Very truly yours,

C. Z. German

C. Z. German, Chief
Suspension and Revocation Section

Attachment

On September 3, 1941, the first registered letter arrived in Ghost Alley addressed to: Howard Poberezny, Route 11, Box 129, West Allis, Wisconsin. Its contents indicated the local CAA office was recommending Mr. Poberezny forfeit his pilot license. Working at typical bureaucratic break-neck speed, the suspension became effective December 5, 1941...two days before Pearl Harbor! It read, "That the careless disregard for the lives and safety of others and the disregard for the CAR's manifested by the Respondent would constitute sufficient cause to justify refusal at this time to issue to Respondent any type of pilot certificate." In other words, Paul could not hold a flying license of any kind for a period of one year. He was grounded! This lesson from the "school of hard knocks" confirmed that his aviation "degree" was not only costly, it was downright painful! But that didn't stop him from flying!

Waukesha Airport is located approximately twelve miles west of Milwaukee and today boasts two paved runways, a control tower and several other facility upgrades. But in the late thirties and early forties....

"Waukesha Airport began as a hayfield from which Jennies and other old OX-5 powered biplanes flew. Located a mile or so north of the city of Waukesha, it was at one time some ten or twelve miles west of the outskirts of Milwaukee. As one looks down from the air today, it seems as if Waukesha has merged with Milwaukee into one massive community.

Waukesha Airport

"The airport had a beautiful old hangar made of lannon stone carried from the nearby cities of Lannon and Sussex, Wisconsin. Built in 1934 by the WPA (the Work Projects Administration, a depression-era government 'make-work' program), it housed many famous airplanes during its lifetime. The airport had two grass strips: one running in front of the hangar on a westerly heading, the other on an uphill slope heading toward the city in a southerly direction. It was not uncommon to see airplanes start at the hangar and roar full power in the direction of the pilot's choosing. This is something one normally would not see today, what with having to taxi to the end of a fixed concrete runway or, on a controlled field, move step by step to the commands of someone never seen, only heard through your headset."

Airplanes that were not built by an approved aircraft company were seen by many (even some within aviation) in a negative light. As they became increasingly unwelcome tenants at the major airports, the owners of these modified and homebuilt airplanes sought refuge in outlying fields. Waukesha was one of the first homebuilt "reliever" airfields in the Milwaukee area, and Paul remembers it well....

"In the early thirties, Waukesha Airport was known for its many homemade airplanes that were built in the Milwaukee area. There were creations of all shapes and sizes—reflections of man's imagination, with motorcycle and airplane engines of various names powering what the newspapers then called 'crates.' This was hand and mind building aviation, and it was these activities that left such a great impression on me. I admired those who produced the designs, performed the woodworking or welding, and used whatever materials were then available to build their airplanes. All too often our society expects something to be produced perfectly at the first attempt.

"I am very proud of the homebuilt movement. It has caused airplanes to be smaller, faster, and better, although maybe not quite as comfortable at first! The movement has provided industry with engineers, mechanics and pilots who have a real appreciation and a love for aviation. It was a wonderful feeling to be around and watch men such as Bob Huggins, the Crites brothers, Irv Miller, Al Luft and others. Some, like Herman R. 'Fish' Salmon, went on to attain national attention ('Fish' became a very famous Lockheed test pilot). Indeed, being around these people as a young boy made a great impact on me."

The public has always been susceptible to influence from the media. In turn, the media can easily be swayed by well-intentioned, yet too often, retrospective, individuals. When it comes to airplanes, which are a popular target anyway, there are few things more fragile in the vicious world of public opinion than a homebuilt or experimental airplane....

"After several fatal accidents at Waukesha airport involving homemade airplanes, our well-meaning citizens and city officials began to take a harder look at homemade planes on homemade wings. Soon, both the Milwaukee and Waukesha airports banished unlicensed airplanes. However, five miles north at Sussex, Wisconsin, stood a little grass field with old, tin-covered hangars that appeared to be stuck into the side of a wooded area. It was called Outlaw Field. Although not very large, it had a certain touch of nostalgia to it. More important, it provided a place where we could hide from the public eye and fly! Along with many others, I moved my Eagle to Outlaw Field. From there, Slim Schobert, Bud Perry and I had much fun.

Flying out of Outlaw Field

"When I lost my license, it was not legal for me to operate my licensed American Eagle. Airplanes either had to have an NC number, which meant the airplane could be maintained for commercial purposes, or an identification number from the Department of Commerce. I sent a telegram to the Department of Commerce telling them to remove the 'NC' from its registration, keeping only the numbers 211N.

"Al Luft, an early day homebuilder, owned a number of airplanes; one of them was a Kari-Keen. The little monoplane had a Comet engine that was made in Madison, Wisconsin, and a control stick that hung from the ceiling —a rather unusual arrangement! One day, Bud Perry and I took off from Outlaw Field, I in my Eagle and Bud in the Kari-Keen. After taking off to the west and reaching an altitude of about 200 feet, Bud's engine quit. The airplane stalled, did a half turn spin, and crashed into the railroad tracks. I quickly landed and ran to the scene. The airplane was totally demolished, but Bud was still alive, having received severe cuts around his face and head and nothing else. Someone called an ambulance and off he went while a number of us towed the wreckage off the track in the event a train came through. Bud later went on to serve in Ferry Command along with Freddy Mattson, another pilot from Outlaw Field. Sadly, both men lost their lives in aircraft accidents during World War II."

Being an "outlaw" had its pros and cons, much like any other non-approved occupation. The positive side was that Paul was still flying airplanes, although there weren't any logbook entries to verify it! The negative side was having to constantly worry about getting caught by the CAA....

"Though we didn't have licenses, we frequently took our friends for rides from Outlaw Field. We were brave because we figured we knew Mr. Goddard's car. One day, a gray automobile pulled up while Bud Perry was circling the airport. He was flying his boss from Presteel Tank where Bud worked the third shift, as I now did for Allis-Chalmers. Bud quickly flew northwest for three or four miles, landed, in a farmer's field and dropped off his passenger, telling him he would be back shortly to get him. He returned to Outlaw Field and landed, only to find the car was not Mr. Goddard's, just a curious spectator who had stopped to look at the airplanes. Bud wheeled around and took off again, heading northwest to find his passenger. Unfortunately, he couldn't remember in which field he had left him! Returning with an empty cockpit, Bud wondered what was going to happen next. Several hours later his boss arrived—on foot! I don't think he will ever forget his first airplane ride!"

As this chapter draws to a close, Paul reminisces about having the opportunity to participate in what is affectionately called, the "Golden Age" of aviation. He and his fellow aviators were fortunate to have been a part of this era. Like so many other things, aviation soon would change forever....

"We had so many enjoyable times at all the smaller local airports and farmer's fields we dropped into—those were the days when aviation was really fun. You could look across the fence or walk behind it to see, touch, and smell the airplanes. You were welcomed with enthusiasm, for you were looked at by those who flew as another potential pilot and friend, not as a threat! In turn, you looked at them as heroes of the sky. How different it is today!

"But that is progress in the eyes of many. Yet when one compares the performance specifications of today's basic, factory-produced airplanes to those of many years ago, the actual improvement is not that great. Those early biplanes powered by 90 horsepower OX-5 water-cooled engines burned six to seven gallons per hour and carried three people at 85 mph. They also could land and takeoff in a third of the distance. Certainly the factor of reliability has improved, as has comfort. But not so performance, considering the large number of years in which to do so. The final test might be to answer the question, 'Would you buy an automobile that starts like an airplane engine?' "

The days of personally accepted risk and reward were rapidly disappearing. Soon the country would be embroiled in another world war. This war would, by its very nature, compel the nation's industrial complex to achieve staggering technological advances, many of which were not yet on the drawing boards. Such an impressive increase in activity would eventually drive society into a never-ending search for improvement at almost any cost. The end would always justify the means, as long as it meant the final result was going to be faster, cheaper...or more deadly. But even worse, the Golden Age of aviation was about to be lost to history!

The Wings Club

Before we enter the wartime period, a brief look at Paul and Audrey's senior yearbooks might add insight into the innocent times they were about to leave behind. The 1941 edition of the West Milwaukee High School Yearbook pictures Paul, at last a graduating senior, wearing a coat and tie and looking very much at ease as he posed with fifteen fellow members of the Wings Club. The way he projected himself into the camera lens gives an early indication of the strong sense of purpose waiting to be unleashed.

It was common practice for the senior class to "will" something of a personal nature through the pages of the yearbook…a lasting reminder in print of those wonderful years spent at high school! This written legacy was called the "Senior Will." Across from Howard Poberezny's name was written, "wrecked glider to anyone who needs a bed sheet!"

Why there was no mention of his attendance record after his sophomore year is unclear, for it certainly was an unusual one. On his own, Paul had decided that Mondays were reserved for the pursuit of his own personally directed, aviation "college degree." He or his mother would write notes excusing him from school—a procedure that continued unabated until his delayed graduation. (In addition to mandatory summer school, Paul needed one extra year to complete high school.) Of course, Audrey had her own opinion....

"Howard skipped school every Monday, which I thought was terrible. I believed that when you were of school age, you went to school. I certainly would never have thought of doing such a thing; in fact, I rarely missed a day—even for illness!"

A year later when Audrey graduated, her Senior Will proclaimed, "stylish and fashionable clothes to Miss Wendlandt!" Whether Miss Wendlandt's lack of interest in her own apparel justified this verbal lashing, is of little interest. Its' importance lay in documenting Audrey's high standard of dress, standards that she justly defends....

"I admit I was always pleased to receive the compliments of teachers and students alike because my mother had put a lot of time and effort into keeping me dressed as nice as she possibly could—and I was proud of that!"

For Paul and Audrey and many others, this era of innocence would never be repeated. True, it had been sprinkled with a few cruel lessons, but it was a time of more personal freedom, latitude, and hope. It was growing up, courting, flying, making friends, and planning for the future. Yet all of a sudden, many of these things were out of step with the world situation. It was time to go to war!

Private Poberezny checks out an L-1.

Chapter Fourteen

The War Years (an overview)

The war years brought disruption and upheaval to many American households as families watched their loved ones go off to war. But not all of them. Most Americans actually worked at home, contributing to the war effort in common, ordinary, even boring ways. Not everyone could be a war hero or a fighter ace because most of them were behind the lines building the ships, tanks, guns, and airplanes. Someone had to convert the farmers, plumbers and accountants into soldiers, sailors and airmen. Someone had to deliver the massive supplies of personnel and equipment to the battle zones, take care of the sick, handle the paperwork, and generally keep the country going. Our story is about the "average" person who got caught up in events far beyond his or her control, yet pitched in and did whatever it took to overcome this threat to their way of life. They weren't national heroes, nor did they stand out individually as much as they did collectively. But they were as valid a reason for victory as anyone who participated in this mammoth war effort.

In this chapter, we discover some of the experiences endured by other members of the Poberezny and Ruesch families during the war years, then conclude with a brief outline of Paul's wartime tale. The complete details of his escapades unfold in the following three chapters, but the reader might find the erratic path taken by our tireless aviator less confusing by first reading this preview.

AUDREY & LILLIAN RUESCH

Audrey's mother, Lillian, remained with the Wisconsin Telephone Company throughout the war, as did Audrey with Northwestern Mutual Life. Because Paul was gone, she and her mother spent more time together. They shared household chores, followed the war's progress, planned for the future...and remembered the past. Audrey also maintained her relationships with Paul's family, apparently getting along with Peter much better than Jettie. Peter would utilize this to his own advantage, as Audrey recalls....

"Grampa Pete more than once used me to scheme against Gramma Jet or Paul's sister, Martha. But his 'schemes' were skillfully executed and always done for the good of everyone concerned."

Audrey continued working her way up the corporate ladder. Hired as a clerk in the mail room, she ended up as secretary to the unit president; the skills she was learning would serve her well in the future. Of course, she always found time for a daily letter to Paul, and each month she would deposit into their savings account the money he sent with his letters.

MARTHA POBEREZNY

In 1941, Martha married her childhood sweetheart, Bill Marolt. Martha was eighteen years old and had been going with him for about two years. Before Bill went off to war, the couple found time to have a child, a daughter they named Eileen. Martha dismisses the war years with this terse statement, "The war came and went. My life continued, doing what was fit at the time." Bill was a Navy man, a seaman by trade, and almost lost his life while serving on an aircraft carrier that was torpedoed in the South Pacific. After the war, he and Martha enjoyed many years together before Bill died from a fatal heart

Howard, Martha and baby Eileen

attack, a few hours after his own mother had passed away. Their daughter, Eileen, married and produced four sons of her own. They, in turn, made Martha a great-grandmother—six times, at last count! Martha lives in Milwaukee with her second husband, Jim.

NORMAN POBEREZNY

Paul's younger brother, Norman, was apparently infected with his father's wanderlust—at about the same age! In 1941, the thirteen-year-old boy slipped out his bedroom window with one small suitcase and ran away with his equally adventurous cousin, Bud Burnett. Together they rode buses, hopped freight trains, and hitchhiked south to Texas and into Mexico. After Norm was robbed south of the border, the boys decided to head west to California...no doubt looking for more secure surroundings!

Norman, Audrey, Howard & Jettie

They survived by performing menial jobs for food. When there was no work, they raided nearby gardens for vegetables and fruits. Movie theaters often provided a convenient place to sleep whenever they felt the need for a roof over their heads. By chance, the boys became separated in Northern California and completed the remainder of their journey apart. They were eventually reunited in Milwaukee with many a tale to tell!

Later in the war, the Poberezny family awoke to another of Norm's disappearing acts. This time it was several weeks before they were made aware of his whereabouts—he had joined the Merchant Marine and gone off to sea! Norm describes his adventure:

> During the summer of my sophomore year in 1944, I got my first opportunity to sail on a boat. It was a car ferry, and I was very impressed by the experience. During the beginning of my junior year in high school, I decided I should go into the marine service. I changed the year I was born on my baptismal certificate from 1928 to 1926, got my Coast Guard papers and joined the Merchant Marines in early 1945. My cousin Bud was already in the Coast Guard. He helped me sneak out again and we left for New York harbor where I signed on with a freighter.

Its boiler blew up before we ever left the harbor, so I signed on with a T-2 tanker that was carrying fuel for other ships.

We traveled the Atlantic south to the Gulf of Mexico, through the Panama canal and into the South Pacific. We continued following a westward track to a series of island stops at the Marianas, the Carolinas, the Admiralty Islands, New Guinea and Australia. Next we went to the Persian Gulf and stopped at a port in Iran. From there, we backtracked to ports in Ceylon and India, and then across to the Philippines where we celebrated V-J Day. Finally, it was back to the United States, having to fight a typhoon along the way. It was a most memorable voyage!

Upon returning to Milwaukee, I went back to school, but felt so much older than my classmates that I soon quit. I drove cab and worked construction with my father—until he fired me! I got my GED and went to school to become an aircraft mechanic, eventually working for my brother, Paul, in the Wisconsin Air Guard.

Norm settled down, married and remained in aviation until he retired. His relationship with Paul turned out much better than the brief one with his father; the two brothers worked together in the Air Guard for many years. They still visit on a regular basis, although to reminisce, not to work! Norm and his wife, Betty, live in Milwaukee.

PETER AND JETTIE POBEREZNY

Paul's parents spent the entire period contributing to the war effort in Milwaukee. Unlike their male offspring, neither parent strayed far from their home in Ghost Alley. Peter worked as a laborer in the shipyards, building liberty ships. He became involved with labor interests, being concerned about the plight of the common man and deciding to do something about it. Local politics was the next step, and he was instrumental in getting city bus service to the outlying areas of the city. Jettie worked in the Allis-Chalmers factory, building superchargers for B-17s, P-47's and others. She continued to sell her baking at the local fairs and exhibitions, and did quite well—her cooking never lost its appeal! Both Paul's parents have since passed away.

PAUL POBEREZNY

Because of his unrelenting desire to fly, Paul ended up with a rather complicated wartime career. To him, flying airplanes was more important than rank, prestige, career path—or anything else, for that matter! As a result, there were three phases to his wartime career: glider pilot training, primary instructing, and ferry pilot duties. This brief overview is intended to provide a basic understanding of how it all happened.

At the beginning of the war, Paul applied to the military as a potential pilot candidate. He was rejected because of his lack of formal education, so he successfully applied for entry into the War Training Service program (WTS), which was the only flying option available to him at the time. WTS schools were similar to primary flying training schools. They were designed to select candidates for additional training, either in gliders or, if the applicant was qualified, to undergo flight training as an aviation cadet. WTS programs were run by civilians at civilian flying schools under contract to the government.

After completing WTS, Paul was assigned to a glider pilot training school in Roswell, New Mexico, now a private in the US Army. Upon arrival, his group was canvassed for pilots with prior civilian flying experience. With almost 200 flying hours in a variety of aircraft, Paul easily made the cut. By successfully completing a flight physical, a flight check, and an Officer's Board of Review, he could qualify for a direct commission as an officer and earn service pilot wings. This wing indicated the holder did not go through military training, but had qualified for and passed all required military qualifications and check-outs.

While waiting for their orders, Paul and another friend, Slim Schobert, tired of the constant delays. They wanted to fly for their country *now*, not hang around waiting for the war to end, so they volunteered for glider training. Once again, Paul chose flying over a career path—a trademark that would follow him throughout his life.

After completing glider training and receiving his wings (the first of seven military wings he would earn!), the program was canceled. It was a fortunate twist of fate, as flying gliders into battle zones was not considered a low risk occupation! Along with some of his classmates, Paul was then transferred to a large pilot pool in Albuquerque, New Mexico. Once again the direct commission was offered and once again he accepted and passed

all qualifying phases. While waiting for his orders, an opportunity arose to return to Milwaukee and do some flight instructing with his commanding officer, Captain Bass. There, Paul met a old friend who offered him a civilian flying instructor position at the US Army Primary Flying School in Helena, Arkansas. He accepted and returned to Albuquerque to tell them, no thank you, I found my own flying job!

Instructor Pilot Poberezny

Honorably discharged from the US Army as a Staff Sergeant, Paul reported to the draft board in Milwaukee to advise them he had accepted a position as flight instructor. Because he was of draft age, he was enlisted in the US Army Reserves as a private. It's beginning to read like a game of career snakes-and-ladders, but as was said before, flying airplanes has always been more important than rank or station to this unusual man.

After twelve months as an instructor pilot, he applied for a position ferrying airplanes with Air Transport Command. At the same time, he was courted by United Airlines to become a DC-3 copilot. He chose to stay in the military and underwent several advanced training courses, at last receiving his commission and service pilot wings.

Thus began the ferry pilot phase of Paul's wartime duties. Here, he would fly a variety of aircraft, including many of the latest transports and fighters. After Germany surrendered, he was assigned to a C-47 training school in California, with the prospect of being sent to fly the "Hump." But the war ended before his course, so he spent the remainder of his commitment ferrying airplanes. He was released from the Army in the fall of 1945.

Throughout Paul's story run a few common threads: his love of flying, people, and country (his love for Audrey is understood!). He was a patriot and a participant, doing whatever his country asked of him during the entire span of the war. There was never anything but a sincere desire to serve—except maybe to deal with the frustration of not being able to convince the authorities he could do so much more!

For the complete story, we now return to a fateful day in December 1941....

Chapter Fifteen

World War Two - Phase I (Glider Pilot Training)

By the time the United States entered World War II in late 1941, Adolph Hitler's Nazi war effort was reaching its peak. Their successful Blitzkrieg tactics had, with considerable ease, swallowed up most of Europe, Scandinavia, the Balkans, and even parts of Africa. But signs of German vulnerability were beginning to show. The highly touted Luftwaffe was unable to force England to surrender during the Battle of Britain and so the Fuhrer, mistakenly anticipating an easier diversion to the east, proceeded to attack his former ally, Russia. He only succeeded in adding another miserable front to his spreading woes and in less than a year the tide would turn. Meanwhile, a small island-nation half-way around the globe managed to do one thing Hitler had not—it became the catalyst that activated the untapped potential of the American war machine. Paul remembers the day well....

"So many of us will never forget December 7, 1941. It was a Sunday afternoon and I had flown a Waco 10 earlier in the day. (My Eagle was without a propeller after Slim Schobert taxied a bit too fast toward the fence one windy day. With no brakes available to stop, he knocked the moving propeller against a fence post—I still have the

remains of that propeller.) I had borrowed Dad's car to pick up Audrey and her mother at her aunt's home. While driving down Fond du Lac Avenue, we heard President Roosevelt announce the attack by the Japanese on Pearl Harbor and that we were declaring war on Japan. Those words changed the lives of millions of people, mine included."

Not only did the attack on Pearl Harbor awaken the industrial capabilities of this previously isolated nation, it opened the doors of the armed forces recruiting offices to a surge of American youth, all eager to prove themselves in this fight against the demons of democracy. The gloves were off! In less than twenty-five years, a second "war to end all wars" was about to begin in earnest for the people of the United States of America....

"There was a rush by many young men to the Recruiting Stations. I had about 175 flying hours, a tremendous amount by the day's standards, so I went to the Federal Building to join the Aviation Cadets and become an Army Air Corps pilot. I was told I must have some college education and pass an exam—I needed more knowledge about English, chemistry, and especially algebra and arithmetic, which seemed to be the magic words used by those who flew. I couldn't understand why all this was so important, for it certainly never hindered me in any way with my seat-of-the-pants flying. I pestered the Recruiting Officer and told him I already was a pilot and that I could be of some help. He said I definitely could not qualify as a cadet, but if I would like to go to Chanute Field in Rantoul, Illinois, and talk to them, possibly there might be some other way.

"The trip to Chicago on the North Shore electric train was my first train ride. From Chicago, we switched to a steam engine and another 'first'—the smell of the smoke, cinders and soot, and the clicking of the wheels along the rails. It was something I will always remember. Checking in at Chanute Field that Saturday afternoon and being assigned to the barracks was also quite an experience. Along about 11:00 P.M., the Army Air Corps guys began to come back to their bunks, feeling no pain after leaving the Enlisted Men's Club. It was my first indication of life in the Army. However, I returned home a few days later, saddened by not being able to convince the officers I could fly and that I was just wanting an opportunity to do so."

Rejection by your country when you are eager to come to its defense is a tough pill to swallow—more so, when you know you have a skill that is badly needed! It is difficult to be cast aside by those who are entrusted with public safekeeping and yet are unable to grasp the "big picture." It got worse....

"The word was out from the government that all civilian flying must cease. We were in a state of war and they were afraid of airplanes being used to drop bombs on government facilities by pro-German or pro-Japanese people; today the term is 'terrorists.' My Eagle came apart for storage, as did many other airplanes, and we settled down to find our spot in the world of aviation. I never flew the Eagle again and eventually lost track of it during the war years."

Slim and Paul taking the Eagle apart

The fate of the Eagle during the war

"Our country was totally unprepared to fight a war. When one reads the history of those who fought for airpower, such as General Billy Mitchell (and many others), it is apparent that they were well aware of our needs. But the politicians and much of the public were harshly critical of their stands, calling them war mongers. As a result, our country paid dearly! It paid in the needless loss of many thousands of lives because the people didn't understand...or didn't want to listen."

"The heads in Washington were busy trying to figure out how to train more pilots— we needed them now! There already were limited Civilian Pilot Training Programs (CPTP) sponsored by the CAA. Primary courses were given in Cubs and Aeroncas, with secondary training and some aerobatics in Waco UPF-7s. Someone along the line had anticipated the needs of our aviation community.

"The government finally began to act more aggressively: orders for Piper Cubs, Taylorcrafts and Aeroncas were being written. Civilian pilot training schools, now operating as War Training Service, or WTS, began to show up under the supervision and operation of airport fixed-base operators. It was a shot in the arm for these financially-strapped people, and the beginning of a massive effort to train candidates as aviation cadets or prepare them for glider training.

WTS - Spring City Flying Service - Waukesha Airport

"As I didn't have the educational qualifications for cadet training, I applied for one of the War Training Service programs. Since my pilot license had recently been revoked by the CAA, emergency action was required by the Department of Commerce to reissue me a student pilot license so I could fly in the program. I joined the WTS at Waukesha, operated by Dale and Dean Crites of Spring City Flying Service. We were stationed at Carroll College and put under the leadership of a ground school instructor, Professor Batha. My mom, along with Audrey and her mom, would pick me up on weekends from one of the homes near the campus that served as dormitories for the student flyers. On Sunday evenings they delivered me back. Most of the people in the program had not flown before; however, Harvey Siegert, Slim Schobert, Bud Perry and myself had been flying for some time.

"Rodney Williams, a World War I ace who had shot down at least five German airplanes, was the airport manager and our commandant. He was a stern, but fair gentleman who didn't put up with my antics of kidding, teasing or, what he termed, 'crazy flying.' He was a man I learned to love and respect. Rodney was from Lake Mills, Wisconsin, and in later years returned to that same city where he is buried."

Strict air discipline was a quality noticeably lacking in Paul's early disposition. By receiving a large dose of it during this impressionable period, our young pilot would overcome many obstacles later on. He eagerly began the three-month WTS program....

"It was the summer of 1942. We flew our Cubs with precision and grass-roots talent; the flight instructors were also learning as they instructed. We did our ground school and bookwork at night and our flying during the day. Even though I was only fifteen or so miles from Audrey, I became very lonesome for her.

"The day soon came when we completed our training and were awaiting orders to go to a glider pilot pool. But where? The orders finally came and Professor Batha, along with several Army Air Corps personnel, arranged our transportation. He announced we were going to an Army Air Corps base in Roswell, New Mexico. Where was that, we asked? Out came the maps and we finally located it. It seemed to be hundreds of thousands of miles away, somewhere in the great southwest. One part of me was thrilled to be heading out on this new adventure, the other terribly disappointed, knowing I would be leaving Audrey behind."

As expected, Paul's departure was an emotional occasion. His family, along with Audrey and her mother, went to the train station to say farewell, joining many other recruits and families doing the same thing. Few of them knew where their departing loved ones would end up, or if they would ever see them again; only that they were leaving on a train for some distant war they had read about in the newspapers....

"There was a tearful good-bye to my family and then I, along with many other recruits, departed Milwaukee on the North Shore electric train. We arrived in Chicago in less than two hours and transferred to a much slower troop train operated by the Atchison-Topeka-Santa Fe Railroad. It seemed that we stopped a thousand times along the way to let off civilian passengers and pick up more Army troops. It was not a comfortable ride sitting on the hard seats for so many hours. It was also quite warm and, with the windows open, we could always smell the smoke from the train—a smell that people of that era will never forget. Nor will we forget the clickety-clack of the wheels on the steel rails, the toilets that were nothing more than chutes for human waste, and the wooden ties below going by in a blur. Times certainly have changed."

Roswell, New Mexico. A sprawling air training base so situated because of its good flying weather. It was Paul's first military base and the beginning of his long and distinguished military career....

Private Poberezny

"We arrived in Roswell several days later. It was very warm and the sandy, flat land was scattered with mesquite and other small trees. We left the railroad station for the base and my mind soon began to whirl as I gazed at the many twin-engine Cessna UC-78 'Bamboo Bombers' lined up on the ramp. Roswell was only a staging base for us; its main task was as an Army Air Corps multiengine, or twin-engine training center. We got off the buses and joined ranks with the other glider pilots from the train, lining up as best we could. As we really hadn't had much in the way of military training, we certainly were a motley sort, as the English would say. Roll call was taken by several corporals—corporals

from the old school of the Army Air Corps with their shiny shoes, sharply creased trousers, and shirts with three, crisp creases down the back. Their pith helmets reminded us of old Jungle Jim movies, and the sticks they carried were called 'swagger' sticks.

"After roll call, the corporal in charge, who had the authority of a captain, asked if there were any in the ranks with more than 100 hours total flying time in aircraft with 125 horsepower or more. Out of the two hundred or so present, six of us stepped forward, including my friend, Slim Schobert. The corporal told us to wait while the others were marched off to the barracks. When they left, he told us that with certain other qualifications (the passing of a flight physical, a flight test in a BT-13, and an Officer's Board of Review), we might qualify for a direct commission and service pilot wings—a plain Army Air Corps wing with an 'S' on the shield. This wing identified you as a pilot who did not go through military training, but who, because of prior flying time, was able to pass current military flight testing standards. At age twenty-one, all of this was very confusing, but I was extremely happy nonetheless.

UC-78 "Bamboo Bomber"

Vultee BT-13

"We were assigned to the barracks along with the glider pilots. It was there I learned more of the antics and horseplay of soldiers and the establishment of good friendships. One of them, John Lorita, was an airplane mechanic from Hightstown, New Jersey. He and I formed a strong friendship during the five weeks we were at Roswell. After the war, I learned that John had lost his life on the way to Africa when the troop ship on which he was a passenger was torpedoed and sunk.

"I passed my physical and the flight check in the BT-13. Never in my whole life had I seen so many instruments nor felt such power as that of the 450 horsepower Pratt & Whitney. After flying airplanes like the American Eagle, Piper Cub, Eaglet and Waco 10, it was like having the fastest racer at one's fingertips. The First Lieutenant Army Air Corps check pilot said I did extremely well. I was very pleased and went on to easily pass the Board of Review."

BT-13 Check Ride at Roswell

Much of one's military duty time is spent waiting: waiting for food, waiting for leave, waiting for transportation, waiting for immunization shots, waiting for a paycheck. For some, the worst wait of all is waiting for mail from home. For others....

"We were told to wait for our orders transferring us to Mather Field in California where we'd be given additional training and assigned to flight instructor duties as second lieutenants. We didn't have to do KP (kitchen duties) and so we had a lot of time on our hands. Several of us built model airplanes in the barracks and often times

became a bit too noisy, at least according to the corporal at the end of the hall. He'd walk outside his room and bellow orders for quiet—to which most of us complied.

"Other times we walked to the flight line to watch the many 'Bamboo Bombers' landing and taking-off. The airplanes were being operated with wooden propellers and one day we saw a student and his instructor 'belly-in.' They had problems getting the landing gear to come down, and whatever emergency procedures they tried hadn't worked. We watched it land in a cloud of dust and splintering wood, followed by the well known 'meat wagon,' an Army ambulance displaying the famous red cross.

"Each evening I wrote Audrey a letter. After each payday, which was once a month, I also enclosed twenty of the twenty-one dollars in cash that we were given. This caused things to get pretty tight between paydays, so I also wrote to my parents and complained about being broke. Sometimes they would mail me a little extra spending money, but even more welcome were the packages Mom made up with her fine baking inside. Mom's cooking was another thing I sorely missed...besides Audrey!"

At Roswell, Paul enjoyed his first exposure to the USO. This admirable program was appreciated by all the young soldiers who came from homes across the country to train for their biggest personal challenge....

"The days dragged on. Every so often we were told to get ready—pack your clothing, you're off to California! After several aborted alerts, Slim and I became disenchanted. As the days and weeks rolled by, we decided that no matter what, we were going to fly—even if it was a glider! The other four said they were going to sit it out. We later learned their orders came the next week. They went to Mather Field, received their wings and commissions, and ended up as captains and majors after the war.

"Slim and I, along with six truckloads of potential glider pilots, left Roswell for 'dead-stick' training at Artesia, which was also in New Mexico. It wasn't quite a day's drive and we soon arrived at the quickly prepared field—a square area hacked out of the desert in the middle of nowhere! It was another contract school run by civilians, and we viewed the assortment of raggedy air-

Artesia, New Mexico

planes with more than a bit of distrust! The L-2s, L-3s and L-4s in their olive-drab finishes reminded me of what I had imagined some of the flying aces of World War I had flown.

In front of the barracks in Artesia

"We quickly found the overall condition of the flying field to be as poor as the airplanes. Even the barracks had been moved here from somewhere else. They were very old and crude, the mess hall being tacked on to the end of one of the buildings. The lavatory facilities were especially primitive...and for waste water? Nothing but holes in the ground!

"After a checkout in the airplanes, we began training for glider operations. We would slowly climb over the field until reaching an altitude of two thousand feet. This took several minutes, as the engines in our machines were very tired—they had eaten the sand and dust of New Mexico for a long time! Once over the field at altitude, we throttled back, cut the 'mag' switch to 'kill' the engine, and practiced our (power off) landings. We'd glide back to earth in a spiral descent and attempt to hit a mark on the sandy runway...the military version of a 'dead-stick' spot landing contest! Our propellers continued to whirl during the descent; the compression of the engines long ago reduced by the sand and the poor maintenance that was accomplished outdoors by what few mechanics the school could locate.

"At night we followed the same procedure: climb to two thousand feet, cut the switches, and glide to a landing. The runway was lit up by smudge pots, as there were no runway lights. I suppose this also served to simulate lighting conditions in a war zone. After night flying, most of us were extremely hungry—the rations were very poor and really not enough. It was not uncommon for us to break into the kitchen to find whatever supplies we could. Of course, we eagerly awaited packages from home with the fresh cookies and candies!"

Christmas 1942. For the first time in his twenty-one years, Paul spent Christmas away from home. But he wasn't the only one stuck at this remote location during a time when most families are together....

"My first Christmas away from home occurred while I was at Artesia. Another pilot and I hitched a ride some twelve miles to town in one of the GI trucks and went to church that Sunday morning. As we were leaving, a family with two pretty daughters approached and asked if we would like to have Christmas dinner with them. What a pleasant and wonderful surprise—one we certainly did not decline! I corresponded with the family a number of times after the war…just a postcard here or there. Eventually the relationship was lost, but never forgotten."

Paul told Audrey about the "two good-looking daughters" in his evening letter—another indication of how honest their relationship had become in spite of the distance and uncertainty that was facing them.

One adjustment that new recruits must make to life in the military, is to adapt to its nomadic lifestyle. This is especially true during the first few months when bases often serve as stepping stones to additional levels of training—training that not only increases in intensity, but also in risk....

"Many complaints rolled in to the Air Corps about the living conditions and maintenance standards at Artesia and shortly after Christmas it was closed, which meant more traveling orders. We soon departed on a train for our next base, one we were told had just been built in Wickenburg, Arizona. After a long and beautiful ride through cowboy land, the new flying field was, indeed, a pleasant surprise. It was well laid out in the mountains, with near-perfect temperatures, clean new barracks, and only two of us to a room! BT-13s were used as tow planes, and TG-5s, -6s and -8s were our training gliders, having been converted from Aeroncas, Taylorcrafts and Piper Cubs.

"Except for having to be towed to altitude, glider training procedures were similar to what we had done in the airplanes at Artesia. There would be two of us on a tow. Sometimes we would aggravate the tow pilot by flying our gliders from side to side, causing the tow airplane to skid. Our 'funning' took a serious turn one day as we watched one of the students and his instructor get tangled up in the tow rope of the second glider. Their glider broke loose, its wings folded, and it fluttered to the ground. Both lives were lost."

Search and Rescue. In order to become qualified for a position in a search and rescue squadron, highly experienced pilots must graduate from demanding advanced courses. Paul hadn't even finished glider school when he and a fellow student pilot were involved in one of the most amaz-

ing bovine rescues of the war. "Save the beef," was the cry that followed the eagerly awaited details of this daring aerial adventure: a war story with a happy ending....

"We also had L-4s at Wickenburg, in which we practiced 'dead-stick' landings and did some cross country flying. Harold Tuft, from West Allis, Wisconsin, and I met at Wickenburg and often flew together. It was on one such flight into the hills just north of the base that we noticed a cow standing in a catch basin: a concrete arrangement designed to capture water from the frequent thunderstorms that would cause the creeks to suddenly rage with water. With its steep sides, I wondered how the cow could ever get out. What could we do?

"Just then an automobile stopped nearby...a family possibly deciding to have a picnic. I quickly took a sheet from my 'Form 1 - Aircraft and Pilots Log' and scribbled a note saying approximately two hundred feet east of their position was a cow stuck in the ravine, and could they help? I added our names and noted that we were from Milwaukee, Wisconsin. We began circling overhead and waving at the people below. When they waved back, I came in very slow and dropped the paper. One of the family members ran for the note, picked it up, read it, and waved. We watched them walk several hundred feet to the east; when they saw the cow, they waved again.

"Several months later I received a newspaper clipping from Audrey and my mom. It was from the Milwaukee Journal and it gave the story of how two Army pilots had saved a cow. Apparently the family on the ground wrote the paper to tell them about their adventure and my note."

One would think after such a "noteworthy" deed, the last thing to distort this heroic aviator's glorious future would be another dead-end military training program. But such is the fate of lesser heroes! After completing his advanced glider training on the large CG-4A, the program was discontinued. At least Paul received his wings!

It's open to debate as to how many of these young men realized what they were getting into when they volunteered for military programs such as glider training. In Paul's case, he just wanted to fly...something—anything! Did he suspect how dangerous it was to be a glider pilot? Probably not...there was no hint of it in any of his records, including his letters. Had the program not been canceled, or had he been involved in it sooner, he could easily have been sent to Europe where his career might have ended at an obscure landing zone.

Saving Trapped Cattle Adds 'Fun' for Milwaukee Fliers

It's hard to say what these Milwaukee boys we have sent away from home will be up to next. Take Staff Sergt. Harold J. Tuft, 22, and Staff Sergt. Paul Poberezny, 21. The other day, while flying in an army plane over the Arizona desert, they rescued three head of beef cattle, trapped and starving to death.

The incident was described in a letter to The Journal from Jewel Evans of Buckeye, Ariz., which is 30 miles west of Phoenix.

"You will be interested in knowing that two of your local boys, Staff Sergts. Paul Poberezny and Harold Tuft, did an excellent piece of work in helping to conserve the beef supply on the home front while preparing to do active duty abroad," said the letter.

Tuft *Poberezny*

"While they were doing routine flying or just sightseeing over the foothills of northern Arizona, the boys chanced to see three helpless bovines trapped in a small basin, not more than 10 or 15 feet in diameter. The animals had descended the sloping cement walls to get a drink of water and were unable to get back out. The boys saw the cattle again three days later. This must have caused the boys a great deal of concern, and quite a lot of scheming as to how these valuable brutes could be saved.

Drop Message From Plane

"Their opportunity came on a sunny afternoon Feb. 27. By chance, we had stopped to prepare a late lunch within a stone's throw of the impending tragedy. As we gathered sticks for a campfire, we were startled by an approaching army plane, flying far too low for our comfort. As it passed over, we saw the two occupants leaning out and we could hear them shouting something, but we were unable to make out what they were saying.

"They circled over the canyon and wrote a message. When they were in just the right position, they dropped it. Their bombsight must have functioned properly, for the paper floated directly into our hands.

"The message asked help in rescuing animals from their slow but certain death. Hastily we planned what could be done, and after a short trip up the road and a short trip down the road, the owner of the animals was located. You can be sure he was very appreciative of the information.

"All the while the boys were watching from their comfortable seats in the 'balcony,' and when they saw that everything had been taken care of, they decided to say 'thank you.' They dropped another message, expressed their thanks, gave their former and present addresses, and told us that they didn't like our state.

Stunts for Spectators

"Then began a series of stunts. They kept up their show for quite awhile, and we looked on in wonder. When the acrobatics were over, we received another note asking how we enjoyed it. Of course, we wanted to express just how much we had enjoyed it but found ourselves powerless to do so. Then someone had an idea. We ran out on the sand in the middle of a dry creek bed and began to work. When we had finished, there were the letters 'O. K.,' large enough to be seen for a mile.

"No sooner had we finished than we saw the plane swooping low, and when the fliers were close enough, they both yelled, 'O. K.' Then we watched until the horizon swallowed them."

Tuft, writing to his parents, Mr. and Mrs. Thomas J. Tuft, 2214 S. 83rd st., adds this foot note to Jewel Evans' story:

"Incidentally, keep your eyes open for any articles in The Journal. Another fellow from West Allis, Paul Poberezny, and I rescued some cows out of a basin in which they were trapped. We spotted them and dropped notes. The farmer got them out by using a truck and pulley. We then dropped another note with our names and told him to write to The Journal. He scrawled a big O. K. in the sand—some fun, huh!"

Sergt. Tuft, who is a graduate of West Allis high school, was an attendant at the soldiers' home before he joined the army in February, 1942. A brother, Russell, is in the navy.

Sergt. Poberezny, who attended Carroll college at Waukesha, has been in service about a year.

The flying "cowboys" are now stationed at Kirtland field, Albuquerque, N. Mex. At the time of the rescue they were stationed at Wickenburg, Ariz.

Maybe it was the times; maybe these young men truly did believe in the cause. It really doesn't matter now, because our hats are raised in solemn salute to those fearless men who flew airplanes without engines into combat. It wasn't a glamorous job—but it sure was a dangerous one! They did what they were trained to do, and they suffered high losses. As there were no "kills," there was little glory and they were soon all but forgotten.

But not here…we salute you, Army Air Corps glider pilots!

Waco CG-4A Glider

Meanwhile, back in Wickenburg, Arizona, Paul was again perfecting the art of waiting....

"Instead of flying the gliders we had trained so long for, we were now to be sent to a pilot pool being formed at Kirtland Field in Albuquerque, New Mexico. By then we were staff sergeants, a part of the four thousand or so pilots being assembled in this pool. It was not uncommon to see staff sergeants doing KP, with a corporal or private first class in charge! We now drew $144 per month, including flight pay—a fortune in those days! I continued to send the majority of it home to my bride-to-be, Audrey.

"Slim Schobert and I arrived at Kirtland Field, a very busy base with bombers and fighters continually flying over our heads. We were assigned to a tent along with two other glider pilots. It was still winter, so it wasn't uncommon for us to have snow blow in over our blan-

kets and fill our shoes during the night. I was again offered the familiar options—a direct commission as a Service Pilot or to become an Aviation Cadet and go through pilot training. Once again I chose to be a Service Pilot and successfully completed my flight test (in another BT-13) and passed the Board of Review. (I didn't need another physical, as I had just had one during glider pilot training.) I was again accepted for a direct commission and told to await my orders.

"Kirtland Field was also a bombardier training school, so while I was waiting, I volunteered to fly as camera man on the twin-engine Beechcraft AT-11s. When the airplane reached 10,000 feet, my task was to open the camera door and place the camera in position. As the 100-pound practice bombs fell from the aircraft, I put the camera in motion to score the bombardier's hits in the large target circles that were seen so frequently throughout the deserts of the southwest.

Waiting at Kirtland

Beechcraft AT-11

"Traffic at Kirtland was always busy. One hazy morning we taxied out for a routine 'bombing' mission and our pilot began his takeoff roll. Because of the heavy traffic, airplanes often took off and landed at the same time on crossing runways. As we reached a runway intersection, we almost collided with another aircraft that was also taking off. It was a very close call and required some abrupt control movements by both pilots. But there was no contact and the airplanes continued their departures, their crews alive but badly shaken! With our hearts in our throats, we completed the flight with little conversation…but I'm sure there was a prayer or two said in private!

"One day while walking by Headquarters, there was a note on the bulletin board stating that anyone knowing where one could rent 100 hours in an airplane with 125 or more horsepower should please see Captain Dorsey M. Bass. I reported to the captain and he told me his predicament: he was not a rated pilot and needed the time to secure his service pilot status. I said I thought I knew where such time could be rented at a reasonable price, and that I could provide the necessary instruction. Of course it was not very far from Audrey!

Capt. Dorsey Bass, Howard and Audrey

"A telegram was sent to Dale Crites of Spring City Flying Service at Waukesha County Airport, asking if the 220 horsepower J-5 Waco biplane would be available, and what was the cost. A positive reply was received, and Captain Bass and I were soon on our way to Indianapolis in a C-87 (a B-24 bomber converted to carry passengers). From Indy we took the train to Milwaukee, and the next day were at the airport ready to fly. We flew constantly for the next three weeks getting the required time, but all too soon it was time to return. Because he was appreciative of what I was able to do for him, Captain Bass gave me another week's leave. After that, I was to report back to Kirtland Field. Captain Bass is from Columbia, Missouri, and we have stayed in touch over the years.

"While I was at home, I met my old civilian instructor, Ben White, who was also back for a short visit. He was in charge of aircraft maintenance at Helena Aero Tech, a Primary Flying School located in Helena, Arkansas. I told him I had finished my glider pilot training, received my glider pilot wings and was eligible for a direct commission. He asked if I'd be interested in a job in Helena as a flight instructor teaching aviation cadets in Fairchild PT-23s. I told him I was very interested and would let him know after returning to Albuquerque. By then, Audrey and I were beginning to accumulate a sizable amount of money, anxiously waiting for the time when I could ask her mother if we could get married.

"Upon returning to Albuquerque, I requested the status of my Service Pilot Rating. It was still not forthcoming, so I was allowed to take a discharge and return home; they told me they would let me know when and where to report. I bid good-bye to the friends I had made in the glider program and boarded a train that wound its way back through New Mexico, Texas, Kansas, Missouri and Illinois to Chicago. From there I took the old reliable (and much quicker), North Shore electric train home to Milwaukee."

Strike three! And the end of the glider phase of Paul's wartime career. He was released from the US Army in April 1943...without the twice-promised commission....

"One of my requirements was to report to the West Allis Draft Board. I still remember the puzzled look of surprise on the faces of the ladies and gentlemen as I stood before them in 1943, a Staff Sergeant in full uniform. The war had really just started and here the Army was already discharging its soldiers! I was put on a special list (I think it was 4-D), and Audrey and I had some time together before I left for Helena, where I spent the next year as a primary flight instructor."

Paul was only trying to prove to the bureaucracy that his abilities could—and should—be better utilized. It was unfortunate "the system" was unable to recognize his potential. However during his next duty, more than a few fledgling student pilots would come to appreciate their good fortune at being assigned to this new instructor pilot, Private Paul Howard Poberezny.

Chapter Sixteen

World War Two - Phase II - Instructor Pilot - "Hitched!"

Becoming an instructor was quite a change in roles for our once "boyish and irresponsible" pilot, the same young man whose motivation once centered around absorbing the pleasures of flight. Soon he would fulfill the most important role in the development of any aviation student, that of flight instructor. In this capacity he would be giving the joy of flight, not taking it. But first, he had to get to Arkansas....

"Helena was a small town on the Mississippi River, some fifty to sixty miles south of Memphis. It was a town of old buildings and very high temperatures in the summer. I took a bus from Memphis that motored its way through Forest City, Mariana, and then into Helena. It was a rather lonely experience, as it was the first time I had to depend on myself for all my travel and living arrangements.

"The ninety-degree plus temperatures hammered me as I got off the bus at the old hotel. I told the desk clerk that I was to be a flight instructor pilot and got a room. Later, as I walked up and down the street some four or five blocks long, I noted a group of flight instructors in front of the Post Office Cafe. Having finished eating, they were milling around in front of the restaurant, passing the time away. I could tell they were flight instructors because the area on their faces where their goggles would sit, was all white. I too would soon have those 'owl-like' eyes.

“Ben White said he would pick me up in front of the hotel first thing in the morning, Sure enough, he was right on time. It was good to see Ben again, and we talked about old times on the way to the flight school at Thompson Robbins Field, a few miles west of town. He dropped me off at headquarters where I was interviewed by Mr. Vanderveer, operator of the school, and Mr. Sam Williams, who was in charge of all the pilots. They told me I would have to complete the flight instructor refresher course before I could start instructing.

“I moved out of the hotel after finding a room at a boarding house where several other flight instructors were staying. It was a block off Main Street and was run by the two ‘old maid’ Kaplan sisters. Our perception of age was much different then—the oldest Kaplan girl was twenty-nine and the youngest, twenty-six!”

When compared to fighter aircraft, training airplanes are slow and unglamorous. They are built for another, equally important purpose: to teach people how to fly. Besides, you couldn’t fly fighters or bombers until you had mastered the trainers....

“I checked out in a Fairchild PT-23, a low wing monoplane powered by a 220 horsepower Continental. I then flew it some twenty-five or thirty hours, dual and solo, front and back seats, and completed my instructor checkout in less than a month.

Checking out in the PT-23

"I was assigned my first class of five aviation cadets. To say I was nervous would be an understatement! How was I to teach these men, some of whom seemed so old to me? Again, when one looks back at being twenty-one years of age, another five or six years makes a big difference! But it was such a thrill for me to sit in the cockpit of a PT-23 and look out at the star on the wing. I still couldn't believe it! I was being paid to fly and I just couldn't get enough of it!

"Our schedules rotated between two weeks of morning flying and two weeks of afternoons. We held ground briefings and performed other assigned duties outside the scheduled flying periods. I flew as much as could: I volunteered to 'slow time' the aircraft coming out of maintenance (fly them at reduced power settings to properly break in a new engine); I went on morning weather checks; I even accepted some 'washed-out' (failed) students from other flight instructors—whatever it took to keep me in the air!"

There are instructors and there are *instructors*. The good instructors develop a few common, and exceptional, qualities: they maintain a high level of personal skills; they establish and retain the respect of their students; and they truly care for those they are entrusted to teach. Paul Poberezny would become a *great* flight instructor....

Instructor Poberezny in the cockpit

"I am proud to say that during my flight instructing days, *all* my students graduated from Basic and Advanced flying—including the former wash-outs! I learned that if you were sincere, took the time—and had patience—you could teach almost anyone to fly! I also learned that it was not uncommon for some instruc-

tors to wash out two of their five students so their workload was lightened. This was certainly not in the best interests of the young men who dreamed and desired to fly—nor the country!"

Paul and his students by a PT-19

No matter how busy it got, Paul always found time to write....

"All during the time I was gone, Audrey and I wrote to each other daily. It was a familiar sight to see 'SWAK' (sealed with a kiss), along with a lipstick mark from her lips on the back of the envelope."

Audrey adds....

"I enjoyed receiving Howard's letters and I knew he felt the same about getting mine. While I wasn't directly involved in the war, I stayed busy and the time seemed to pass by rather quickly. Most of the young men were gone, so it wasn't like there was a whole lot of things to do anyway. I kept very busy at work, learning new jobs as I continued to be promoted. Mom and I spent much of our spare time doing things together—including the housework! I certainly never had a problem finding something to write about."

"Owl-eyes" Poberezny was now earning his keep as a flight instructor. As was previously observed in our former barnstormer, one of the more difficult spirits to harness in a young pilot is the spirit of adventure. In a war zone, we demand aggressive behavior from our warriors. But back home, discipline is more rigidly enforced, especially within the training environment....

"I enjoyed doing aerobatics, and sometimes more adventuresome things like rolling my landing gear on the levees of the Mississippi River! I was doing just that one morning when I noticed another airplane following me. Not knowing if it was one of the Army lieutenant check pilots or another flight instructor, I started climbing for some distant clouds and soon found myself outside our flying area. It turned out I was being followed by a lieutenant. Upon landing, I was called before Sam Williams, a fine, but firm gentleman from whom I received quite a lecture! He said, 'We were told by your old flight instructor, Ben White, that you were full of 'pee and vinegar.' But your record here has been very good. You've done a lot of extra flying for us by taking on extra students at no additional salary, flying maintenance test hops, and even doing weather checks. However, we don't ever want you rolling your wheels on the levee again...is that clear?' It was to me!"

Although it was the middle of a war, people still found time to escape reality—if only for a short while. For Paul, it meant returning to Audrey whenever he could. During one visit, something special happened....

"Every two months between classes we had three or four days off. I'd go to Memphis on the bus and catch the Illinois Central to Chicago and the North Shore to Milwaukee, there to spend some time with Audrey. She was now a secretary with Northwestern and I always felt proud to be waiting for her on the steps at quitting time in my flight instructor's uniform. While standing there watching for her, many of the other girls would come out and give me 'the eye'! I suppose it was because I was in uniform, which was quite popular at the time. When Audrey came out, we'd walk hand-in-hand down Wisconsin Avenue to catch the trolley to her home.

"On one trip, I picked out a set of rings from the jeweler and asked Audrey to become my wife. We were going down National Avenue, the streetcar swaying from side to side, when I asked her to marry me. It was a subject we had talked about many times, ever since we passed notes to each other back in high school. She said 'yes', and I slipped an

engagement ring on her finger. As she looked down at the five-and-dime store, ten-cent ring, she almost started to cry. I quickly took out the real one, placed it on her finger, and her concern was gone."

Audrey didn't think his proposal was so funny at the time....

"Howard was waiting for me when I got off work. We got on the streetcar and soon he hauls out this ring (she laughs). ***It's funny now, but I was quite upset and hurt when he handed me that cheap ring and the so-called diamond fell out on the floor—I was pretty close to tears! But after he gave me the real one, which was very nice, I calmed down. You never knew what to expect from Howard...at least he could have picked one with a securely attached stone!"***

Paul continues....

"When we got to her mom's apartment, we happily announced our engagement. But when I asked about marriage, her mom gave us a dollar figure of $3300 that we must have in the bank before she would give her approval. We had been saving our nickels and pennies and dollars ever since high school. As a flight instructor, I was making very good money, sending the majority of it home to Audrey so she could put it into the bank. I would continue doing so, anxiously waiting for the day when we reached the goal set by her mother."

Audrey shows off her ring in front of her apartment on Pierce Street

Lillian Ruesch and her future son-in-law

Audrey recalls Paul's unusual display of trust and faith in their future together....

"Now that I think about it, Howard went off to the service and would send his money back to me, even before we were married, and I would put it in our bank account. Nowadays, you wonder whether you could trust somebody that much; but I guess that thought must not have entered his mind because he kept sending it!"

Paul continued to fly students and add to a growing list of acquaintances....

"I made many friends at Helena and was soon spending my evenings standing around in front of the P-O Cafe with them, tossing pennies toward a crack in the sidewalk or occasionally going to the show (movie) across the street. One of my new friends was 'Muleshoe' Jennings, who roomed at the same boarding house. His real name was Elvie Tipton Jennings, and he really was from Muleshoe, Texas. His 1939 Chevrolet coupe provided us with much appreciated transportation.

Paul, Jack Wismar and Muleshoe Jennings in front of the P-O Cafe

"Another good friend, 'Pappy' Hughes, was a longtime pilot and magician by trade who had traveled the country with a dog act prior to the war. One time he picked up a stray dog and taught it to do tricks, like standing on one leg and balancing on Pappy's hand—sometimes his head! Pappy was always entertaining! Then there was Tommy Shepke, the base photographer, and Chet Wellman, one of the ground school instructors. Today, Chet is an active attorney and provides some of the legal assistance required by the Experimental Aircraft Association."

Stories involving military experiences can be very interesting, especially aviation stories. There's something unique about the camaraderie that goes

with being a member of the armed forces—any branch, really. The tales involve endless recollections of adventure, misadventure, and humor....

"We had a number of auxiliary fields where we practiced landings and takeoffs with the students, and from there we would sometimes solo them. Many good times were had buzzing the fields and performing all sorts of antics. One afternoon I landed at Wooten Field, one of our auxiliary fields located beside a dike that ran parallel to the Mississippi River. When I saw another flight instructor on the ground, I got out and told my student to go back up and practice his aerobatics. I would observe him from the ground while the other instructor and I sat and chatted. After he took off, I remembered that my parachute was still in the front cockpit. It wasn't long before my student made his first slow roll and we saw an object fall to the earth. It was my parachute—another embarrassing situation! Fortunately, the parachute was retrieved.

Paul (middle) and his fellow instructors monitoring their students at Wooten Field

"Another day, one of the students came back to the main base and reported to Flight Operations that he had lost his instructor. The dispatcher, thinking the student couldn't find his instructor on the base, failed to realize he'd been lost in flight! About an hour and a half later, the instructor, speaking in his German accent, arrived by truck from the cotton fields of Arkansas...holding his deployed parachute!

"In Operations, he explained what had happened. The speaking tube, or 'bitching' tube as we called it (we didn't have radios or intercoms), had unknowingly caught on his safety-belt latch and unhooked it as he was talking his student through a slow roll. Suddenly he felt himself leave the airplane! As he was going out, he saw the star on the wing pass by and realized he was in trouble! As he fell toward mother earth, he said it was just like being in the movies. Then he got upset with himself, wondering why he was thinking about movies at a time like this! He found the rip cord, pulled it, and his chute blossomed some five hundred or so feet above the ground!

"We had over a hundred airplanes at our school, initially PT-23s, and later, PT-19s. It was amazing how well our traffic moved, with no radios, hundreds of students—and no midair collisions! One wonders why today, with much less flying activity, the worry is so great and the devices needed to separate the machines so complicated. During World War II, we had a great many more airplanes flying in the same airspace with less experienced pilots. And we call this progress?"

Paul could never be satisfied by flying just one or two types of aircraft...he liked them all. In spite of the considerable extra flying he did for the Army Air Corps, he found plenty of time to keep his hand in the civilian aircraft scene....

"Back home in Waukesha, there were two Waco 10s powered by 90 horsepower, OX-5 engines that we thought would be wonderful for barnstorming and fun flying during our off-duty hours in Helena. Early in December 1943, I came home between classes and arranged to obtain one of them. After a quick local test hop, I started out. My route remained close to the Illinois Central Railroad line—in case I had to leave the airplane and catch a train back to Helena.

"On my first leg from Waukesha to Bloomington, Illinois, I had four forced landings due to carburetor ice, water pump leaks and other problems. This increased my knowledge of maintenance and allowed me to meet some wonderful farmers! I finally made it as far as Decatur, Illinois, before I had to leave the airplane and return to Helena on the train, so as to be available for my student flights the following day. The next weekend I returned for the Waco. Several more forced landings and unplanned meetings later, I arrived in Helena with much more experience as a mechanic and a pilot, having used my tools and a road map all the way. We decided to wait for spring before getting the second airplane.

"We kept our Waco at a little field adjacent to one of the auxiliary fields. Sometimes we got permission to fly it from the auxiliary field on Sundays, carrying those with fifty cents or a dollar. One advantage we had, was that obtaining fuel for airplanes was more liberal than it was for automobiles. We could buy aviation fuel in fifty-gallon barrels, giving us plenty of fuel for Muleshoe's car."

Pumping gas from Muleshoe's car

Paul was becoming well known around the squadron as a pilot who would fly just about anything....

"Chet Wellman bought an old Rearwin Sportster down in Alabama and asked if I would ferry it back some weekend. I said I would and picked it up in Auburn in early March. I remember landing for fuel at Tupelo just after it rained. The red mud had turned to gumbo and I had quite a difficult time taking off. After reaching Helena, we took the wings off and put the airplane in the old barn Chet had rented for its restoration. I had hopes of flying it home to pick up Audrey for our wedding day, as our bank account was growing near to the sum her mother had set."

In April 1944, Paul returned to Milwaukee for the second Waco…and an even more exciting trip to Helena. Actually, it began on the way to the airport....

"Obtaining gasoline for automobiles during the war through gas

rationing was not easy. People were issued stickers and coupons that allowed them a certain amount of fuel. With the meager gas available to them, Mom, Audrey and her mother drove me to the Waukesha Airport—almost! Within several miles of our destination, we had a flat tire; fortunately, the spare was good!

"It was early spring and the ground was still covered with patches of wet, soggy snow. After some hugs and kisses good-bye with Audrey, Dale Crites swung the Waco's prop and I headed south on another adventure! This trip would also take two weekends to complete, due to even more forced landings than I had encountered on the first one—I believe there were nineteen in all! But none were of a serious nature and I finally made it back to Helena, giving us two Wacos in which to fly and have fun."

Heading for Helena in the Waco

Although their savings account was approaching the financial goal set by "Mom" Ruesch, Audrey still had one seemingly insurmountable objection to taking that final step....

"I didn't feel comfortable about leaving my mother alone. But when I mentioned this to Howard, he immediately said, 'Well then, she'll live with us!' He said it without hesitation or uncertainty, and that surprised me. I guess I thought nobody would want to do that."

"Ever since Audrey's father died, I felt I always wanted to take care of both her and her mom. I never thought it would be any different."

"Funny, but Mom ended up taking care of us!"

Almost every incident of note in Paul's life involved aviation—including his marriage. Paul and Audrey were wed; but not in Milwaukee as we might have expected....

"We finally arrived at our financial goal and Audrey's mother said we could get married. The Rearwin was ready and I was going to fly it home on the weekend to pick up Audrey. My landlady worked at the courthouse in Helena and made arrangements for the marriage license. In fact, she bought the license and arranged for the preacher too! I arranged for the 'bridesmaids,' who all happened to be close friends—male flight instructor pilots!

Elvie "Muleshoe" Jennings
Audrey's "Man of Honor"

Paul returns the Rearwin to Helena and his bride-to-be

"I started off in the Rearwin, but after several forced landings, turned back and parked it at West Memphis Airport, a small grass strip along the highway leading to Forest City and Little Rock. Once again I caught the train to Milwaukee, and the next morning, Audrey and I headed back to Memphis. Muleshoe met us at the station and dropped me off at the little airport so I could fly the Rearwin back to Helena while he drove Audrey. I had arranged for our accommodations at a little motor court where some of the other flight instructors were staying. It was hot outside, the temperature hovering between ninety and ninety-five degrees! That afternoon in May, we all met at the preacher's house...and Audrey and I were married.

Our Wedding Day - May 28, 1944 - (left to right) the Minister and his wife, Mr. & Mrs. Paul Poberezny, Muleshoe Jennings, the "oldest" Kaplan sister, Ben White's girlfriend, Ben White, and the "youngest" Kaplan sister.

"After the ceremony, some of the flight instructors quipped that my flying days would soon be over; I immediately drove out to our little field and went for a couple of good buzz jobs in the Waco. With that out of my system, and with me now having oil on my dress uniform, we all returned to the base for our wedding dinner in the mess hall. One thing I do remember was having to get up at 5:00 A.M. the next morning to instruct!

"The next evening, my class of cadets took Audrey and me to dinner at the P-O Cafe and presented us with a fine set of dishes which we still have today. Audrey was to have remained there for a week, but stayed for almost two before returning home to her job at Northwestern Mutual."

Why did our young couple go all the way to Arkansas to get married—especially when both of them were tied to family roots in Milwaukee? We know they didn't have to elope, so they had nothing to hide…or did they? It turns out they did! Audrey's employer enforced a company regulation that required all female employees to be single (try doing that in the nineties!). If they discovered she was married....

"We got married in Arkansas mainly because I wanted to keep my job. Everyone in the family agreed it was the best thing to do—including Gramma Jet,

which surprised me. Had we been married at home, we could not have kept it a secret for very long, and I would have been forced to quit.

"It really was a good job. It paid well and I enjoyed the work. Northwestern looked after its employees—we even had our own cafeteria staffed with waitresses! Because most of the young men were being drafted into service, I was being promoted very quickly. Everything seemed to be in favor of my remaining there as long as possible, so when I returned from Arkansas, I didn't say a word about the events of the past two weeks and went quietly back to my job."

Paul (center) and PT-23 students.

Meanwhile, her "secret" husband was flying more and more aviation students; they kept arriving from all over the country and from all walks of life. Because of this increase in aerial activity, it was reasonable to expect the accident ratio would also rise. It soon did....

"One morning several of us flight instructors had solo students in the pattern. We were standing in the field and monitoring them when a young cadet came in for a landing. He leveled out much too high and the airplane stalled, falling off on its left wing and gear and striking the ground with such force that the spar in the center section must have broken. Just as he was taught, the student added power to go around and try another landing. What he didn't realize was that he had incurred great structural damage—the left wing was now pointing skyward at least ten to fifteen degrees! We watched him go around the pattern with deepening concern. On the downwind leg, he throttled back. The airplane immediately stalled and entered a three-quarter turn spin into the ground, killing him instantly upon impact. We felt so helpless during all this. If we'd only had a way to tell him to climb straight out to a sufficient altitude and bail out...but those were the days without radios!"

A tragic day…

The military was not the only operation with pilots; the airlines were still flying and they too needed airplane drivers....

"Finding pilots to fly for the airlines was quite a chore during the war. By June 1944, things were beginning to slow down in the training programs and a representative of United Airlines visited our field. He talked to a number of us, asking if we'd be interested in applying for a position with them. He said they had also heard that things would soon be slowing down and they were looking to the training schools as a source of experienced pilots. At the same time, Air Transport Command (ATC) was looking for ferry pilots. I knew my current position could soon end, so I had to make a decision as to where to go next: United or ATC."

Which career path would it be? The answer becomes our next chapter. But before we find out, there is one nagging flaw in Paul's character that should be exposed! True, he did everything he could to serve his country with the skills he knew best; and he was doing a wonderful job at Helena, including flying all those extra sorties without being asked. And yes, he diligently sent his money home to Audrey and maintained a daily letter writing campaign.

What he fails to admit, though, is that he also sent his dirty laundry home in a specially made black box! Small wonder he could accept extra flying assignments and do all those "fun" things—he didn't even do his own laundry! It should also be noted that this curious habit would later pass down from father to son.

...a wartime diversion!

Chapter Seventeen

World War Two - Phase III
- Ferry Pilot
- Wings and Commission

By mid 1944 the war had turned decidedly in favor of the Allies. Eighteen months earlier, German forces at Stalingrad were annihilated by the Russian counter-offensive, thus reversing Germany's fortunes on the eastern front. In Africa, the Allies had regained their lost real estate and were now fighting German troops on Italian soil, following Italy's surrender in September 1943. The Battle of the Atlantic was won, although it was certainly not over. And on 6 June 1944, the Allies successfully landed their mammoth D-Day invasion force at Normandy, France. The push to Berlin was underway from several fronts.

In the Pacific, Japanese invincibility had also been reversed. This was primarily due to US naval air actions during the Battle of the Coral Sea, and later, the decisive US victory at Midway where the Japanese carrier fleet was decimated. This ensured that American airpower could now provide proper air support, thus allowing Allied commanders to switch from defense to offense with increasing success.

Back in the United States, the war support effort was incredible. The production of goods and services and training of personnel was far outpacing that of its enemies, as Americans engaged in an all-out effort to defeat the tyrannies of aggression.

With the war apparently on its way to a predictable, yet still costly, conclusion, Paul was faced with a career decision: stay in the military or go with the airlines....

"During one of my breaks in June of 1944, I visited Midway Airport in Chicago where I was interviewed and accepted by United Airlines. I was to fly copilot on a DC-3 after completing an instrument course in Denver, Colorado, in their Stinson SR-9s and 10s. The starting salary would be $180 per month. However, I was already making $375 instructing, which certainly was good for that time, and Air Transport Command would pay about the same to ferry pilots, plus per diem. I notified United that I was going to go with Air Transport Command and went back to Helena to say farewell."

Paul's decision to turn down a career with United Airlines led him to Air Transport Command, or ATC, where he would soon have the opportunity to fly many different military aircraft, including transport, bomber, liaison, trainer, and fighter types. He signed on as a private in the Enlisted Reserves, his commission now hinging on the satisfactory completion of the ATC training programs....

"In July, I joined the 4th Ferry Group of the Air Transport Command in Memphis, Tennessee, along with several other pilots from the flying school at Helena. During the first month I ferried PT-23s around the country, checked out in the AT-6, and flew as copilot on several flights in C-47 and B-25 aircraft. I then received orders to report to Greenwood, Mississippi, to attend a four week instrument training course flying under the hood in the back seat of a BT-13. 'Flying the beam' and the 'cone of silence' were terms used to describe the instrument and approach procedures of the time. They were quite challenging, yet when mastered, became an effective approach in instrument (bad weather) conditions...although much more tedious when compared with today's procedures!

C-47

"Having previously been a Staff Sergeant during my glider days, I was given the responsibility of Section Commander for two flights of thirty-five pilots each. Most of the pilots were a little older than I and had no previous military training; they were quite a sight to see! They often heckled me as I assembled them in front of our tarpaper bar-

racks to march the six or seven blocks to the flight line. Sometimes the songs about their Flight Commander (me) meant an extra block or two of marching (for them)! But it was great fun and all taken in stride.

"Having completed our instrument training, we were transferred to Blytheville, Arkansas, for multi-engine training in the AT-10, Beechcraft's all wood, twin-engine trainer. Although similar in outward appearance to the Cessna UC-78 'Bamboo Bomber,' the AT-10 had more of a blunt nose and only two side-by-side seats for the instructor and student. It was much like another twin trainer, the Curtiss AT-9 Jeep. The AT-10 was a delight to fly, its two Lycoming radials providing sufficient power for its duties."

Although he was in Air Transport Command, home of the multi-thousand hour aviators, Paul was one of the more experienced students taking the course. His total flying hours were considerably higher than those logged by many of his instructors. More important, his time consisted of short, high-activity flights in numerous different aircraft, rather than straight and level, cross-country ordeals in a few. Sometimes his skills advantage caused him to appear condescending....

How "not" to do a short field landing in an AT-9 (pilot unknown)

"Some of our young lieutenant flight instructors only had four or five hundred hours, while many of us students had considerably more. On one flight, my instructor asked me to practice a short-field landing at one of the auxiliary fields. Undaunted, after having taught this so many times in a variety of different

airplanes, I approached the field in slow flight. Just before coming to the fence that bordered it, I chopped the power and flared out, stopping very, very short. The surprised instructor told me that was not the way to do it. He said you should fly well into the field, touch down on a spot and let the airplane roll out. If I had used his method I would have been well off the landing field and into the cotton!"

In addition to demonstrating his considerable flying skills, Paul also found time to inject his special brand of humor—another trait he carries on to this day....

"We had radios in the AT-10s, and often times the 'Green Hornet' would speak over the airwaves. It didn't take long for some of my buddies to learn the identity of the scoundrel—this 'kilroy of the air' was yours truly!"

At long last Paul was to be commissioned as a Flight Officer in the Army of the United States. He would also receive his second military pilot badge, the elusive Service Pilot Wing. It was late October 1944, and it was cause for another celebration....

Audrey pins on Paul's Service Pilot Wings

"Audrey and my brother, Norm, took the bus to Blytheville to attend my graduation and appointment as Flight Officer. I was very proud of my 'pinks and greens,' and especially the wings with the 'S' on them. After the ceremonies and the celebrations, Norm returned home. Audrey and several of the other wives and girl friends went with us by train to Memphis and the 4th Ferrying Group, where we were processed for our assignments. Bill Ralston, a close friend from Milwaukee, and I decided to request a transfer to the 3rd Ferrying Group, as they were more active in ferrying fighter type aircraft. While our requests were being handled, Audrey returned home to work."

What was it like to be a "war bride"? Audrey tells us....

"Of course the war years were lonesome years for me, as they were for the many other girls whose husbands or boyfriends were gone. I spent my weekdays working and my evenings writing letters, reading, and making items for my 'hope chest.'

"Because Mom worked for a telephone company, she sometimes had to work on weekends. I would then spend time with Ruth Wickert, a friend I had met at work, and her family. On Sundays, they would pick me up and take me to their home for dinner; later that evening they would drop me off at home again. Sometimes we went for a sightseeing trip around the area. They were a very nice family and treated me like one of their own. Ruth had a younger brother, which was a new experience for me as I was an only child. He always answered the phone, 'Wickert-summer-home-some-are-not!' I liked him and he treated me like another sister.

Audrey and Ruth Wickert

"On the weekends that Mom didn't have to work, we'd do our household chores or go shopping together; we were so lucky to have each other during that difficult time."

Paul's flying story continues...

"Bill Ralston and I were reassigned to the 3rd Ferry Group in Romulus (Detroit), Michigan. When we arrived, I spent some time in the link trainer and then checked out in the C-47, which later became one of my favorite airplanes. While we were waiting, an assignment came through for a trip to India in a B-24 Liberator (a model 109 used for carrying fuel over the Hump). Bill and I flipped a coin to see who would take the trip as copilot for this new adventure. Bill 'won' the toss and left to join the rest of the crew at the factory, which was just west of Detroit at the Willow Run Airport. They picked up the airplane and soon left for India. A few days later I learned they had crashed after takeoff from Bangor, Maine, killing all aboard.

"I was saddened to learn about Bill and his crew, and often thought of him and the many other friends I had lost to aviation and the war. But I had little time to ponder as I already had orders to go to Uvalde, Texas, to take a PT-19 up to Minneapolis. After delivering it, I was to go back to San Antonio, pick up another and take it to Vernon, Texas, just west of Wichita Falls. I was privileged to see so much of this beautiful country of ours while flying airplanes with stars on their wings!"

The Women Airforce Service Pilots, or WASP, was a blend of two women ferry pilot organizations: the Women's Auxiliary Ferrying Squadron, initiated by Nancy Harkness Love, and the Women's Flying Training Detachment, headed by Jacqueline Cochrane. Although they differed in their methods to accomplish their goals, both ladies believed that qualified female pilots could be trained to ferry airplanes and perform other flying duties behind the lines in order to free more men for combat duties. One can only imagine the resistance they encountered while promoting their programs!

WASPs eventually ferried all types of aircraft, from the slowest liaison, observation and training aircraft, to the largest bombers and the fastest fighters. A WASP flew the Army's first jet, the then top-secret Bell YP-59A; they flew B-17s and even the B-29. Commanding officers began to prefer WASPs over their male counterparts. Why? They delivered their airplanes faster! The women also trained pilots, performed test pilot duties, flew target tows, and trained with anti-aircraft battery, radar and searchlight tracker crews—virtually every type of flying duty except combat and overseas. They were unsung patriots, and their accomplishments have only recently been properly recognized.

During his time in ferry command, Paul crossed paths with these talented ladies....

"Occasionally we flew with some of the WASPs who ferried fighters as well as trainer and bomber type aircraft. They did an excellent job and we respected them. They never expected or asked for anything more than any other pilot. They always carried their own parachutes and luggage, did their own pre-flights, and were treated, at least by our pilot group, as equals. We thought it was pretty neat that women were flying these aircraft, particularly the fighters; yet I know there were officers of higher rank who were envious of these ladies. I think rank sometimes blurred the vision of a lot of people. It seems they felt the higher their rank, the more they should have a say in what airplanes they flew!"

The WASP program ended abruptly in December 1944, a victim of politics rather than a shortage of enthusiasm, dedication or ability. In 1977 their military service was finally recognized by the US government and they were granted veteran status. In 1993 they were honored at the annual EAA Convention, with more than twenty of the original group in attendance. EAA Founder and former ferry pilot, Paul Poberezny, participated in this memorable tribute by flying a special airborne salute in EAA's P-51D Mustang, one of many aircraft the ladies had flown some fifty years earlier. As the powerful Merlin engine pulled the graceful fighter through the bright, afternoon Wisconsin sky, there were no dry eyes in the little group of WASPs watching on the ground.

The pressures of a war situation tend to dilute peacetime safety procedures. In war, you do whatever it takes to get the job done—within reason of course! It is also true that there will always be a measurable degree of risk in any operation involving man and machinery, no matter what our benefactors in Washington may tell us! The politically acceptable level of risk is allowed to increase—sometimes dramatically—when the future of the country is at stake....

"I was soon called back to Romulus and given orders to report to 'Peashooter' school, a name given the pursuit (fighter) training school at Brownsville, Texas. The idea was to check me out in more airplanes so I could be of greater use to my command. First came a four week course in instrument training and back seat landings in the AT-6. The thinking was that if you could land a T-6 from the back seat, you could fly pretty much anything! As I had flown many similar aircraft, including the BT-13, I had no trouble passing the course. However, what came next was far more challenging!"

While it is true that modern aircraft are more complex in comparison, being tasked to fly five different high performance fighters in a matter of days— aircraft you had not even started before—is a daunting challenge in any era. Early in January 1945, Paul did just that. In less than a week's time, he checked out in five different fighter aircraft....

"After completing my T-6 ground school and back-seat landings, came a time I will never forget. I was assigned to fly five different pursuit (fighter) airplanes: P-39, P-40, P-47, P-51 and P-63. It was a short course designed to prepare us to ferry any type of fighter—even some not in the school's inventory! I went through a hasty ground school and sat in each cockpit to become familiar with the locations of the landing gear, throttle, mixtures, and switches. Many times I went over all the emergency procedures, but I must admit that it was difficult to remember everything. Then it was time to fly!"

Day One

Paul's first flight in a fighter type aircraft: the mighty P-47 Thunderbolt....

"The staff sergeant crew chief assisted me in starting the first airplane, the massive Republic P-47 Thunderbolt, or 'Jug' as it was affectionately called. It was an early model, a razorback, so named because the sliding canopy was a fastback style, rather than the bubble canopy seen on later models. What a huge airplane it was and possibly the reason for its nickname. Sporting a big cockpit, it grumbled a deep-throated sound from its radial engine. The exhaust was routed through two large tubes to the rear of the aircraft where it operated a turbo-supercharger located ahead of the tailwheel.

"I taxied out, swung onto the runway, opened the throttle and lumbered into the air. I retracted the gear and soon felt like I was a mile behind the airplane. I climbed out over Mexico and swung around to the east, circling the airport as I continued on up to 10,000 feet. The canopy was still open. As the speed built up to around 220 mph, I decided to close it—but I didn't know how! Each time I had gotten into the airplane for some cockpit time, the canopy had always been open and there was never any reason to close it. I flew the entire hour and forty minutes with it open!

"I found the P-47 to be quite a nice flying machine and was thrilled by the massiveness of it. I came back for some approaches and landings, and discovered it was also very easy to land with its wide landing gear. It had been quite a day."

Day Two

The second P-47 flight: a long one, almost four hours, during which the logbook entry indicates the aircraft reached 400 miles per hour....

"While on this flight, I was east of Brownsville over a swampy area. All of a sudden I saw a flash of light and a big cloud of smoke ahead of me—two B-26 Marauders had run into each other! I couldn't tell if anyone made it out, but later learned that all had lost their lives."

Day Three

Two more "first" flights in two new aircraft: the P-39 and the P-40....

"Unlike most other fighters, when you get into a P-39 you enter through a door. Slamming the door shut was like slamming the door on a Studebaker—it even had roll up windows! Of course, being a little thinner back then, one could fit in it fairly well. Another unusual design of the P-39 was that the Allison engine was installed behind the pilot. A driveshaft ran forward under the floorboards, through a housing and into a gear box, from which it drove the propeller in the nose. Upon starting the engine, the vibration of this driveshaft assembly would cause the instrument panel to shake like mad. Many pilots felt uncomfortable having all this mechanical activity going on between their feet!

"We had two run-up areas at the end of the runway: one for air-cooled engines and one for liquid-cooled. The liquid-cooled area was basically for the P-39 and P-63 aircraft, which would easily overheat on the ground. I taxied out toward the runway, closely watching my coolant temperature. I was instructed that if it got to 125 degrees, the pop-off valve would blow and steam would come out. This meant you had better get airborne as fast as possible to get cooling air through the radiators. The temperature was getting very close to that point and I was becoming extremely concerned. When I called the tower, they cleared me for an immediate takeoff. That's when I discovered the P-39 and P-63 aircraft always had priority for takeoff.

"I had never flown an airplane that rolled so long and so fast on the ground. At 80 mph, I applied some back pressure and the nose-wheel lifted off; at around 90 or 95 mph, the airplane finally left the runway. I retracted the gear and climbed out—my head cocked with one ear listening to the sound of the engine, the other to the whine of the gearbox...always thinking about that driveshaft under me!

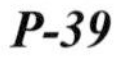

P-39

Curtiss P-40 Warhawk

"I flew for an hour and thirty minutes and began to feel good with the airplane. I'd heard a lot of stories about it flat-spinning, or even tumbling, if it was stalled. But nothing like that happened, and I brought it back for some nice landings. I taxied up to the ramp and got into a Curtiss P-40 Warhawk."

His third fighter, the famous P-40, had by this late in the war relinquished its front line status. Still, it was an impressive airplane, one with a historic background that would later be properly eulogized....

"While flying the P-40, I imagined myself as one of the Flying Tigers. We all admired the men who had flown with the American Volunteer Group in China—the famous Flying Tigers!

"You can always tell a P-40 pilot, for he or she knows one of the little secrets of this fine machine: when retracting the landing gear handle, your little finger is used to operate a small trigger on the control stick. This trigger operates the hydraulic system that raises (and lowers) the landing gear."

Day Four

The fourth new fighter: the P-51 Mustang, and a second flight in the venerable P-40....

"The North American P-51K Mustang was very much like the more famous D model, each having a Rolls-Royce engine, four-blade propeller and a bubble canopy. The early A and B model Mustangs had the lower powered Allison engines with three-blade propellers and were called razorbacks because of their fastback style of canopy. I was thrilled to be sitting in any Mustang, as I had built so many models of the airplane. I cranked this one up and flew it for two hours and twenty-five minutes!

"I heard that if you bounced the Mustang upon landing and then applied too much power while recovering, the torque from the powerful Rolls-Royce engine would cause the airplane to roll—you could not hold it level with the rudder. This was certainly true; however, I was able to make very good three-point landings and immediately felt more comfortable. I taxied back to the ramp to once again fly the P-40 Warhawk.

"There is quite a difference between flying a Mustang and a P-40. The P-40 is much more docile and also a bit tail light—at least the model I flew felt that way...and I did see several up on their nose on the runway when the brakes were not used sparingly!"

Day Five

A "review" day that included a short twenty-minute flight to practice landings in the P-39, and a much longer local flight in the P-47.

Day Six

The fifth and final new fighter, a close relative to the P-39: the P-63 Kingcobra....

"The P-39 and P-63 were quite similar, the latter being an improved airplane with more power, better brakes, a much better cooling system (due to larger radiators), and a larger fin and rudder (a dorsal fin was added later). As in the P-39, the Allison engine with its long driveshaft caused the airplane to shake noticeably. But I enjoyed flying the P-63; it was easy to fly and more comfortable than the P-39. Of course, both had tricycle landing gear which certainly made them much easier to land than either the Mustang or the Thunderbolt where you couldn't see over the nose."

Imagine soloing five different high-performance fighter aircraft in six days! That would be akin to asking a current military pilot to check out in a F-14, F-15, F-16 and F-18—starting with a T-38 for good measure! Paul's feat justified a minor celebration at the Officer's Club...then it was off to the barracks for a quick letter to Audrey.

For the next four days, Paul flew additional familiarization flights in each of the fighters, after which it was time to leave "Peashooter" school. A hurried graduation picture was taken in front of the barracks and then it was off to Grand Prairie, Texas, and the North American P-51 manufacturing plant. Upon arrival, he was confronted by an awesome sight—row upon row of brand new, shiny P-51D Mustangs, some sporting the markings of the Netherlands and Australian air forces. His assignment was to ferry a new Mustang to Newark, New Jersey, which was a shipping point for fighter aircraft going to England. It was the first of many hours Paul would spend in this legendary gunfighter. Ironically, the P-51 would also be the last military airplane he flew prior to being discharged at the end of the war. But for now, he had lots of airplanes to deliver....

"I had many wonderful experiences ferrying aircraft, having the opportunity to fly all the liaison models, the basic and advanced train-

ers (both singles and twins), and many of the fighters. Our orders allowed us a very high priority while riding the airlines using our TR books (Transportation Requests), which were just like checkbooks. We often rode in the famous DC-3, and occasionally a bus or train.

"I ferried many of the fine, newly modified for long range, P-47Ns from the plant in Evansville, Indiana, to the west coast. Whenever I could, I stopped in Milwaukee to see Audrey. Sometimes my control officer (whom we always called upon arrival and again before departing each stop), would question my stopping there, but I usually had an excuse that satisfied him.

"On one occasion, while taking off from Evansville in a P-47N, I was departing to the north when the engine began misfiring at about 500 feet above the ground. I was losing power, but still able to maintain altitude. Not knowing if I was going to make it back to the field, I unbuckled my seat belt and shoulder harness in preparation for a low-altitude bail out. I remember hearing another test pilot tell the tower over the radio, 'He's still going...!' After what seemed like ages, I was able to return the airplane to the field and land safely.

Another P-47 ferry flight

"I was then assigned another P-47 to take to the same destination, Long Beach, California. It was only natural to be a bit concerned on my next takeoff. But it went well, as did most of the trip, until I was approaching to land at Winslow, Arizona. After a long three hour and forty-five minute flight from Oklahoma City, I encountered landing gear problems and had to put the gear down using the emergency system. After waiting a few days while the aircraft was repaired, I delivered it to Long Beach. Next, I picked up a new P-51D at the main North American factory, which was located at Mines Field in Los Angeles (now known as Los Angeles International Airport). As my final destination was Newark, I decided to make a special appearance along the way, so I flew by way of Winslow, Denver and Omaha to Madison, Wisconsin. I chose Madison in order to have enough fuel to make it to my next scheduled refueling stop—with one diversion!

"As I was in the area, I 'naturally' had to swing by Waukesha County Airport, my pre-war stomping grounds. After some low passes, I did a few rolls and then held the aircraft on its back for a bit. Suddenly my windshield was covered with oil. I quickly recovered to level flight, landed at nearby Milwaukee airport and taxied up to the old Pennsylvania Central Airlines hangar. Even with the problem, it was quite a thrill to bring one of our country's top fighters back to the hangar where, as a young lad, I had looked through the windows to see the airplanes inside. My problem was that an oil cap had come off, something that has happened to many a Mustang pilot (including myself) over the years. As always, it pays to do your own checking!

Paul's unscheduled stop in Milwaukee provided an opportunity to see Audrey; meet up again with old friend, Eddie Holpher (lower left); and spend some time with brother, Norm (lower right).

"While the airplane was being cleaned by the chief mechanic for Penn Central, I was able to spend some time at home with Audrey and get my clothes washed and pressed before resuming my trip to Newark. My stop had inadvertently provided me the privilege of flying the first P-51D into what is now General Mitchell Field. I could not have known it then, but I would soon be flying P-51s out of there on a regular basis!"

Paul has always enjoyed flying the Mustang and many of his more memorable moments would be that aircraft. But during his ferry pilot days, it was the P-47 Thunderbolt that provided most of the challenges....

"A week or two later I was assigned to ferry a P-47N to Sacramento. While flying from Amarillo to Albuquerque, I began to encounter some very bad weather, including snowstorms and poor visibility. The weather really closed in near a place called Otto, New Mexico, some seventy or eighty road miles east of Albuquerque. I decided to land on their 3500 foot, sandy, east-west strip.

"I had no problem landing the 'Jug' with its wide landing gear and the sand to help me slow down. The buildings at Otto contained the Radio Range and its now familiar 'beam' and 'cone of silence.' I taxied up to the headquarters shack and shut down. Next to it was a small house that provided living quarters for the husband and wife who operated the facility. They greeted me as if they hadn't seen anyone for a long time—which may very well have been the case, being so far out in the open country. We went inside and talked for a while.

P-47D

"Soon we began to hear other airplanes calling in, also having difficulty with the weather and wanting information about the airstrip. I encouraged them to land, advising them I didn't have any problems with the P-47N. A short time later, two other P-47Ns landed; fifteen minutes later, a P-63 Kingcobra. We all rode the twenty-five miles to the nearest town with the radio station manager's wife to buy extra food. They had enough blankets and allowed four grateful pilots to sleep on the floor of their little house. We had a grand time that evening.

"The next morning was a bit cloudy, but VFR. I departed first, turning north towards Santa Fe, then west around the mountains and south to Kirtland Field in Albuquerque for fuel. The other two P-47s also took off, but the pilot of the P-63 had trouble with the short, sandy runway. With only some 3500 feet available, he was unable to get up enough speed to make a safe takeoff. I later learned the aircraft had to be disassembled and trucked to Kirtland Field."

United States aircraft production facilities were scattered all over the country, providing plenty of work for those in ferry command. Paul picked up North American Mustangs in Dallas and Los Angeles, and Republic Thunderbolts in Evansville, Indiana. He visited the Bell aircraft plant at Niagara Falls, New York, to deliver P-63 Kingcobras destined for the Lend-Lease Program arranged with our ally of the moment, Russia. Hundreds of P-63s (and P-39s) were ferried across North America to Alaska where they were accepted by Russian pilots. The airplanes were painted in Russian colors with a big red star outlined in white. Paul was involved in the initial leg of this mass transfer of American assets, his task being to get the aircraft from Niagara Falls to Great Falls, Montana. Doing so involved plenty of low-level flying across the midwestern states....

Paul brings the first P-63 to Milwaukee

"I remember many long flights in P-63s, often at low levels. The two 60-gallon drop tanks allowed us to remain in the air for up to three hours—more than enough when it was hot and bumpy! We navigated by VFR, depending on our sectional maps with course lines drawn on them because the (radio) beams didn't cover much of our route. At times, the visibility was poor and you had to be very accurate with your navigation skills. This type of flying wasn't unusual for most of us back then; today it probably would be.

"One incident that happened to me during the ferrying of a P-63 involved a start truck. It had been positioned too close to my airplane, allowing the tailgate to brush up against the side of the fuselage. I guess my nosewheel was turned in that direction too, although I didn't realize it at the time. After the engine was started, I began to ease forward. As the tailgate touched against the side, I thought I had a dragging brake, so I added more power. The tailgate tore a 12-inch gash in the fuselage! My punishment was two hours in the link trainer for not making sure my airplane was 'clear' during the pre-flight inspection!"

Though his orders originated from Romulus, Paul often flew around the country without returning between assignments. The telephone would tell him where to go next....

"I didn't spend much time at Romulus, other than to occasionally check in. When I first arrived, I stayed in the tarpaper shacks on the east side of the field. We had German prisoners based there who worked in the Officer's Club and did other odd jobs around the airfield. Later I shared the beautiful home of Mr. & Mrs. Harry Rudd in the suburb of West Dearborn. Audrey came to visit me there when one of my trips brought me back to the base for a longer period of time.

"As did most of us in this command, I was able to fly a number of different aircraft. One was the A-24, an Army version of the famous Navy Douglas Dauntless SDB dive bomber. I remember E. J. Meyers and I being told to pick up two of them in Windsor Locks, Connecticut, in April 1945. 'E-J' flew with me quite often and was a very congenial pal.

"We took the bus from New York City, lugging our parachutes and flying clothing, and living out of a small briefcase. After changing clothes in Operations, we placed our uniforms in the pillow cases that were 'borrowed' from the hotels and BOQs to keep our clothes clean while they were in the aircraft. We then took off for our first stop at New Castle, Pennsylvania. Upon arriving I realized my wallet was missing.

I remembered leaving it on top of a locker, so I turned around and flew back to Windsor Locks. But the wallet was gone and no one had seen it so I refueled and flew on to Langley Field, Virginia, arriving late in the afternoon...with no money.

"Since I also had no identification, I was unable to get into the Officer's Quarters. I went over to the Enlisted Men's Club where a sergeant and a WAC were more understanding and allowed me to wire home for some money. That night I ate in the Enlisted Men's Mess Hall and stayed in their barracks. The next morning my money arrived and I took off for Bush Field, south of Augusta. Many months later, my wallet and its contents were returned to me—but no money!"

As we have already discovered, Paul joined the service to fly—certainly not to be in a parade....

"On another occasion, I delivered a P-63 to Great Falls, Montana, and returned to Romulus in a DC-3 late one Friday night. When I saw an order stating that everyone was to muster for a base parade the next day, I hurried over to Ops and told them I'd ferry any kind of airplane to any location—just so I didn't have to go on parade! The Ops Officer said there was an L-4 at the Piper plant in Lock Haven, Pennsylvania, that had to go to Ft. Sill, Oklahoma. I quickly packed and went to Detroit to catch a bus.

Note 'Poop Deck' on cowl

"After checking out the aircraft the next day, I threw my gear in back, jumped in the front seat, and took off with my map and compass, flying along at 600 or 700 feet above the ground. It was early summer and it began to get a little choppy in the afternoon. All of a sudden there was a big 'bump' and my parachute fell forward onto the rear seat, jamming up against the rear stick. I couldn't pull my stick back and the airplane began to descend. Quickly, I unbuckled my safety belt, turned around and lifted the chute back onto the rear seat. I was down to less than 200 feet above the trees before I was able to climb again. I climbed until I reached 2,500 feet before taking time to

recheck the parachute. At the next airport, I landed to properly secure my baggage…continuing my flight more than a little wiser!

"When I landed at Ft. Smith several days later, I went to see a rodeo…the first time I had ever been to one. On the way back to my hotel, I stopped at the bus station to see if anyone was going west; if so I'd give them a ride in my airplane. There was a sergeant going to Ada, Oklahoma. As he was on leave, he didn't have too much stuff, so we packed it in and took off. I landed on a dirt road just north of Ada to let him off, and then continued on to Ft. Sill. In all, the trip took eleven days and almost thirty hours flying time! Happily, my next assignment was to take a P-47D from Evansville to Abilene, Texas. Even with the weather, I did that in a day and a half—a welcomed change of pace!"

By now the war in Europe was in its final throes, the allies having pushed the once mighty Wehrmacht well back onto its own soil. Victory was a matter of hours away, which meant the demand for support in the European theater had eased dramatically. On May 7, 1945, Germany surrendered; the United States could now shift all its resources to the Pacific campaign.

"I recall being at Evansville to pick up a P-47 when President Roosevelt died, and I was in Little Rock ferrying another P-47 when Germany capitulated. But the war was still going on in the Pacific and so our efforts turned to the west and the Hump in India—that vast range of mountains that claimed so many lives and airplanes while ferrying food, fuel, ammunition and other supplies into China. I was called back to Romulus at the end of June and issued orders to report to Palm Springs. There I would train and check out in the Douglas C-47 prior to going to India to fly the 'CBI' (China, Burma, India) routes.

While on leave, Paul visits with his dad (center) and brother, Norm

"I took the opportunity to spend a few days at home before heading to California. When it

was time to leave, Audrey went with me on the North Shore to Central Station in Chicago and watched many of us board the train before returning to her home. We spent five days on that train: stop-start-stop-start, all the while listening to the constant clickety-clack of the rails. We finally arrived in Palm Springs about midnight, a little depot out in the middle of nowhere—nothing like the Palm Springs of today!

"Several dozen of us got off the train, but no one was there to meet us. It was dark and we could see the lights of the town and the airport beacon off in the distance. We began to get impatient and considered walking to the base—at least we did until someone mentioned scorpions, a crab like creature with a tail poised over its back that was said to have great stinging power. We stayed put, and soon the bus came and took us to our barracks.

"The next day we reported for duty and learned just how hot our tour in Palm Springs would be, with temperatures up around 100 degrees each day. Our barracks didn't have air conditioning—not even the old water-cooled type of air conditioner, or swamp cooler, as

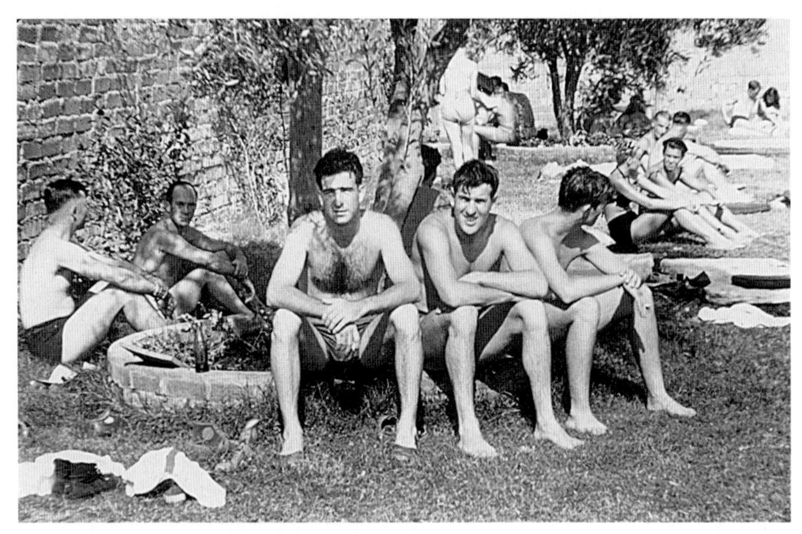

Outside air? — trying to find a cool breeze

they are also called. We envied the Italian prisoners whose quarters on the north side of the base were air conditioned. We also wondered 'why?' "

Why indeed!

Checking out in the once familiar C-47 "Gooney Bird" was nowhere near as difficult as coping with the burning-hot days in Southern California....

“Ground school and checkout was very easy for me, having already qualified in the C-47. We had many nice flights, just a pilot and co-pilot, often going over to Los Angeles, Hollywood and Lake Arrowhead. Most of us flew in shorts and I recall how uncomfortable it was trying to sit in the seat prior to start-up. The leather burned the back of your legs and the control wheels were so hot to the touch that it was uncomfortable holding them until long after we were airborne. I made several trips to LA and Hollywood, admiring the many orange groves and palm trees that began at Banning Pass and continued westward to the ocean. What a change today: a concrete jungle.”

Paul continued his training, preparing for those long flights across the Himalayas into China. It meant day and night practice missions....

“One of my more interesting flights occurred at night. I took off to the north and made a right turn, observing what I thought was another C-47 on a downwind leg with its cabin all lit up. I began a diving turn to cross underneath when my co-pilot and I were quickly jolted to our senses—we realized that ‘it’ was a train, not an airplane! Another learning experience...this time in vertigo and mistaken identity.”

And another close call! Wartime fatalities are not always caused by the enemy; many occur during training and in the development of new weapons. One of the latter involved the most celebrated American fighter pilot of World War II, Richard I. Bong....

“We were at Palm Springs when Wisconsin ace, Richard Bong, lost his life during a test flight in a P-80 Shooting Star jet fighter. I later learned about the I-16 pump situation while flying the P-80. It was an extra boost pump added to ensure that fuel could still get to the engine in the event the regular fuel pump failed. A great pilot died and a tragic lesson was learned for others to benefit.

“This day, August 6, 1945, was also noted for the first wartime use of an atomic weapon: the dropping of the atom bomb on Hiroshima. After hearing the news, we all suspected the war would not last very much longer.”

Indeed, World War II was all but over. Three days later a second bomb was dropped on the city of Nagasaki and the Japanese capitulated. The Tripartite Pact had been defeated and their historic challenge to democracy overcome. On September 2, 1945, World War II officially came to an end on the deck of the battleship, USS Missouri....

"V-J Day was a memorable day for all of us. Another pilot and I were scheduled for night missions, so we flew down to Hollywood and circled it at some 800 or 900 feet, watching the search lights bounce off the mountains and the buildings. The streets were jammed with people waving and shooting skyrockets in every direction. For them, the war was finally over. But not for us.

"I returned to Romulus from California to ferry fighters once more. After delivering a P-51D to Phoenix on September 27, I was sent to Sioux Falls, South Dakota: then an air base, now a municipal airport. I was to pick up a doggy P-63 and take it to Kingman, Arizona, probably to be scrapped. When I arrived, I called Operations at Romulus to tell them I was ready to takeoff. The Operations Officer told me to forget about the P-63 and return home as soon as possible. Out came my TR book and my orders, and I returned to Romulus. A few days later I was discharged from the Army and headed home to Milwaukee for a new and different kind of life.

"Although I enjoyed the flying, I was glad the war was over. It was a great joy to be able to go home, this time to stay. I wanted to settle down and be with Audrey—after all, we'd been married for a year and a half and hadn't been with each other for more than a few days here and there! Maybe we could look into the airplane repair business…or do whatever else I could to stay in aviation."

Paul's last military logbook entry reads, SO ENDS MY ARMY FLYING. DAMN IT. Which meant that for him, Audrey, and their world in Milwaukee, Wisconsin, the war really had ended!

TIME INTO CLASSIFICATIONS			REMARKS INSTRUCTOR SHOULD ENTER IN THIS COLUMN THE NATURE OF EACH MANEUVER IN WHICH INSTRUCTION IS GIVEN, AND THE TIME SPENT THEREON, AND SHALL ATTEST EACH SUCH ENTRY WITH HIS INITIALS, PILOT CERTIFICATE NUMBER, AND PERMANENT RATING.
	Dual	Solo	
	477 50		
	2	20	Ferry
	1	35	— So ends my army flying Damn it
	1	30	Instruction
	2	10	"

Chapter 18

The Early Post-War Years

The greatest war in history was over. Tens of millions had died, supposedly to make the world a better place for the survivors and their offspring. But scientific advancements in weaponry had increased man's destructive powers to where entire societies could now be eliminated! The atomic bomb hailed the dawning of the nuclear age and the potential for widespread devastation. Huge air forces were capable of quickly delivering tons of effective explosives to multiple targets. Soon there would be supersonic aircraft, thermonuclcar bombs, intercontinental ballistic missiles and much more. Current advances in weaponry and delivery systems were unprecedented.

No longer could a major power like the United States isolate itself from the world. The end of the Second World War actually meant the beginning of a broader search for power and influence, natural resources, and even national identity. This worldwide quest precipitated a confrontation between two former allies with vastly different ideologies: the Soviet Union and the United States. It would be called, "The Cold War."

In the long run, World War II solved little, at least insofar as settling differences. Man would continue to fight and within five years the United States would be involved in another war: Korea. After that would come the Middle East, Vietnam, and so on. In order for positive things to happen to humanity, it seemed that individuals remained our primary hope—individuals like Paul and Audrey Poberezny, working together as a team!

In less than a quarter of a century they had grown up through a depression and a world war, stubbornly clinging to their dreams. He served his country while courting and marrying his childhood sweetheart; she supported his passion while gaining skills in the business world. The diverse experiences they encountered created a wealth of knowledge and ability that would serve them well in future endeavors. But for now, like so many others, they had to cope with the reality of a post war environment....

Paul and Audrey celebrate war's end

"Babe" Ruesch welcomes her son-in-law home

"It was a happy time for the many families throughout the world whose sons and daughters, husbands and wives, returned to their homes and loved ones. I arrived home in October 1945, ready to start a new life with my lovely wife and our wonderful families. Audrey and her mother had moved into another apartment on 32nd and West Pierce in Milwaukee. Mom Ruesch rented a room next door in a private home in which to sleep at night so that Audrey and I could have the apartment to ourselves. The house at 3801 South 56th Street remained rented, as it had throughout the war years. Audrey was still working at Northwestern Mutual Life Insurance, her mom with the Wisconsin Telephone Company.

"Like so many other servicemen coming home, it was time to find a job...but what to do? The war-machine factories had come to a standstill as production now began switching to much needed civilian

products. Ration stamps needed to be replaced with great quantities of product for the free-market system. But Audrey's mom felt that airplanes were not here to stay. To her, driving a city bus or getting a job with the telephone company offered job security and a good retirement for her son-in-law. However, I could not imagine a life without aviation, so I went out to the Waukesha County Airport to talk with my old acquaintance at Spring City Flying Service, Dale Crites.

"I asked Dale if he needed a flight instructor and mechanic. He did, so I began teaching students in PT-19s, Piper Cubs, Aeroncas and Taylorcrafts, occasionally flying his Waco Straightwing or Stinson SR-7 for passenger hopping. I met another longtime friend, Wilbur Schelfeffer, who had gone through the glider pilot program with me. He was an excellent mechanic whom Dale had hired to convert a number of TG-8s back into J-3 Cubs (TG-8s were Piper Cubs previously modified into gliders for the military). I learned much about maintenance, covering, and welding while working with Wilbur.

Dale, Paul and Wilbur

"Several other airmen came home from the war and established operations at our airport; one of them was Captain Jimmy Bruno and Bruno's Flying Service. Yet as more and more soldiers returned home and used the GI Bill for flight training, Dale's operation continued to be successful, even with the additional competition on the field. Perhaps the advertisements by Cessna and the other airplane companies that depicted a great need for privately owned airplanes for the homecoming airmen would come true. Sadly, this was not to be the case."

If only we had realized that the immediate post war period was the last opportunity to enjoy unrestricted access to inexpensive, surplus military aircraft....

"As the war was winding down, airplanes began to accumulate at some of the bases now shut down. What one wouldn't give for that sight today and to have today's dollar to purchase PT-17 Stearmans for $200 or $250, Vultee BT-13s for $400 or $450, North American T-6s for $650, P-51 Mustangs with only ferry time for $1500 to $1800, and so

on. It was said that many B-17s were sold with full loads of fuel, the value of the gas being equal to the price paid for the airplane! How many military museums today wish to acquire one of these aircraft for display but can't, either because of availability or cost? Yesterday they were junk; today they are treasures!"

Hindsight is always "twenty-twenty," which is why protecting our aviation heritage is today such an admirable pursuit for those with the capacity to do so. As generations continue to pass, we will see fewer and fewer of these magnificent machines in the air. Paul was fortunate to have the opportunity to fly so many of them during and after the war. That, along with his lifelong passion for all things with wings, would later manifest itself in his future vocation. But for now he just wanted to keep flying…and maybe take advantage of the current government "fire sales"....

"In December 1945, Dale Crites and I each decided to buy a Stearman PT-17. This meant a long train ride to the aircraft storage and dispersal area in Americus, Georgia. There we saw hundreds of Stearmans for sale; I bought one for $200 and Dale paid $250 for another. We then bundled up and took off on what was a very long—and very cold—flight home.

The Stearman PT-17 parked at Waukesha on a cold winter day!

"At home, we made several repairs to the aircraft. I flew my Stearman until later the next year when I traded it for a Vultee BT-13; the Stearman ended up as a crop-duster for Aerial Blight Control of West Bend. I had my BT-13 painted black with a lemon-yellow stripe, and was continually scrounging for automobile gas with which to fly it.

The Pobereznys' BT-13

"That winter I also flew many trips in the J-3 Cub to Palmyra, located some twenty miles from Waukesha. Landing at this little farm strip always brought out a few farmers with a desire to be flight students; a bonfire kept them warm while waiting their turn. Once again, even though my wages were meager, I could not believe I was being paid to fly!"

A career as a civilian flight instructor has rarely led to monetary riches, even during the best of times. With so much competition springing up after the war, Paul realized he must soon find other ways to supplement his income....

"Even though I enjoyed instructing, I wanted to establish my own airplane business. I had made a new friend, Charlie Gaulrap, an airplane mechanic who often worked out of the back of his car. His regular job was doing maintenance work at an A & P food warehouse. But Charlie was a CAA licensed aircraft and powerplant mechanic and, though I was not, I certainly enjoyed working as one. We decided to go into the aircraft repair business together.

"In March 1946, I landed a Luscombe in a field at Jake Falk's farm in Hales Corners. It was good practice for my student and I wanted to look over the area, thinking it might be a good location for our business. But our plan didn't work out, so Charlie and I continued to look elsewhere.

"The next month we learned that Reuben Miller had an airstrip and a crude hangar some fifteen miles west of Milwaukee. More important, he was agreeable to cheap rent! We made plans to open our aircraft repair shop at Miller's Field while Reuben moved his Porterfield out of the hangar to beside his house. That house still stands today and the airport is known as Capitol Drive Airport.

Our first car–a 1938 Dodge Sedan

"There was no public transportation near Miller's Field, so Audrey and I were forced to purchase our first automobile. Consumer goods were still in short supply and very expensive when you could find them; the few dealers who had vehicles for sale could hold out for top dollar. But we had no choice if I was to continue working, so we purchased a 1938 Dodge sedan. Audrey often drove me the twenty miles to work and helped out whenever she could.

"First the dirt floor had to be converted to concrete—I mixed a lot of concrete with the 'putt-putt' mixer! With enough floor laid to start taking in work, I set out my Sears and Roebuck tools along with a cheap air compressor and spray gun, and opened up shop. A few minor repairs and several covering jobs came in. Our first big job was to convert a Waco UPF belonging to Bruno's Flying Service into a 3-seater by using a kit that was offered back then. One of my flying students, Jesse Norship, later provided us with another significant bit of work—a BT-13 rebuild job delivered to within 150 feet of our door!

"Jesse had a welding company, Wisconsin Welding, located in the heart of Milwaukee. He had purchased a BT-13 and kept it on this little 1700 foot strip. The runway was really too short for his pilot ability—it was barely long enough for someone highly qualified in the airplane. One day Jesse attempted an uphill takeoff in high pitch (low rpm). He lost con-

Jesse's BT-13 (Jesse stands on the left)

trol and ran into the house next door, knocking off a wing and doing other serious damage to the airplane—not to mention the house! Jesse employed us to rebuild his airplane.

"I soon learned that Charlie's daytime job left little time for him to help. Most of the time I worked alone, so our output of work was not great. Even though I was also doing some flight instructing at Miller's, the money was limited and Audrey and I began to see our savings dwindle. I also learned that airplane ownership was too often the last priority when it came to paying bills, even at such bargain rates! Many owners thought that the repair and recovering of airplanes was supposed to be cheap. (I don't think that attitude has changed much over the years either!) We decided I should find a steady job elsewhere and leave what eventually became the successful Capitol Drive Airport to its own destiny."

Audrey had been involved in the ill-fated decision to go into business....

"I thought it was a good idea too—until we didn't get paid! Then I didn't think much of being in business! In the beginning, I thought we would become wealthy, since it would seem that anyone with an airplane had lots of money. Well, if they did, they had it because they didn't pay their bills! But in looking back and considering our own situation over the years—especially the early ones—I can understand how people could own airplanes and have no money. After all, we were a good example!"

Ironically, their aviation business suffered a fate similar to the automobile repair business Audrey's father had left many years earlier, and for most of the same reasons. Paul adds....

"When one thinks back and realizes how these two methods of transportation have evolved—the automobile and the airplane—it is easy to understand that for today's families, the automobile has become a necessity, while the airplane remains a vehicle primarily for recreation and personal pleasure. Apparently we are willing to pay more for repairs to our automobiles than for maintenance on an airplane."

As happened to so many couples after the war, a special event was about to change Paul and Audrey's lifestyle. Although not directly related to aviation at the time, aviation would certainly benefit in years to come. It also proved that life with Paul was not *entirely* focused on airplanes. as Audrey explains....

"I suppose something could be said about having one's own apartment! Actually, it was really the first time we had been together since we were married. But now that we had a child on the way, we were faced with several problems. To begin with, the apartment we were living in was too small and we would soon need more space. Of course, my job could not be continued much longer, as it would be difficult to hide my condition in a few more months. I would have to leave work and we would lose my salary. This led to the third problem, that of Howard needing a steady job, preferably one that paid him regularly so he could support the three of us!

"Mom helped by suggesting we could all move into her house on 56th Street. The tenants were notified their lease would not be renewed and all of us—Mom included—moved in during the spring of 1946. This gave Howard access to a two-car garage and I began to suspect what might be coming next! I suggested that before there were any more airplanes, we should consider finding him a steady, well-paying job!

3801 South 56th Street

"I had still not said a word to my boss about being married—certainly nothing about being pregnant! I knew he would soon have to be told, but before I got around to doing so, he called me into his office to tell me about a better job coming available within the company. He said he didn't want to lose me, but that I deserved the chance to apply as it would entail another promotion. I had to tell him I was planning to leave in a few months...and 'why.'

"He immediately replied, 'So you're finally going to admit you're married!' It shocked me to hear this, for I hadn't suspected he knew a thing. It turned out he knew everything—at least he knew I was married; I had to tell him the part about being pregnant. Somehow he had found out all about our marriage: when, where...he knew everything! Yet all

this time, he never mentioned a thing to me. I told him I would leave now if he wished, but he asked me to stay and help train the new girls in a number of positions that were being filled...mine now included!

"Looking back, I guess I did have a lot of experience there. I worked in just about every position in the company since I started a week or so after graduating from high school. Soon after I was hired, the war had begun. We were an insurance company and our jobs were non-defense related, so all the guys were quickly drafted into the military. I'd been told I would be a messenger for about six months; in fact, I was only there two weeks before I got my first promotion. This happened to me over and over again until I became secretary to our unit president. I really was sorry to have to leave; it was a good place to work. I agreed to stay until it became obvious it was time for me to leave.

"In the meantime, even though our money was becoming scarce, Howard managed to keep flying his airplane. We'd go on weekend 'breakfast flights' in the BT-13—at least I did until my eighth month of pregnancy! Even though it was a large airplane, by then I could barely get in and out of it!"

Paul completes the story....

"On October 3, 1946, our first child was born, a son we named Thomas Paul. I remember first seeing that little red-faced, bald-headed fellow, cuddled in the arms of my beautiful wife: his mother. Like so many other dads, I had patiently waited while Audrey gave birth to a son who has since made his mark in aviation as an excellent administrator and an outstanding aerobatic pilot. How proud we were to have our first child, this healthy eight pound, thirteen ounce son!"

Proud Parents

So many dreams are born without fanfare, only later to become significant. At the moment they occur, we often have little appreciation of their importance or of any future part

Future aviation leaders

they might play. Of course this is best, for if we had access to a crystal ball, we would undoubtedly fail to use it wisely! Neither Paul nor Audrey knew on that day in October 1946 that the birth of their son would one day guarantee the smooth transition of leadership in a great organization that was not even in their fertile minds at the time!

Nor did they know that in less than eight years they would be blessed with a second child, a baby girl!

Wondrous as the event may have been, it also meant Paul's responsibilities had increased. He now had a family of three to provide for....

"Soon after Tommy was born, I asked Jesse Norship for a job at his welding company. He gave me one at a dollar-an-hour and taught me how to electric weld. All day long I sat behind a shield in his small shop filled with hot fumes, welding on the big frames Jesse had sub-contracted from the A.O. Smith Company. At night I came home very dirty and with low morale…my heart was still in the air."

We could have guessed that working as a welder would rapidly lose its appeal, but the need for a steady income had placed responsibility ahead of desire. For the remainder of 1946 and the first six months of 1947, Paul dutifully provided for his family. You do what you have to do; no one says you have to like it! However, if a guy could still do a little flight instructing on the side....

"Less than six months after my springtime landing at Jake Falk's farm, the Hales Corners Airport was born. Bob Moody and Jack Nicoud, both World War II pilots, moved a small filling station office and a few other items to the site, and the airport became a reality. For me, an after work and weekend part-time job doing flight instructing was now available."

Hales Corners Airport

Hales Corners was the second airport (the first being Capitol Drive) Paul had been involved with long before either became an established entity. He simply didn't have sufficient capital to remain at either location until his business could become financially sound. As we now appreciate, this was not to be his fate anyway.

Never having been accused of possessing an idle mind, Paul began to develop an interest in race planes like the Goodyear and Steve Wittman racers. He would draw them for hours on end, fascinated by the designers' ability to squeeze so much performance out of so little subject. The day would come when this interest was augmented by the real thing.

During this period Paul made another wise move, one that later returned big dividends....

"My wartime Air Corps commission as a flight officer and service pilot was similar to being a warrant officer pilot in the Army. Within a year after the war, I had to make an application to change my status and apply for a commission in the reserves. This I did. Effective 12 November 1946, I was appointed a Second Lieutenant in the Officer's Reserve Corps, Air Corps, Army of the United States."

During the winter of 1946-47, Audrey adapted to her new role as mother while Paul remained a reluctant, yet but gainfully employed welder who flew whenever—and whatever—he could....

"In addition to flying my BT-13, I began to fly an F-7F Tigercat in which the owner had installed a crude smoke system so we could do some skywriting. Because the engines ran cool, they didn't produce much smoke. I tried lowering the landing gear and flying at higher power settings and slower speeds, hoping this would lessen the cooling effect and cause them to make more smoke. One day she rolled on me pretty good! It was then I decided that less smoke was better than more stalling —especially in the middle of a word!"

Paul augmented his meager welding salary by flying students at Hales Corners Airport, bringing home two dollars for each hour he instructed in the Luscombes, Cubs, Aeroncas and Taylorcrafts, and even more when he used his own BT-13. By July 1947, he felt he could again make a living from aviation....

Breakfast flights continued throughout the winter!
(Silver Lake, Wautoma, WI)

"Audrey and I became quite active at Hales Corners Airport and spent many hours and weekends socializing after I finished my flight instructing. We enjoyed wonderful times there, including breakfast flights, picnics and several air shows that were quite successful. Harold Gallatin, one of Wisconsin's early homebuilders, built a hangar and brought his single-place Mooney to the airport. Harold was another man I admired for his wisdom and ingenuity. He and his brother were well known for their homebuilt airplanes back in the thirties when Wisconsin was first noted as a developing hotbed of homebuilt flying activities. Unfortunately, his brother lost his life back then in a fiery crash a few blocks from their house: he was flying one of their creations when the wings folded!"

Paul's lifestyle was aided in great part by "Mom" Ruesch. She was always there for the struggling young family, as Paul remembers....

"My enthusiasm for homebuilts and antiques continued to grow during the period when Audrey and I lived with her mother. Mom Ruesch was called 'Babe' by her close friends and family. Every morning, no matter what the weather, Babe left for work at the telephone company. I can still see her walking down the street to the bus stop on the corner and coming home each evening. She was a wonderful woman who gave Audrey and me so many opportunities. She was like a mother to our child; her extra care and love for us enabled me to spend more time with aviation, and allowed Audrey to share my building enthusiasm during those early days."

Paul and "Babe"

To which Audrey adds....

"Mom really was a big help to us. She would baby-sit and make meals—and in effect became a mother to all three of us, always ready to help in any way she could."

More pieces of the puzzle were fitting into place as Paul's persistent pursuit of flight continued to be driven by his undying love of airplanes. Now that he was gainfully employed as a two-dollar-an-hour flight instructor, aviation had reentered his life on a full-time basis. This time it would never leave...although it might change course a few times!

Paul and Tommy astride the "Monstrosity"
(Consolidated L-13)

Chapter Nineteen

Back With "Uncle"

World War II ended too soon! At least it did according to military planners at the time. The deployment of the atomic bombs had caused Japan to surrender much earlier than expected—by as much as twelve to eighteen months in some estimates. The net effect was a significant saving of lives on both sides, although the sudden and unplanned end to hostilities imposed a rapid and often chaotic demobilization on the American forces.

During this period of post-war downsizing, discussions continued regarding the future makeup of the US military. There was no doubt the airplane had emerged as a primary weapon, and this may have helped to push decision-makers into finally agreeing to establish a separate air force. On September 18, 1947, the United States Air Force (USAF) was formed, thus ending aviation's turbulent forty-year relationship with the Army. It also signified a new era where airpower became our country's first line of defense and its primary deterrence against war.

American forces remained in disarray for some time after the war. Troop strengths were so low that in many cases minimum assigned duties could not be carried out. In order to shore up the nation's ability to respond to an emergency, a growing dependence was being placed on the network of Guard and Reserve units. Many of these units had struggled with second-hand equipment and inadequate supplies; now they were being faced with

a new challenge—technology! Their biggest problem, as it was for the active duty forces, was a lack of qualified personnel, which became more critical as modern technology produced increasingly complicated and technically advanced weapons.

During this period of turmoil and uncertainty, circumstance created an opportunity for Paul to return to a military career in aviation. At first, it was not exactly in the manner he had hoped....

"I heard that an air unit of the Wisconsin National Guard was being formed at General Mitchell Field and that they were looking for mechanics and pilots. The pilot positions were mostly for part-time, weekend duties; few in number, they were available mainly to those of higher ranks. On the other hand, air technicians were to be employed full-time. I went down to the airport and was interviewed by an Air Force Advisor who was given the task, along with several state representatives, of organizing the 128th Fighter Wing. I then was told to see Colonels Fojtik and Peterson.

Paul can be seen leaning against the far wall...debating whether or not to join!

"I suppose I could have become a 'weekend warrior' pilot, but the part-time pay was not sufficient to provide for my family so I inquired into getting on full-time as an aircraft mechanic. My experience was reviewed and I was accepted in the fall of 1947 as a Staff Sergeant, a rank I held twice previously. My starting pay was to be $160 per month. As I needed the work, title became unimportant, and I joined the Wisconsin Air National Guard.

"Lt. Col. Paul Fojtik was my commander. He'd been a P-39 pilot during the war and was a good leader. We were just beginning to receive our allotment of twenty-two P-51D Mustangs and would later have a C-47, B-26 and several T-6s. Having flown all these airplanes during the war, it was heartbreaking for me to be preparing them for other officers, knowing I had so much more flying experience and

Paul and Tommy check out the Air Guard P-51

hours than many of them. But I had chosen not to fly in order to have the benefits of a full-time salary…although I quickly found a way to do both! I moved my black and lemon-yellow striped BT-13 next to the guard ramp and often used it to pick up parts and paychecks or for other duties that involved my flying it.

"I kept busy with my maintenance duties. Though there was a great amount of surplus equipment available, it didn't seem to get to our unit. Once we had to use our coffee fund to purchase two 50-gallon barrels of much needed hydraulic fluid from a local war surplus store. We sold one barrel to recoup our money and had the other left for our use.

"During the war, our hangar had been converted into a shop where batteries were made by German prisoners of war. Their barracks were located a short distance away and were no longer in use. We were in need of maintenance stands and so I, along with Sergeants Holsten, Krause and Terlizzi, went to the POW barracks, tore out some water pipes, and returned them to the welding shop. As I had considerable experience in electric welding, I made up several stands. A few of those stands followed me to Oshkosh, many years after they had fulfilled their usefulness with the Guard."

Not only would the stands follow him, so would people. Paul continued to meet and surround himself with those who shared his love of aviation. People like Bob Nolinske and his wife, Lois, became very important to Paul and Audrey, and to sport aviation within a few short years. Bob Nolinske recalls their first meeting:

> I met Howard at the Wisconsin Air National Guard in either 1947 or 1948, where we both worked in aircraft maintenance. I think what attracted us to each other was that we both had BT-13 aircraft and enjoyed flying them. One summer afternoon after work, Howard was going to fly his BT-13 to Hales Corners Airport and suggested I follow him with my airplane, and I did. He introduced me to a lot of nice people at that airport. It was an active flying group which I was happy to join. It was known as the Whitnall Flying Club.

Tommy is ready for breakfast!

> Lois and I flew to various fly-in breakfasts, air shows, etc. with another couple, but invariably we would meet Howard, Audrey and sometimes Tommy at the same functions. We were always impressed with Howard's sense of humor and outgoing friendliness. Over the years we enjoyed many social functions at the Hales Corners Airport with Howard and Audrey.

In an effort to broaden his range of skills, Paul used the GI Bill to take flying lessons in a Republic Seabee at Anderson Air Activities in Milwaukee....

"Every pilot dreams at one time or another of flying an amphibian aircraft off land and water, but for me the experience fell short of my expectations. Bouncing off the waves in Lake Michigan in this underpowered aircraft provided far less enjoyment than I had imagined. Also, having to remember to place the landing gear 'up' before landing in the water was an unnatural procedure. But I kept at it, soloed, and got my seaplane rating."

Even though he was not employed by the US Air Force, Paul wisely maintained his reserve pilot status....

"In order to keep my pilot status, I was required to take a check ride in a military T-6 aircraft. I flew my BT-13 down to the air force contingent based at Orchard Place, Illinois, now O'Hare Field. The first time I went, I arrived at base ops and made it known why I was there. As I was filling out the ever-present paper work, the pilot who was to give me my flight check asked how I got there. I told him I had flown my own BT-13. After looking over my flight records, he completed the paperwork without requiring the normal check ride. Within several months I received my commission as a Second Lieutenant in the USAF Reserves and was re-rated from Service Pilot to Pilot, thus earning my third military wing, the plain 'Junior Birdman' wing.

Paul and his BT-13

"I continued with my Air Guard tasks and flight instructing on evenings and weekends at Hales Corners Airport. The tools from our airplane repair shop sat on the benches in our garage on South 56th Street where Tommy, Audrey, Babe and I were adjusting to our new life. Things were looking much better for us—at least I wasn't driving a bus!"

"While at work one day, an L-17 (Navion) and two Aeronca L-16s arrived at the base. More kept coming until we had tucked away a total of two L-17s and fourteen L-16s into our hangar. Rumor was that these were Army planes assigned to the famous Wisconsin Red Arrow 32nd Division of the Army's newly formed Light Aviation Division (later changed to Army Aviation).

"About a month after the aircraft arrived, I was called into Colonel Fojtik's office. I couldn't help but wonder if the fuel we had drained from the fuselage tanks of the Mustangs to service my BT-13 on its

trips for payroll and other supply runs had caused concern. Or was it the pipes we scrounged from the POW camp? Colonel Fojtik opened the conversation by calling me 'Poop Deck' (a nickname I carried throughout my military career, yet one that actually started during my time on the high school wrestling team). He told me the State Adjutant General and two 32nd Commanding Generals, General Hill and General Briedster, were looking for someone to take over and lead the formation of Army Aviation units for the Wisconsin Army National Guard. They wanted an officer who was a pilot with aircraft maintenance experience, particularly in light aircraft. They felt I had the proper qualifications...and he noted the position would mean an increase in pay!

"To say the least, I was pleased and immediately said 'yes.' I could not wait to get to a phone and call Audrey. Then the colonel added that the aircraft and the position would operate from Camp Douglas (later renamed Volk Field, located in the western part of Wisconsin, near Tomah). My heart sank! I was familiar with Camp Douglas, as I had often flown there in my BT-13 to pick up paychecks for our detachment. One hundred and forty miles from home would mean moving to a new area. What about Audrey's mother? And our home? My head was swimming. Colonel Fojtik told me to talk it over with my wife and let him know the next day. If we were interested, we could drive to Camp Douglas and talk with Colonel Ralph Birkness, Colonel Everett Roberts and later, Colonel Williams, who headed the central location of supplies and materials for the entire Wisconsin State Guard.

"Audrey and I discussed the opportunity and decided to drive to Camp Douglas for the interview. There was much uncertainty along the way; many 'what-ifs' dominated our conversation. Audrey and her mom had always been very close, especially with her being an only child and losing her dad so young. We were still unsure of our answer when we arrived.

"Meeting Colonel Birkness was a pleasant surprise. He was a soft-spoken and sincere officer who had seen battle in the Pacific. Colonel Everett 'Foxy' Roberts was another veteran of the 32nd Division and the war in the Pacific. He gave the appearance of being stern, but I soon found he had a heart of gold. Our meeting went very well and my responsibilities were outlined. I was to move all the aircraft in Milwaukee up to Camp Douglas and find the necessary employees and mechanics to support them. The aircraft would then be assigned to various infantry and artillery units throughout the state. I was to arrange for hangar and shop space, hire and supervise the employees,

and deliver and coordinate all the necessary supplies. My headquarters would be at Camp Douglas and my unit assigned to the 32nd Division Headquarters under the command of General Fritz Briedster.

"It was a real plateful to swallow...but there was more! They added that as part of my duties, I would have a new L-17 at my disposal, and L-16s in which to tour the state. They also didn't feel I would have to move, as it was only about an hour or so flight to work. What happiness I felt upon hearing that statement—we accepted the position!"

Other than the distance separating his work from his home, this job was ideally suited to Paul's abilities. Now that the relocation problem was solved, especially since the answer meant more flying at government expense, the couple eagerly accepted. They could remain in their home in Milwaukee while Paul embarked on his next aviation adventure. Effective February 24, 1948, he was commissioned a Second Lieutenant in the Field Artillery of the Wisconsin National Guard. Even more important was his classification, "Pilot, Ground Forces." Once again, Paul was being paid to fly, albeit with a distinctive Army flavor....

Another meeting with General Briedster later in my military career

"Since I was now in a Field Artillery unit, it was necessary for me to learn about such things as artillery firing—I had to hit the books! When General Briedster gave you that bulldog look of his and spoke, his point was well made. He was a fine gentleman and a great leader...a credit to our country. Many years later, after leaving the military with failing health, General Briedster asked to be driven to my EAA office, which was then located in Hales Corners. He told me how proud he was of my flying for him and also of what I had done in starting EAA and the museum we had built. It meant a lot to me and taught me a great deal about this man who was both firm and fair, yet possessed an extremely soft heart!"

"The L-16s in the Milwaukee Guard hangar were stacked on nose blocks off in one corner. The Air Advisor from the US Army, Captain

Anderson, arrived with his assistant, Sergeant Ward. Between us, we prepared, inspected and ferried all fourteen L-16s to Camp Douglas, where we temporarily stored them in an unused hangar. Next I checked out in the Navion. It was built in San Diego, California, where they also held a school on maintenance of the aircraft. Colonel Birkness ordered me to attend and said that if I drove, they would pay mileage and a per diem of three dollars per day. I accepted, knowing it would offer Audrey a chance to see some of the country I had been privileged to see under different circumstances.

"We soon left for San Diego and had a wonderful time. In addition to the beautiful countryside, we saw a Stearman propped up on its nose in front of a filling station in San Diego, and a Mustang, a B-17 and several old biplanes on rooftops in other cities. Such was the fate of many wonderful airplanes that had already become a novelty—in my mind, too soon after they had fought so valiantly!"

Audrey adds a gentle reminder....

"Mom agreed to take her vacation days and look after Tommy so we could both go to California. She was always doing things like that...giving up her time and vacation so that Howard and I could do things together. Mom's enjoyment came from spending time with Tommy."

After completing the L-17 maintenance course, Paul and Audrey motored their way back to Milwaukee and the 140 mile commute to his new job....

"I would usually get up around 4:00 A.M., file a military flight plan, and then fly to Camp Douglas. I became very friendly with the people at the Air Force Flight Service Station and Operations at Wright Patterson AFB with whom I had to file my flight plans while flying the Guard airplanes. The early hours were not a drawback for a young man who loved flying so much. Looking back, I recall many days when I took off in 200 and 300 foot ceilings with visibility one-half to three-fourths of a mile, skimming over the wires and treetops. Flying above the same farms, roads and intersections every day made it easier to navigate when the visibility was poor. Only on occasion would I have to land in a farmer's field and wait for the weather to improve.

"In spite of the distance and the weather, I fulfilled my responsibility of getting to work through rain, fog, snow and ice. I often used the L-17 or my own BT-13. The BT made the trip in less than an hour while the L-17 took about an hour and twenty minutes. L-16s took even longer, so I avoided using them. (One advantage an L-16 did have over the others was that in case bad weather forced me down, I had many more suitable places in which to land!) My responsibilities at Camp Douglas involved a considerable amount of travel, yet I rarely missed a day's work. I was also assigned a jeep that many times took me to outposts in Superior, Chippewa Falls, Kenosha, and to and from Milwaukee during periods of inclement weather."

Delivering an L-16 to Superior ("Paul's" L-17 Navion in the background)

Was Audrey a part of the early morning departure routine? You bet she was....

"There were many early mornings when I would get up with Howard, fix breakfast and then go with him to his airplane. In the winter, I helped chip ice off the wings and turn the hand crank on the small gasoline heater that he used to warm the engine for those cold starts. But I always kept in mind that I must return home before Mom left for work so Tommy wouldn't be left alone."

In March 1948 Paul was assigned as an Aircraft Accident Investigating Officer; in May he was awarded his fourth military wing, the Liaison Pilot wing. The next month, the USAF followed suit and changed his Air Force Reserve pilot status to Liaison Pilot….

"Initially I had two L-16s based at Chippewa Falls. Another L-16 and the second L-17 went to General Jim Dan Hill, Commanding General of the 32nd Division at Superior (I operated the other L-17). Two more L-16s went to Kenosha and two to Milwaukee. I was busy renting hangars, hiring and supervising employees, and delivering supplies to the units. I began to fly more cross-country flights; as the number of units increased, I got many more hours in the air."

Since Hales Corners airport was only about five miles from his home, Paul began using it as a remote base of operations. This made sense because he was responsible for picking up and delivering a growing number of aircraft that were on loan to some of the smaller units scattered throughout the southern part of the state. One such unit in Monroe, Wisconsin, was scheduled to return their airplane. Paul requested they fly it to Hales Corners where he would meet the pilot, fly him back to Monroe, and then return the airplane to Camp Douglas. The pilot agreed, but the airplane never arrived….

"It was early spring and there was still snow on the ground. The weather was a bit foggy, although for us low flyers, not of great concern. However, I did begin to worry when the pilot was over two hours late! Then the telephone rang…it was the Lieutenant. I was greatly relieved when he said he was OK. He said he'd bailed out and didn't know where his airplane had gone. I asked what had happened. He said he had gotten caught in the fog and was trying to climb out of it when the airplane stalled. As there were no flight instruments for blind flying, it was apparent to him that he could get killed—so he bailed out!

"He landed in a pile of snow and was at a farmer's house, saying he would notify the sheriff in case anyone found the wreckage. I got directions and jumped in my jeep. Two and a half hours and several phone calls later, I located him. The sheriff said the airplane was about five miles away in a snow-covered field, and then escorted us to the scene. What a surprise it was! There sat the silver L-16, with less than 100 hours total flying time on it, in a small, snow-covered field. The airplane was level and intact, lying on its belly with the gear and wheels pushed out to each side. The bottoms of the engine cowl and firewall were damaged, but repairable; the prop was undamaged. How's that for luck? We hauled it back to Camp Douglas where the repairs were quickly made. Within a month the airplane was back in the air!"

Paul continued to add to his flying time, now approaching 2000 hours thanks to numerous flights between Hales Corners, Camp Douglas and other units throughout Wisconsin. Of course, more flying meant more stories....

"Whenever I flew my BT-13 from Hales Corners to Camp Douglas, I wanted everyone else coming to work to know that I, too, was on time. I'd come in between the cliffs on the east side of the camp and, by putting the prop into low pitch at full power, make that Pratt & Whitney 450 beller like no other! It was a real attention-getter for the camp and, of course, the town's people. But in the opinion of Colonel Williams, a short, snappy officer of long service, this young air corps kid was making too much noise. One morning, as I taxied up to the hangar and got out, he came up to me and snapped, 'That's enough noise!' Then he got back into his car and left. That was all he said…but I got the message!"

"Neil LaFrance had worked with me in the Air Guard at Milwaukee and was now working for me in the Army Guard at Camp Douglas. At times we rode to work together in one of the airplanes. I'd pick him up at the end of the bus line at 43rd and Oklahoma Avenue. He usually had a Milwaukee Sentinel in his hand. After he read it, he'd pass it to me. When I was done, we'd slip a couple of rubber bands around it and drop it off at a farmer's house northeast of Portage. I was sure the farmer wondered about the airplanes that flew back and forth, occasionally dropping off the morning paper. Some time later while flying an L-16, I landed in his field to introduce myself. He and his wife and kids came out, saying they wondered who the pilot was that so often brought the paper and waved to them."

The job was challenging and Paul was enjoying it. He flew many hours, checked out in new types of aircraft, met more people—even delivered a few newspapers! Life was good: comfortable, yet busy. At the same time, another pattern was developing in the world of civilian aviation. An increasing number of surplus military aircraft were being sold to anyone with a little money in their pockets—cash being the only qualification for ownership. Soon the accident rate began to rise; pilots were flying airplanes in which they had never been properly trained. Paul witnessed the following....

"Hales Corners, as was the case at many small airports throughout the country, had an influx of surplus airplanes after the war. Vultees, Stearmans, 'Bamboo Bombers' and more could be bought at a very reasonable price, and the young men who purchased them were eager to try out their new wings. As many had never flown these airplanes in the service, the growing toll in lost lives and injuries was great.

"One tragedy I shall never forget involved a young World War II ex-Navy pilot who decided to go into the banner-towing business. One hot, summer day, he took off at noon with a banner strapped to the wing walk of his surplus PT-17. In the front cockpit was a young lad. With the nose high in a climbing turn, the 220 horsepower Continental was struggling just to keep the airplane aloft. Finally, it couldn't hold on any longer and settled in a nose-high attitude on top of a new Taylorcraft on the ground. The propeller was slashing through the Taylorcraft's fuel tank when the Stearman went over on its back. Almost immediately, there was an explosion and a huge ball of fire. Both individuals managed to crawl out of the flaming wreckage, only to give their lives to aviation: one at the scene, the other shortly after in the hospital.

"Unfortunately, in the years since, many more accidents would be caused by inexperienced, non-military pilots flying the higher powered military airplanes such as Mustangs, Thunderbolts, P-40s and even T-6s, without obtaining the proper training. They joined those whose experience, or lack of it, took them to their final destinies!"

We suspected that the empty garage at South 56th Street would soon find itself occupied by airplane projects. Actually, it was a tribute to Audrey's father that his old workshop was again being put to use by another skilled craftsman....

"Living at home allowed me great flexibility of travel, although it occasionally meant an overnight stay at Camp Douglas in the small room

at our hangar. I began to think about building faster transportation that also had aerobatic capability and in the spring of 1948, purchased a disassembled 1938 Taylorcraft. I picked this design because it was lighter and faster than most similar airplanes. Soon our garage was full of airplane parts, and a clip-wing Taylorcraft was under construction. This marked the beginning of a new era for me—homebuilt aircraft...the spark that ignited my first real 'airplane factory.'

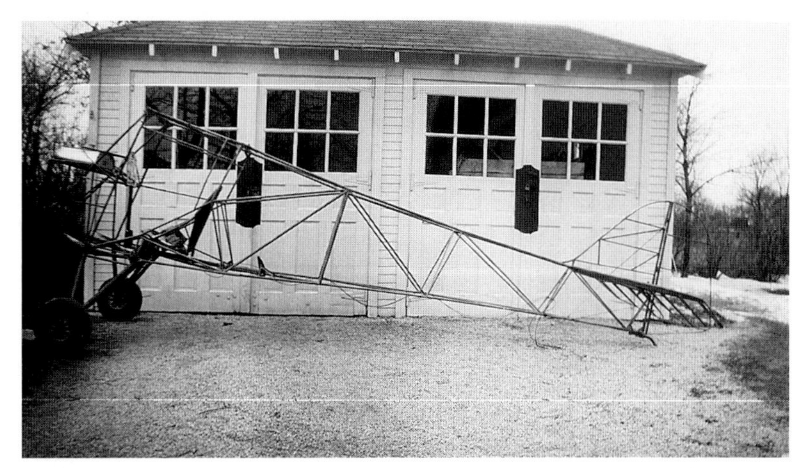

The 1938 Taylorcraft project in front of the airplane factory (garage)

"The influence of the Milwaukee Lightplane Club of the thirties had never left me; our garage quickly became a hangout for builders from that era, as well as those who currently frequented Hales Corners Airport. During this period, my idea of forming a Milwaukee airplane homebuilder's club was generated. Our garage soon became a place for freedom of expression relative to aviation matters and new designs of the homemade airplanes of the future.

"My after-hours flying at Hales Corners as a flight instructor also continued. I enjoyed the flying, and the extra income always helped out at home. Friends such as Gil and Bruce Pitt, Ed and Ruth Falk, Joe Dann, the Nolinskes, the Gardners, and many others, became familiar names to us. We had good times at the Hales Corners airport, as it had become a part of our social life.

"Tommy grew bigger and was given the nickname 'Poncho.' Little towhead 'Poncho' soon became a favorite around the airport with his unique vocabulary. He called the Navion, 'Va-von'; the windsock, 'windblow'; the runway, 'runfield'; and the airport, 'plane-a-port.' When the Army Guard later acquired one of the large L-13 liaison airplanes that was designed and built by Consolidated, Tommy promptly named it the 'monstrosity!' "

The Va-von (Navion) and the Monstrosity (L-13)

Little Tommy on the tail of the Monstrosity

GONK! Another word that became part of young Tommy's early vocabulary, and one that now lives on in his father's. It all started one day when Paul picked the little boy up to greet him. Tommy squeezed his dad's nose and said, "GONK!" pretending it was a toy horn; it was great fun! As the game continued, GONK! grew to mean many things; its use quickly began to encompass everything from "hello" to "goodbye"—as long as the word or action had a pleasant meaning. GONK! can still be heard to this day; Paul uses it regularly when he is among friends. Even Oshkosh tower has been known to say it over the aircraft radio after "Red One" touches down in an airplane. (Paul's radio call-sign is "Red One," Audrey's is "Diamond One") If you have ever been "GONKED!" then you'll know what we mean. It's another of Paul's special trademarks—a four-letter word with class!

While Tommy's vocabulary continued to grow, his father became more involved in the world of homebuilt aircraft. The clip-wing Taylorcraft was his first attempt at modifying an existing design of an approved airplane manufacturer. This was significant because the experience eventually led Paul to believe there were other ways to create a better flying machine besides modifying an existing design. The seeds of creativity, long a characteristic of the homebuilder, had been planted....

"My clip-wing Taylorcraft was coming along quite well. We also recovered the Whitnall Flying Club's 65 horsepower, Lycoming powered Porterfield in my garage and began rebuilding a 1936 E-2 Cub. Behind the garage stood a beautiful Waco 10 that was given to me by Ben Turna, along with another Waco 10 fuselage and tail group on its gear, a Super Cruiser fuselage, and many other parts and aeronautical oddities I had accumulated. I knew that Audrey and her mother were not too fond of this growing airplane junkyard behind our home."

In the summer of 1949, the Army Guard base of operations moved from Camp Douglas to Milwaukee's Curtiss-Wright Airport, although Paul had actually been working out of there for some time. An old metal building was rented from Schwarzberg Chevrolet Company to house the Milwaukee-based Army pilots. The move presented Paul with one of his rare "missed" opportunities....

"Merle Zuelke then operated the Curtiss-Wright Airport under the banner of Milwaukee Fliteways. On the edge of the airport was an old barn containing what was referred to as 'junk.' When I moved to our new quarters, it brought me closer to this barn—although not with the vision I should have had! Merle sold his operation to an ex-Navy pilot, Bill Lotzer, who changed the name of the FBO to Gran-Aire. Merle told me that since I seemed to like old junk, I could clean out the barn and have its contents. Included were a large variety of Continental A-65 and OX-5 engines and props, as well as wings, tail-groups and other parts for Cubs, Travel Aires, Wacos, etc. Much of it had been left over from the days of the pre-war CPTP and wartime WTS programs. The barn was to be removed so I saved what I could over the next few days and a match was set to what would now be so valuable!"

In October 1949, Paul was promoted to First Lieutenant in the Army National Guard. As the Liaison category had been discontinued, he also received the new Army Aviator Wing—his *fifth* military wing.

Now that Paul had a "regular" job, one that paid a reasonable wage with some weekends off, he and Audrey attended a few nearby air shows. One particular act caught Paul's attention....

"I had seen the clip-wing J-3 Cub with the 85 horsepower Continental engine that Duane Cole used in the Cole Brothers Airshow. During one of my trips to Superior, I ran into Duane who, with his wife Judy, operated a resort in Minnesota. We became good

friends. I was impressed with their show and later had the opportunity to fly his airplane called, *Little Bit.* Finding it to be a snappy airplane, it gave me more enthusiasm for my own project...and to think I might possibly go into the air show business myself! I recall my biggest problem was designing an inverted fuel system so that I could fly upside down without the engine stopping. When completed, it operated satisfactorily, but it looked like a Tennessee still, with pipes, tubes and tanks running every which way."

Paul and Tommy in northern Minnesota, visiting with Duane & Judy Cole and their son Rolly

Along about this time, Paul got involved in producing a local air show at the Hales Corners airport. It was scheduled for September 3-4, 1950. Duane Cole describes the event in his book, *This is EAA*:

> We (Cole Brothers Airshow) had long before learned that to contract for air shows on a percentage of the gate receipts was an unsound practice. Unfortunately, we had been the victims of some real 'Flopper-roos' and vowed never again to enter into a contract except for a guaranteed amount. Yet, we had entered into a contract for this one with no guarantee simply because Paul said that he and the rest of the Whitnall Flying Club could stage a financially successful event.
>
> Our trust in Paul was justified. The results were greater than we could possibly have hoped for. The gate receipts, tallied at the end of the second day, showed that our share would be the largest amount we had ever received for any performance. In addition to the monetary satisfaction, there were two other self-satisfying benefits: first, that my friend Paul proved to be a great organizer, and second, the enthusiastic response to our performance by the people of Milwaukee restored my faith in air shows as an entertainment media.

Success often breeds failure. Paul (and Audrey) witnessed the following tragedy....

"The following year, remembering the success of the Cole Brothers Show, some promoters from the Waukesha Airport staged another event at Hales Corners. It was to feature a plane-to-plane transfer by a proclaimed former Hollywood stuntman. When the pilot of the first airplane inadvertently hit a rise in the runway on takeoff, the stuntman lost his balance and ended up hanging by one foot wedged between a strut and a flying wire. The crowd gasped as he eventually fell to his death into nearby Whitnall Park from an altitude of 200 feet. There was a great silence. We later discovered many of the spectators thought it was all part of the show—that it was just a dummy falling from the airplane!"

The Taylorcraft project shows progress

The small nucleus of friends with an interest in building airplanes began to hold informal meetings in Paul's garage while work continued on his Taylorcraft. The aircraft was named *Little Poop Deck*, a tribute to the nickname that had followed him all these years. Actually, Paul often wrote *Poop Deck* on many of the aircraft he ferried during World War II, so the term has an even longer tradition on the sides of airplanes he has touched....

"Wayne Rowley and I bought a Stinson 108 together and traveled around the state in it with our families. At home, my clip-wing Taylorcraft and other projects were being worked on in my garage. All the spray painting going on caused fog-like fumes and thick spray dust. With the oil stove roaring away nearby, one wonders why there never was an explosion! I guess luck again played into our hands. We covered the Taylorcraft with Grade A cotton, followed by many coats of dope. On several occasions we invited some of our friends to join us,

but mostly it was Audrey and I who hand rubbed the finish. When done, the finish looked as good as that on a new Beechcraft or Waco—all shiny and glistening in the sun.

Paul and his flying friends in front of the Stinson 108

"Our little group continued to grow: Ed Effenheim, Dave Franz, Harold Gallatin, Bob Huggins, Elmer Kleigel, Irv Miller, Ed Pietrzak, Wayne Rowley, Roy True and myself would meet and talk about what might be the future of our homebuilding movement. At the time it was only talk; there was no real structure."

Tommy at work

Speaking of "talk," little Tommy became an unwitting victim of the homebuilding environment in the Poberezny garage....

"Young Tommy would often spend evenings in the garage with us. Gil Pitt and his son, Bruce, were also there building their low wing airplane, *Yellow Jacket;* long evenings were spent working on it and other projects. Tommy was small enough to walk around under the wings we were doping, apparently getting quite a whiff of the fumes. I have to admit that some of the language used in the shop was not always appropriate for young ears and it seems our

words were being repeated by Tommy to his mother and grandmother as he was being put to bed. More than once we were severely reprimanded!"

As one might imagine, Audrey played a key role in this story....

"I was shocked to hear those words coming out of Tommy's little mouth and I was embarrassed that my Mom would also have to hear them. Of course, Tommy didn't realize what he was saying—he was just repeating what he had heard. It wasn't long before I was in the garage informing the guys that I didn't like being called all those unsavory names by my little son, and that their language had better change when he was in the garage!"

Tommy wanted to try his hand at building his own airplane ...Audrey suggested he do it away from the garage!

Finished...at last!

Chapter Twenty

I'd Rather Switch...and Fight!

On June 25, 1950, North Korean troops invaded the Republic of Korea (ROK). Within two days, President Truman ordered US air and naval forces to support the ROK army against the communist invasion; three days later, he called in the ground troops. Less than five years after participating in the second war to end all wars, the United States was taking up arms. And once again, the country was not prepared! Throughout the nation, troops in Regular, Guard, and Reserve units were placed on alert. Some units immediately rushed personnel and equipment to Korea and other strategic points in the far east. Others, as was the case with the Wisconsin Air Guard, began preparing for the time when they too would be called into action. The game of "catch-up" had begun....

"At that time, the Milwaukee unit of the Wisconsin Air Guard, the 126th Fighter Squadron, operated early F-80 jet fighters. Word was out that the unit would be ordered to active duty and moved to Madison with the 176th Fighter Squadron, then operating Mustangs. I recall lying in bed that night and talking with Audrey about America, Communism, and the need to again serve my country—I wanted to go! I told Audrey that I was going to ask General Olson, Adjutant General of the State of Wisconsin, if I could transfer from my current position in the Army Guard to this newly activated Air Guard Unit—at least for the duration of its Korean tour of duty.

"General Olson said he would consider my transfer if I found a suitable replacement. I soon found a candidate, a 32nd Division Air Officer named Major John Sarkow. John lived in Superior, Wisconsin, and said he would give it serious thought and discuss it with his wife. Although they had just built a new home and he had a good job with a brewery, John did accept my position. In turn, he was approved by General Olson, and in January 1951 I was transferred to the Air National Guard and the 128th Fighter Group at Truax Field in Madison. The wing was placed on active duty status in February and remained active until the end of October 1952.

"Truax Field was a ninety-minute drive each way from our home. Sometimes I'd stay overnight in the Officers Quarters on the base, which were World War II barracks, but most of the time I drove home. I wanted to be with Tommy, Audrey and her mother...and work on my airplane projects in the garage!

"My time at Truax was quite interesting. I had several duties, including Flight Test and Reclamation Officer. As Flight Test Officer, I was able to fly many hours in the airplanes coming out of maintenance; as Reclamation Officer, I learned the dark side of aviation. Often I would be kidded by the airmen about 'Poop Deck's junk pile,' as it hadn't taken long for my fenced-in area next to the hangar to be filled with the wreckage of F-80s and Mustangs. Many of the parts thrown away would be treasured today."

"Little Poop Deck"

Paul finished building *Little Poop Deck* and began flying his modified Taylorcraft with the "Tennessee still" smoke system. Because the aircraft had been changed so extensively, the CAA licensed it in the "Experimental Exhibition" category. The inflexible restrictions placed on aircraft in this category caused Paul and his friends to have many conversations about changes they hoped might come about in the future. More seeds had been planted, which in Paul's case translated into more projects....

"Now that *Little Poop Deck* was completed, I decided to purchase the remains of the famous Howard 'Pete' Racer that I had found while visiting Duane Cole in Kewaunee, Illinois. On several occasions it raced at Cleveland as the Baker Special, its original Cirrus engine having been replaced by an 85 horsepower Continental. Since then, the airplane had been through a hangar fire and there wasn't much left of the wings, other than fittings and wires. The fuselage, tail group and landing gear were all intact and in restorable condition. I considered making it into a mid wing sport plane.

"Audrey and I towed a trailer to Kewaunee, purchased the remains for fifty dollars and brought them back to our garage. My first task was to disassemble the fuselage, then sandblast and paint it with primer. I often took parts to the Officers Quarters at Truax Field to work on during the evenings I stayed in Madison."

By the 1950s, the jet engine had become the powerplant of choice, though its potential was still a long way from being fully realized. The speed of sound (Mach 1) was first exceeded in October 1947 by US Air Force test pilot, Captain "Chuck" Yeager, in the Bell XS-1 rocket-powered airplane. Shortly after this momentous accomplishment, a soon-to-be-famous production jet fighter, the North American F-86A Sabre, would join the supersonic fraternity on a regular basis. In the early fifties, NACA test pilot, "Scotty" Crossfield would exceed Mach 2 in another rocket plane, the Douglas D-558-2 Skyrocket. The jet age had begun....

"I had the opportunity to check out in the F-80, a Lockheed design known as the 'Shooting Star' and our first operational combat jet fighter. I clearly remember my first flight, as my intentions were to also fly over our home in Milwaukee. Being accustomed to low altitude flying, I stayed low in the F-80. The aircraft didn't have drop tanks and I was amazed at how fast the fuel low-level warning lights came on! I managed to get to Milwaukee and back, but learned that with only internal fuel you don't stay up very long in a jet—especially at low level!

The F-80 Shooting Star with - and without - drop tanks

"One usually found me in the cockpit of the more familiar Mustang. Since we were an active duty air defense squadron, we always had a minimum of two F-80s and two F-51s on alert. It was never a problem for me to fly extra missions for those local pilots who had other things to do; I flew every chance I could get. In spite of performing my regular duties, I believe I stood alert and flew as much as some of the pilots whose *only* duty was to fly!"

The unit was frequently asked to perform fly-bys for special events such as University of Wisconsin football games, and Paul volunteered for them on a regular basis too. But the primary task of the 128th FW was to defend

the northern sector of the country against air attacks—intercept and knock down the enemy threat before he gets to you. The threat was then Soviet bombers; later it would be their missiles. To do this effectively required hours of coordinated practice between flight crews and those operating the ground-based radar tracking units. The "scope wizards" would locate potential targets on their scopes and then guide the interceptors to a point where, if it was for real, they would fire their guns or missiles. But for practice purposes....

"Our intercept targets could be our own F-80s, F-86s, or an occasional SAC B-36 bomber. But most often we chased airliners! GCI (Ground Control Interception) would pick up a Northwest Airlines Stratocruiser, DC-6 or DC-7 that was flying along at altitudes of 15,000 to 18,000 feet. In the Alert Room we were always dressed in our flying suit, boots and 'Mae West' (an inflatable lifesaving device in case we ended up in nearby Lake Michigan or one of the many lakes around Wisconsin). We sat around and talked while some played cards; but when the scramble horn blew, we all ran to the nearby alert aircraft, jumped into the cockpits and took off.

One of the Wisconsin Air Guard F-51's flown by Paul

"Our parachutes were already on the seats. In the summertime, if it wasn't too windy, our helmets were sitting just ahead of the windshields; otherwise, they'd be on the seats. Our crew chiefs were always waiting for us as we reached the airplanes. On occasion, one of them would start the engine while the other helped with your parachute, shoulder harness, and helmet.

"It seemed that I was Element Leader most of the time. As soon as both our engines had started, we made a dash for the runway. Normally before takeoff in the F-51, we allowed the coolant temperature to come up to 100 or 110 degrees centigrade. However, on many

of the scrambles, particularly in the winter, we took off with the temperature as low as 80 degrees. This was pushing the limits a bit, and sometimes white puffs could be seen coming out of the straight exhaust pipes due to the engine not being thoroughly warmed up.

"One such mid-winter scramble went as planned until we were accelerating down the runway on our takeoff run—I couldn't pull the stick back to rotate! I quickly told my wingman to continue while I tried unsuccessfully to stop on the icy, snowy runway. I ended up in a snow bank, causing some damage to the airplane and raising a lot of questions in my mind. What had gone wrong? We found a GI flashlight wedged in the bellcrank under my seat, jamming the control stick! It wasn't mine or my crew chiefs'…was it sabotage? While suspected, it was never proved, although we did have several 'unusual' incidents during this period when the United States was at war."

"On many intercepts, GCI would have us climb to 30,000 feet in what was called a 'Buster' situation, meaning full power, 61 inches of manifold pressure and 3000 rpm. The Mustang engine would begin to lose manifold pressure as we climbed above 10,000 feet. At around 15,000 feet, the automatic boost, or supercharger, kicked in, causing the engine to briefly cut out and send a strong vibration through the airframe. We waited for the boost with anticipation. Since it could vary by a thousand feet or so, we became more than a little apprehensive when it appeared late.

"Some of the pilots I flew with didn't like to go up to 30,000 feet. They'd often call me as they leveled off at 23,000 or 24,000 feet, telling me they'd wait there until I called in at 30,000. If we were directed to go after a Stratocruiser, the wingman, who was supposed to be with me at all times, would track me visually from below in VFR weather. As soon as we were directed to the intercept, I would descend to the altitude of the target airplane and my wingman would join up for the intercept."

"Numbers on the sides of airplane fuselages came about as a result of our air defense missions. We were asked by the GCI 'sights' (controllers) to call back the identification number on the tail of the airplane we were intercepting. Since it was difficult to see it by flying under or above the airplane, we'd fly in formation, often getting as close as 100 feet to the tail so we could read their number! As we flew alongside, we'd wave at the passengers...and sometimes provide them with an extra thrill. After breaking away, we'd drop down below the

airliner, accelerate ahead by 500 or more feet, and then pull up directly in front of their path! They would then fly through our wake, giving the passengers a bit of a shake! As a result of the many complaints from the airlines to the CAA, all civilian aircraft were eventually required to put 12-inch numbers on both sides of the fuselage. And we were told to stay at least 500 feet away!"

"Many pilots who have done a little buzzing, discover that it is difficult for people on the ground to get your numbers, especially when flying right over the audience. This is because the numbers are only placed on the sides of the fuselage. There is still talk by some Customs people that in an effort to further curb drug running, large numbers should be put on the top and bottom of the wings, as was the case many years ago. After that, maybe they will request 12- or 14-inch numbers to be painted on our boats, motorcycles and automobiles!"

One of Paul's favorite airborne mounts was (and still is) the North American P-51 Mustang. He'd fly it any time, anywhere, and he has flown all models from the XP-51 to the P-51H.....

"To most pilots, towing targets was a boring job and there weren't many in the squadron who volunteered to do it. But here was another opportunity for me to get additional flying time in the Mustang. Having towed aerial banners with Stearmans in the past, I found it to be a lot more fun in the Mustang—it also offered me the opportunity to display a little showmanship!

"Normally, the target was laid on the ground behind the airplane, attached by a thousand foot cable to the right wing bomb rack. I was used to laying the banner out in front and to the right of the airplane. Doing it this way shortened the takeoff run considerably, as it allowed time for the airplane to accelerate before having to drag the weight of the banner. Also, the banner would roll and whip off the ground in a much neater fashion. It was a safer and more efficient method for takeoff, as compared to laying the target out behind and dragging it along 2500 feet of runway.

"With the target hooked to the right bomb rack, it had a tendency to pull the airplane to the right. I dropped my left wing to counteract this and the torque of the engine, which made it quite easy to climb straight out. Going to the range 120 miles away at an indicated airspeed of 140 mph took less than an hour; the entire flight took about two and a half to three hours.

"Target practice was generally conducted over Lake Michigan at 10,000 feet and four fighters were usually involved in 'gunnery,' as it was called. They would start their approach and gunnery run from about 13,000 feet 'on the perch,' dive down on the target, and fire when they were within range. Tracers (different colored bullets used to identify which pilot fired what rounds) were mixed in with the regular fifty-caliber ammunition. Whenever I saw tracers going by my airplane—above, alongside or underneath—I really huddled down behind the armor plating. I'd also let the pilots know of my discomfort by telling them their angle was getting too close, and that if it continued, I would drop the target in the lake and go home!"

Ironically, after so many years in the military, the first time Paul was shot at in an airplane was by his own squadron mates during an approved exercise!

Because of the increasing number of hours and the variety of missions he flew in the Mustang, Paul became quite proficient in the aircraft. He even began to enjoy the odd "tangle" with a jet—under certain conditions, of course....

"I enjoyed dog-fighting with the F-80, as long as it was flown by an average pilot! I'd find myself running around with my spinner almost in his tailpipe, although if he ever wanted to pull away and break off he certainly could have done so. Later on, during missions when we were targets for the Sabres, the two of us would be cruising along in our Mustangs at 8,000 or 10,000 feet, searching for a flash of silver or a glint from the sunlight far above. When we spotted one, we'd increase to 'Buster' power and build up as much speed as possible. At the appropriate moment, I'd bring the nose around and upward so we were firing directly at each other—of course, not with real bullets!"

"One evening, we were scrambled in our F-51s to intercept two of our own F-80 jets. The weather was not the best, but we took off and broke out above the clouds at around 8,000 feet. GCI gave us the headings to make an intercept, which we did, and then returned to land. It was dark by the time we changed clothes and got to the Officers Club. Some time later, there was a telephone call from Operations for the CO, after which he came over to me and asked if all the airplanes were down. I knew both our F-51s were back and assumed the F-80s were too, since they had headed back to the base before us and the lead pilot was also in the bar. I said 'yes.' He then said that a farmer had called in, saying an airplane crashed and was burning beside his barn. It turned out to be the other F-80, the wingman: another fatality!"

Although his unit was on active duty, Paul had not received his orders for Korea, so he just kept on flying…and waiting....

"During this time, requests for pilot replacements came in to both the 126th Fighter Squadron, which flew F-80s, and the 176th Fighter Squadron, which flew the F-51. Occasionally a pilot from each squadron would be sent to Korea; so far, my name had not come up."

In order to improve their chances of catching a Soviet bomber, the unit was scheduled to be re-equipped with the latest all-weather, jet fighter-interceptor aircraft....

F-89B Scorpion

"It was the fall of 1951 when we heard rumors that we were to receive the brand new Northrop F-89 Scorpion, a two-place, twin-engine, all-weather, jet interceptor that carried an 'RO,' or radar operator, in the back seat. Shortly after, a Northrop test pilot came to the base in this new airplane, with its long anteater-like nose and wheels that looked like they were off a locomotive. While it was not very good-looking on the ground, it did have a much better appearance in the air, and the factory pilot made the airplane do things that were difficult for us to believe!

"The pilot was a civilian Northrop employee by the name of Robert Love. Bob had flown in World War II and went on to become a jet ace in Korea flying F-86 Sabres. He later became extremely well-known around the Reno Air Racing circuit with his P-51 Mustang race plane, and he was instrumental in helping me acquire the P-51, *Paul 1*, for the EAA collection. Every time I have the privilege to fly the airplane, I think of Bob Love. Bob passed away in 1987.

"Some time after Bob's demonstration we received a few F-89s, although we retained our F-80s and F-51s until more were made available. The squadron pilots went through ground school, which to most of us was quite complicated. We also had a simulated ejection seat trainer that provided quite a thrill! When you raised up on the right hand armrest, a trigger came out and the seat bottomed. Then you squeezed the trigger and up you went about five or six feet—what a swift ride! To think that we had flown the F-80 without ejection seats was not a comforting thought!

"Several of us had a few flights in the Scorpion. We all felt the airplane was underpowered, especially for takeoff, but that it flew very nicely in the air. The split ailerons that also operated as speed brakes were a delight to use—there was no change in trim, no pitching up or down of the nose, and they provided excellent deceleration.

"Then tragedy struck—one of our F-89s crashed! Initial reports came in saying someone saw the tail fall off...maybe it was a wing! The wreckage was very difficult to retrieve from the swampy area on the southwest side of Madison where it had crashed. We went to the funerals for the RO and the pilot, and the airplanes were grounded until a cause could be found."

The culprit turned out to be the wing attach fittings; if they failed in flight, the wing could fold! The problem was supposedly linked to transonic loads that caused the structural failure. It was solved by switching to machined fittings, although other gremlins continued to plague the aircraft after it returned to flying status many months later.

More sad news....

"One morning, our C-47 was scheduled to leave at 4:00 A.M. to pick up a load of supplies at Norton Air Force Base in Riverside, California. Rex Chalker, a good friend of mine from Milwaukee, was the pilot. The copilot was Jack Nicoud, one of the original partners in the Hales Corners Airport; both men were veterans of World War II. We received word later the next night that the entire crew had perished while making an instrument approach into Norton—the airplane crashed near the top of one of the mountains east of Riverside. More funerals to attend!"

Paul continued to travel between his unit in Madison, and Audrey, Tommy and the garage full of airplane projects in Milwaukee. He used the Stinson

108 or *Little Poop Deck* whenever he could, but more often than not, he resorted to ground transportation....

"I drove back and forth to Madison quite often, occasionally driving our Pontiac coupe and, in the nice weather, my brother Norman's

1941 Harley Davidson 74. Audrey and I finally decided I needed my own transportation. An ad in the paper said a lady had a 1941 Chevy for sale; I went to her home, looked at it and purchased it. It was a beautiful machine—an original two-door coupe that had been driven by a fine little old lady. I wish I still had that car today."

"While based at Madison, I stayed in contact with many of my civilian friends in Milwaukee; we either met in my garage or at Curtiss-Wright Airport. One of the 'regulars' was Irv Miller, a prominent member of the 1930s Milwaukee Homebuilders Light Plane Club and the designer and builder of the famous *Belly-Flopper* airplane. Irv was then restoring and rebuilding a Stinson SM8-A."

Irv Miller's "Belly Flopper"

The year 1951 was making its final contributions to history; soon there would be another chapter in Paul's life story....

"The new CO of our squadron arrived from Greenland where he had been flying F-89s. Colonel Victor Milner was a jovial gentleman—a red-faced fighter pilot who, after a few drinks, became well noticed in the Officers Club. I know, because I had recently attended five 'going-away' parties for pilots who were called to Korea. Each time, the engraved wristwatch was passed on to the next person who was due to leave...but none left!

"One morning when I arrived at the base, Captain Bowers, the Operations Officer, said, 'The old man wants to see you.' I walked into Colonel Milner's office in my flying suit and saluted. He asked if I was ready to go to Korea. I said, 'Yes sir, that's why I joined!' He told me that another of our pilots, the fifth in a row, had resigned his Commission so he wouldn't have to go to Korea. I was next on the list. I was saddened to learn that so many of my fellow officers were looking for excuses not to go. Even worse, they were giving up their commissions! I agreed to go, as that had been my intention when I transferred into the unit.

"Colonel Milner said he would give me a 30-day 'basket leave' (I didn't find out this meant a 'free' vacation until after I returned from Korea). He kept my paperwork in his 'in' basket, to be processed only in the case of an accident or other situation that required it for my best interests. He told me to go home and that my orders would be forthcoming to report to Camp Stoneman in California. And from there...Korea!"

Chapter Twenty-One

Korea!

No matter how glamorous war might appear to those who have never been intimately involved in one, and no matter where one's personal beliefs lie regarding being sent into a combat zone, most who are about to participate in hostile activities will experience a feeling of apprehension prior to doing so. And well they should, for war leaves permanent scars on everyone and everything it touches.

The Korean War was one of the bloodiest in history—one and a half million Communist troops and almost six hundred thousand United Nations and South Korean troops either killed, wounded or reported missing. Civilian casualties were even higher, running into the millions killed and several millions more left homeless.

Although Korea is one of the oldest nations in the world, it is doubtful most Americans could have found it on a map in 1950. With completely different language, customs and geography, it was the last place Americans thought they would be going off to fight a war. The "war" officially began in June 1950 and dragged on until an armistice agreement was signed on July 17, 1953.

Most significant variations to the lines of battle took place early; by mid 1951, both sides were firmly entrenched along the 38th parallel, bitterly fighting for small pieces of territory in battles with such diverse names as Pork Chop Hill and Heartbreak Ridge. Meanwhile, huddled safely behind the lines, politicians began "peace talks" that would continue for the next two years. The reality was that there was no reality…and no end in sight.

It was into this land of death and uncertainty that Paul Poberezny was preparing himself to go....

"I went home and told Audrey I was headed for Korea. I'm sure she was not too happy, but I felt it was my duty. I continued to work on my airplanes, meet with my homebuilder friends, and drive back and forth to Madison to fly with my unit, even though I was on leave. I wanted to leave the house and garage in good shape for Audrey and her mom, so I disposed of many airplane parts and projects that had been collected. The partially complete Waco 10 fuselage and tail group on its gear was towed to the dump—another victim of my cleanup. I later regretted some of these actions taken at a time when life was measured in much shorter terms."

On a lighter note, almost everyone in the Milwaukee area had heard about, if not visited, The Sunflower Inn, a famous bar owned by an infamous and ribald lady known as "Dirty Helen." Her clientele ran the gamut of the local social structure: from the famous to the infamous, the honest to the not-so-honest. There were no tables and chairs, just a clean, carpeted floor and a few stools by the bar. You either sat on the floor or you stood. And if you didn't like Fitzgerald bourbon or House of Lord's scotch, you could leave. The place became a favorite Poberezny hangout....

"During this period, Audrey and I made a number of visits to Dirty Helen's—an improper nickname as the place was kept in immaculate condition. It was a well-known local saloon at 18th and St. Paul, in Milwaukee's gas house district. The owner was a woman whose real name was Helen. 'Dirty' came from her past exploits, which were rumored to have been very risqué. She was a real character, her trademark being a colorful and clear language. Helen said whatever was on her mind and didn't care what you thought of the way she expressed it! It was considered a privilege to get into her place because if she didn't like you, you were out! She was partial to service personnel and took a liking to Audrey and me.

"Helen served only scotch and bourbon and she only kept two bottles of each in stock. When she needed more, she'd call a taxi to bring it to her; sometimes I went after it too. A favorite trick of us regulars was to encourage a newcomer to ask for a martini or a beer. This would send Helen off into a flurry of her choicest words, causing much embarrassment to the person...and many laughs for us.

"We went there often—even more so once I knew I was going to

Korea! While the piano player was making soft music in the background, we sat on the floor and talked, sometimes by ourselves, sometimes with friends. On my last visit before leaving, Helen spent quite a bit of time with us, giving me a bible and a rosary. It was a very special evening. Today, Korea is pretty much forgotten as other wars have taken its place."

It was time for Paul to leave....

"The day I left for Korea there was a lot of hustle and bustle at our house, with many friends stopping by to wish me well. My flight was scheduled to takeoff at 7:00 P.M. from General Mitchell Field, and a number of people were on hand to see me off: the Cole Brothers, Mom and Dad, Audrey's mom, little Tommy and, of course, Audrey. Even 'Dirty Helen' called the airport to say good-bye! When it came time to board, I got on the United Airlines DC-3 carrying my crash helmet...wondering if I would ever see Audrey again!"

Duane Cole recalls the evening, once again from his book, *This is EAA*....

> The night he (Paul) left for Korea, I wondered if he would return. My doubts may well have been mental telepathy. Paul was his usual cheerful self during dinner, but afterward, out in his workshop away from Audrey, he seemed depressed and was not the least bit interested in discussing the future of our homebuilt group. I got the impression that he felt he was not going to be around to be involved in it.
>
> At the airport, he laughed and joked with his family and relatives and repeatedly consoled his Mom and Dad with the assurance that he would take care of himself and come home safe and sound. But it was all an act. After the last hug and kiss, he walked toward the airplane with his crash helmet in his hand and he didn't look back. He told me later that he was so certain he would never return that he was afraid his feelings would show if he turned around.

Audrey shares her feelings at that time....

"I was unhappy about Howard's decision to go off to war. But he was a determined man and very dedicated to his country, and I didn't have the heart to fight it. While he was away, his brother Norm helped out

with any problems Mom and I had around the house. He put the storm windows on for me and even taught Tommy how to ride his new bicycle. On occasion, he would take me out to visit friends or to a movie.

"Sometimes we would finish the evening at Dirty Helen's. She was always very concerned about Norm being with me—to the point of letting me know that she didn't think I should be out having a good time while Howard was at war! Actually, her place was the safest place for me to be, as she would never let a strange man even talk to me. If he went so far as to try to buy me a drink, her colorful language took over and ended his advance. She definitely was my 'protector' while Howard was gone. Now that I think of it, she was that way even when he was here...and I liked it!"

Dirty Helen, Norm and Audrey

Norm Poberezny joined the Wisconsin Air Guard in 1948, shortly after Paul had transferred to the Army Guard. In 1950, Norm also transferred to the Army Guard and began working for his brother at the new Milwaukee Detachment. At Paul's insistence, Norm started out again as a private to allay any concerns about favoritism. Norm remembers Paul as a fair, but demanding supervisor, saying he always worked harder for his brother than for anyone else! A year or so later, the working relationship temporarily ended when Paul entered the Air Force and transferred to Madison; their career paths would not cross again until 1957.

While Paul was in Korea, Norm remained in Milwaukee. In addition to watching over Audrey and her mom, he found time to take Dirty Helen out to lunch on a few occasions. The sage advice offered by this well-traveled and worldly lady was no doubt worth far more than the price of the food!

Paul was enroute to California, having left family and friends behind, and the homebuilder meetings to Elmer Kliegel and the others. After changing planes in Chicago, he spent the remainder of the night listening to the four engines of the DC-7 as it droned its way to San Francisco. A waiting bus took him to the staging area at Camp Stoneman...and one more quick look at America the Great.....

Camp Stoneman

"At Camp Stoneman I met Paul Dowd, a long-time friend and P-80 pilot from the 126th Fighter Squadron at Truax Field. Paul had also received his overseas orders and he and his wife, Flossie, drove to California to enjoy what I am sure they thought might be the last time they'd see each other. They invited me to ride with them to Yosemite

National Park and I gladly accepted. What a wonderful sight it was! I have always been amazed by the abundance of natural beauty in our great country."

Flossie and Paul Dowd...a last visit before he leaves for Korea

Now what? A mix-up in Paul's orders? Surely, after going through all this mental anguish, the Air Force would show compassion by having their part of the process in order....

"The next day after returning from our short trip, there was some confusion. One individual stated my orders were rescinded and that I was being transferred to another F-51 unit in the United States. I admit to feeling some relief, though I still wanted to be part of the Korean effort. I called Audrey to tell her it looked like I would be transferred to another air base in the States; we both hoped it would be Madison!

"But it was not to be! Within a few hours, the confusion was cleared up and I had my orders to report to FECOM (Far East Air Command) in Tokyo, the staging place for pilots assigned to Korea. However there was one change: I would now be assigned to the 30th Weather Squadron, even though my orders upon leaving Madison indicated I would be attached to an F-51 outfit, the 18th Fighter/Bomber Squadron. They told me there was a shortage of qualified C-47 pilots and that was where they needed me.

"The flight from San Francisco to Japan was long and tiresome. We were in an old DC-4 operated by a civilian carrier who provided none of the amenities people expect today. After landing in Hawaii for fuel, we proceeded to Wake Island where we remained overnight. I

took the opportunity to walk around the beach and was amazed to see remains of the last war, both human and otherwise. In the harbor lay the rusted hulk of a partially submerged Japanese ship.

On board a C-54 en route to Korea

"The next day we landed in Tokyo, Japan. The city was completely different than it is today. It hadn't changed a lot since the last war; there was considerable battle damage all over and plenty of rebuilding to be done.

"I won't ever forget Tokyo and May Day, 1952. I was in a taxi going downtown, dressed in my uniform, when a group of communist sympathizers from the May Day parade spotted me. They ran over to the cab and began beating and pushing on it—trying to tip it over! All the while they were yelling and, one supposes, cursing at me. Fortunately, the cab driver was able to keep moving. As soon as we got clear of the crowd, I paid him his yen and got out. I ran to the nearby American Consulate, wondering if there were any more sympathizers along my route. It sure felt good to see all those American soldiers and airmen gathered at the consulate!

"I spent the rest of the week without further incident and then took the train to southern Japan for my in-processing to Korea. I received my assignment to the 30th Weather Squadron and remember thinking I might have experienced more speed while riding the trains in Japan than I would flying C-47s in Korea!

"I got off the C-54 at K-16, the designation given to the base at Seoul. Standing there in my blue uniform with my B-4 bag in one hand and helmet in the other, I felt very much out of place in this unfamiliar combat zone. The airport looked like it was part of a Hollywood war movie set. Situated along the Han River just outside of the city of Seoul, it had one runway, several bombed-out hangars, and was full of military airplanes, including L-5s, L-17s, F-51s, C-119s, C-46s, C-47s, C-54s, B-26s and T-6s. Some were battle damaged, but most were ready for use in the war.

Images of Seoul, Korea…

"More impressions of those first few days come to mind: bleary eyed soldiers just back from the front some thirty miles away; many wounded soldiers being evacuated; endless convoys of trucks going back and forth along the dusty streets; numerous small huts and shacks; waves of Korean men and women on foot; young boys serving as house-boys; girls doing menial tasks, such as picking up laundry and washing it on the river bank for the troops; airplanes constantly taking off and landing at all hours; an Officers Club that reminded me of a wild west saloon; and, of course, the dust!

"I was directed to a Red Cross tent located on a nearby dusty street (they were all dusty). When I asked for directions, a young lady told me she recalled seeing a sign down the street that said '30th' on it. As I walked in that direction, my shined shoes quickly changed color. I found a small Quonset hut with the sign out front and rapped on the door. A gentleman appeared, looking rather bored. He was dressed in creased fatigue pants and a yellow undershirt stained by the waters of the nearby Han river. He looked at me and said in a monotone voice, 'My name is Captain Phil Gormley and I've been here seventeen months!' When I told him my name, he immediately became excited, exclaiming, 'You're my replacement!' And gave me a long, sweaty hug!"

Captain Phil Gormley

Flying the C-47 in Korea

Now that Paul was in the war zone, he discovered things operated much differently than they did stateside. There was no time allocated to acclimate oneself to this new and potentially dangerous environment—get your feet wet as soon as you can, soldier....

"I was there for less than an hour when Phil told me we had a mission in the C-47. He wanted to take me along to familiarize me with the area, so I dug my flying suit and boots out of my B-4 bag and followed him to the flight line. Soon we were off in the old Gooney Bird for the routine flight. Phil remarked, 'This is what Korea is like! Don't sweat a thing!' But I was still amazed at the 'fast lane' I would be living in for the next few months. Then he told me to fly north to where the action was.

"All of a sudden there was an explosion and the airplane rocked violently—my heart was in my throat! We'd been hit in the left wing, just behind the left main landing gear. Phil says, 'I've been here a year and a half and this has *never* happened to me before!' We took turns going back to survey the damage. There was a hole in the left center

My first day in Korea - May 13, 1952

section where the shell had exploded—fortunately just missing the fuel tank. There also were lots of little shrapnel holes in the side of the fuselage. The airplane still handled fine, so we returned to the base. We suspected there could be problems with the landing gear system, but it went down all right...although we had to land on a flat left main tire. So much for my initiation to Korea!"

Paul's hut (above) and room (below)

Some indoctrination flight! At least Paul was able to make a safe landing—so many others had not! The event provided ample justification for an evening letter to Audrey…after his hands stopped shaking....

"As in World War II, I wrote home to Audrey every day. I took lots of pictures and slides in Korea and later on, used 8mm film."

Paul began to meet a variety of characters from the war zone. The more fascinating were those who had been there for a while, as they often had unusual methods for dealing with the risk and death that surrounded them....

Lieutenant Tagge

"I soon met Lieutenant Tagge, a B-26 pilot who flew a lot of night missions dropping flares along the enemy supply routes and then strafing the roads. The communist troops would often mix in with the civilians, whose only safe movements were also at night. Tagge would often come into my hut at two or three in the morning, shake me awake and say, 'They're trying to shoot me down! They're trying to kill me! Come on over to the mess hall and have some powdered eggs and milk!' I would usually get up and go with him. He'd eventually calm down and be ready to go again the next night."

During off-duty hours, everyone hung out at the "O" Club. Because Korea was a United Nations effort, it was a disparate group that congregated at the old watering hole....

"As I said earlier, the Officers Club looked like a Hollywood depiction of an 1850 saloon. It was an old wooden building built close to the (dirty) street. Along each side stretched covered porches, and on each porch an entrance door was located about a third of the way back. Inside, there was a plain wooden floor with a long wooden bar located halfway across the rear of the building. A small coat room was located near one entrance and a jukebox sat midway along the wall opposite the bar. Several old tables and chairs, a mixture of many different sizes and types, were scattered about the room, occupied by folks playing card games or just sitting around talking. There were also some slot machines for those who didn't send their money home.

"Our bartenders and waitresses were Korean girls. They were dressed in typical Korean fashion: high waisted, long black velvet skirts and blouses, their dark eyes and hair highlighting round faces and high cheekbones. They had to be off the base by eleven at night, so we always knew what time it was when the familiar sound of a six-by-six GI truck came from in front of the club. A crude wooden ladder made out of two-by-fours was extended; the passengers climbed up onto the wooden seats and off they went. When they got to the gate, the guards searched them, looking for items they might have taken from the base. While standing at the gate on a number of occasions myself, I watched the guards go through the bags and even newspa-

pers. Sometimes among the pages they'd find morsels of food the workers had tried to smuggle to their hungry families.

"The Officers Club was the usual evening hangout for the variety of pilots on the base: Australians, South Africans, Turks, Canadians and, of course, lots of Yanks. The Turk pilots also flew C-47s and were very interesting characters. Sitting alone or together in groups, they often brought their own guitars and mandolins. After a few drinks, they would begin to sing. Most of their music was sad, but not all of it. Every so often some of them would get up and start stomping on the floor—long enough to create a hole that had to be repaired two or three times a week! I remember watching one large Turk, at least 6' 3", dancing with one of the barmaids who was only about 5' 2". In his right rear pocket was a revolver, the butt buried out of sight while the barrel, which was about eight inches long, protruded upwards. A long, dark mustache hung down from each side of his mouth, adding to the individual's bizarre appearance. The whole scene would have made for a good movie…'Gunfight at the OK Corral' comes to mind."

A new land with new customs, both severely distorted by the war. As Paul's predecessor prepared to leave, there were the usual good-byes. Tradition reigns even in a war-torn environment....

Captain Gormley and Lieutenant Tagge

"Captain Gormley stayed about a month after my arrival. Having been there so long, he was well known and the club was crowded the night of his good-bye party. It wasn't long before Phil was feeling no pain.

"The barmaids had known him for a long time as he had picked up many items for them while on R & R in Japan—things like clothing and other essentials the girls wanted but were not available in their war-torn country. They had a small gift for Phil.

"When it came time for the presentation, the room suddenly quieted. There was no noise as the lead barmaid shuffled forth, holding a little picture frame made around a very crude drawing of the

Korean landscape. It was something you might find in a dime store, but the meaning it carried was much, much greater. It brought tears to many eyes. At that moment it was hard to believe we were in a land of destruction: the bombed out city of Seoul with its beggars on the street and dead bodies floating in the Han River. Through glassy eyes, Phil quietly accepted the little gift and slowly walked back to his seat. Then, just as quickly as it had come, the moment was gone; the juke box began playing and laughter and noise was again heard.

"The next morning in our hut, Phil was sitting on the side of his bed, not feeling too well and trying to recall the events of the night before. I went over to the wash basin and brought back the little framed picture. He looked at it, studied it for a while, and then broke down and cried! Phil left for home that day and I didn't see him for many years. He lives in a little town just northwest of Oshkosh, some hundred or so miles away. Occasionally he stops by and we reminisce about the time we spent in Korea."

There was one more "tradition" the departing Phil Gormley passed on to his replacement. After all, life goes on....

"When Phil left, he gave a note to the lead barmaid telling her I would continue his tradition. The girls were to give me their list and I would pick up the items for them. On my next R & R they did just that, but there was no mention of who would pay for it. When I got to Nagoya (Japan), I went from store to store picking up blouses, the largest they had—all the while listening to the giggling and laughing of the smaller Japanese girls who would say 'Taksan,' which means 'big woman.' Also on their list was yards of black velvet, lipstick, umbrellas and other items; I brought them all back. In the evening, with the help of my crew chief, John Mahoney, I carried it to the rear of the club. The girls were very happy and, bowing several times, took the goods. However, they made no mention of paying for it, and $230 was a lot of money in 1952!

"The next evening when I came to the club after flying, the lead barmaid called me into the little cloak room and handed me the money along with a kind note stating how pleased they were and thanking me for helping them. I felt much better—not so much for receiving the money, but because of the great appreciation they displayed."

This all sounds wonderful, but try depositing "appreciation" into your bank account! Audrey expected money in Paul's letters—not notes of appreciation. However, everything worked out and the arrangement continued.

"While in Korea I had two house-boys: Scosh and Johnnie. The 'boy-sans' lived with the Sergeants in one of the larger Quonset huts; during the day, they made beds and cleaned rooms around the camp. At first I thought the young lads were probably twelve and sixteen years of age, but later learned Scosh was seventeen and Johnnie, twenty-one! Scosh had a little dog that always followed him around. One day it didn't follow close enough and was run over. We buried it and held a little ceremony. The next day Scosh discovered the grave had been dug up and the remains removed. It was hard for me to accept it was taken for food!

Scosh and Johnnie

"On one occasion I was asked to ferry a C-47 to Clark Field in the Philippines. Not having flown such a great distance over water before, I was concerned. But an experienced navigator was assigned from Tokyo to guide us and we soon left for our first stop: Okinawa. I had read much about its history during the Second World War, a little island out in the middle of nowhere. I was sure it hadn't changed much in the seven years since the war had ended, and I was right. In many of the areas, World War II debris was still there, just as I had seen on Wake Island. There were old shoes, ammunition, pill boxes—even human bones! Of course all this has changed today. Even Seoul is like downtown Chicago! It's sometimes hard to believe.

Many long and boring flights!

"The next leg to Clark Field was some five hours of over-water flying. As we landed at Clark we were met by very high temperatures and humidity. I was scheduled to bring another C-47 back to Korea, but there would be a one week delay before the airplane was ready. It was in what was called IRAN—Inspection and Repair As Needed."

While his first visit to the Philippines may not have been as newsworthy as General MacArthur's return some seven years earlier, it was equally memorable for Paul....

"The R & R base was very pleasant and reminded me of our fine parks in the United States. The Officers Club was also very nice. But we decided to see some of the local area so, along with my crew, we took a GI bus up to Baguio, which is located in the mountains north of Manila. In spite of being alerted to the possibility of attacks by Huks (communist guerrillas that roamed the Philippines), nothing happened. While taking the winding roads through the mountains, one could look down and see more burned-out trucks and debris from World War II rusting away along the drop-offs. It was easy to imagine the many vicious battles that took place there.

"We then went to the Lingayen Gulf. The beaches were beautiful—lots of grayish-white sand with palm trees and thatched huts where the natives lived along the shore of the clear, blue water—water that was still cluttered with the rusting hulks of abandoned American landing craft! With a little imagination, one could picture American troops wading ashore under fire. 'I shall return!' Those famous words were said by General MacArthur when he left the Philippines under much different circumstances."

Tourista? Philippine-style? Paul was having such a good time that his body came up with its own excuse for extending its stay on this idyllic island....

"It was overcast the day we were on the beach, so I didn't think too much about getting sunburned—but I sure did! Along with the burn, I caught a very bad cold; by the time we returned to Clark Field a few days later, I was quite sick. To make a bad situation worse, the Quonset hut I stayed in was rat infested and sustained a steady temperature of 100 degrees with 100 percent humidity! The mattress was still wet from whomever slept in it before—maybe it was MacArthur! Over the bed was a netting. At night I could see rats and other creatures crawling around above my head.

"I went to the Flight Surgeon. He grounded me, saying he would write an order to that affect. I told him my airplane wasn't ready and there wasn't any need to write such an order, so he didn't. A day or so later, the airplane was ready and we began planning our departure. Another navigator was flown in from Tokyo to shoot the sun or whatever else he had to do to ensure we got to Okinawa and Korea. Everything was normal during takeoff, but while climbing through 6,000 feet I noticed the carburetor air temperature on the right engine was in the red. It wasn't wise for us to continue on a five and a half-hour flight over water with this condition, so I returned to land. I told my copilot, Captain Thayer, to take the aircraft back to maintenance, while I went to lie down in Operations. The rapid descent had really hurt my ears."

When the airplane was repaired, Paul's crew woke him up to complete the journey. They were soon confronted by another challenge…and another typical "Paul" solution....

"I went out to the airplane and climbed into the copilot's seat where I stayed during the takeoff and climb. Upon reaching our cruising altitude of 7,000 feet, I went back to lie down again. I must have slept for about four and a half hours before I got up and stumbled for-

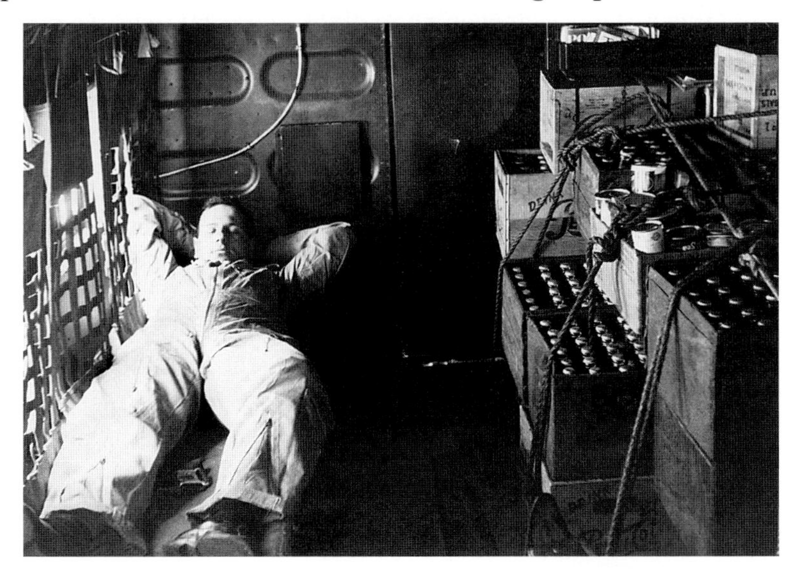

ward into the cockpit. It was getting late in the day and I asked the navigator where we were. He said we weren't too far from Okinawa. I flipped the fuel quantity switches to check all four tanks and found they were extremely low. When I asked Captain Thayer why we were so low on fuel, he said it was such a short first flight that he hadn't bothered to refuel. Even though they'd also flown a second brief test-

hop, he said that with the estimate the navigator had given him, we should still have more than an hour's worth of fuel remaining at our destination. But I was becoming concerned; we were well past our time for arrival at Okinawa! It was then I discovered that our navigator was an administrative type who had only been getting his minimum four hours flying each month in order to stay current. I soon learned he wasn't the world's best navigator either!

"The sun was close to setting before I was finally able to raise Naha Tower at Okinawa on the radio and ask them to give us a DF (Direction Finding) steer. They said their equipment was out of order. By then we had no idea where Okinawa was and I figured that if we were going to ditch, we'd better do it in what was left of the daylight. All of a sudden I noticed two jets at our eleven o'clock position, flying at about 14,000 feet. I quickly told Naha tower that I had two, what appeared to be F-94s, in sight. If tower would get in touch with GCI and ask them to identify the F-94s, GCI could then give us a rough bearing to the airfield. Thankfully, it worked!

"We had already passed Okinawa to the east by some forty or fifty miles. After a 120-degree turn to the left and another twenty or so tense minutes flying time, we began to see in the distance the welcome lights of Okinawa in the deepening twilight. After landing, we refueled the airplane; it took 756 gallons—the C-47 carries a total of 804! Our four hour flight to Seoul the next day was routine."

It was fortunate that Paul hadn't slept for another half an hour or so, otherwise his wakeup call might have been more stressful…and wet!

For most, the initial excitement (if you can call it that) of being in a war zone quickly turns into something you can't wait to leave behind! As his brief tour in Korea drew to a close, Paul recalls some highlights from this period of his life—highlights that will remain etched in his memory....

Paul - the mechanic

"There is much to remember about Korea: the flying; the dog-tired, dust covered faces and

blood-shot eyes of the infantry folks; the ever-present dust; and the never ending drone of airplane engines—C-47 engines for me! One flight in particular stands out more than the others....

"We had to pick up an F-51 pilot at one strip, drop off some weather personnel at another, and then return to Seoul with the pilot. We landed at the first stop without a problem. It was a short strip on the east coast of Korea, below and within a mile of the 38th Parallel…I believe it was K-56, a front line base for T-6 FAC (forward air controllers) operations. We picked up the F-51 pilot, who had barely made it there after his Mustang was shot up by ground fire. Understandably, he wasn't too keen about getting in after I told him I had to go further north before I could return him to Seoul.

"We took off for the next strip, landed, and dropped off the weather personnel with the walkie-talkies they used for weather reporting; they quickly disappeared with the ground troops. There were absolutely no facilities here at all: no ops, no maintenance, no nothing—just a single, sandy runway covered by PSP and located in the middle of nowhere! I went to start the right engine. Nothing happened—the starter was inoperative! What was that about Murphy's Law? There was nobody around; the day was growing shorter and I needed a start! What to do? I didn't want to stay overnight this close to the front lines, fearing for the safety of my crew and my airplane. An idea came to me from my early days of starting airplane engines....

"I primed the engine and ensured the mags were off, instructing my copilot to wait for my signal before turning them back on. I got out of the airplane and pulled the prop through by hand, then yelled to the copilot to switch 'mags hot' and get ready for the start. I gave the prop another sharp pull, and the old P&W 1830-92 came to life! I jumped back into the airplane, cranked up the other engine and took off amid sighs of relief and gratitude from all on board! Later, I would be confronted by those who didn't believe I had actually done this procedure. Several times I would provide proof of my accomplishment, after which those who had doubted were left in a bit of amazement."

"I saw many of my old squadron mates in Korea: Colonel Levenson, my old CO from the Milwaukee Guard…hearing his voice in the air and the conversations we had during his visit to my base to see me; Colonel Smith, also a Maintenance Officer from Truax Field, then based at K-2, an F-84 outfit; Paul Dowd and Jack Mark flying F-80s out of K-13 (Jack later became a key figure in the selection of EAA's first permanent museum site); Captain Sergeant, a pilot and

Colonel Levenson at K-16

Maintenance Officer, also flying at K-13. And Lt. Tagge, who traded his 8mm movie camera and projector for a Russian rifle; he and I flying a B-26 to Nagoya to use the overseas telephone to call his brother in Lake Forest, asking him to deliver the projector to Audrey; a second call to Audrey to tell her what was happening! Today, we make phone calls with ease all over the world, but to stand in line waiting for our turn to use that scratchy telephone system was well worth it."

Paul's time was up—his tour time, that is! Even though Korea was not a place he would have chosen to visit on his own, leaving any "home"—no matter how unsavory it may be—precipitates some regret....

"Knowing I would soon depart, there was sadness in the faces of our two house-boys. Scosh wanted me to adopt him and bring him to America. He got to know and love Americans and America—the land of opportunity, as he had so often heard from us. After the good-byes and the tears, I boarded a C-54 for Tokyo where I was offered the choice of flying home or going on a troop transport. As I had never been on a large ship before, I thought it might be fun, so I chose it. 'They' said they would put me in charge of all Air Force personnel on board if I agreed. I did, later to find out I was the *only* Air Force person on board!

F-80 pilot and long-time friend, Jack Mark

Paul Dowd, Capt. Sergeant, Sgt. "Focus" Vanselow and Paul

"We were trucked to the harbor at Yokohama and soon left with some four thousand of my closest GI buddies and thirty or forty of their Japanese brides. Because there were no facilities for married people, the wives were separated from their husbands at night. My quarters were comfortable, but after a day at sea I wished I was on a C-54. Eleven days later we sailed under the Golden Gate Bridge in San Francisco, my movie camera hard at work. From there I went to Hamilton Field to await orders to return home.

"My discharge paperwork went through quickly. Within a day, I was sitting in a United Airlines DC-6 headed for Chicago where Audrey, Tommy and Audrey's mother waited, having driven there in our Pontiac. It was great to be back! Tommy was dressed in the little Air Force First Lieutenant's uniform that I had the Korean girls make for his small size and sent home earlier. It was a happy occasion for all of us. After the greetings we loaded up and went home.

"It wasn't long before I was out in the garage looking at the remains of the Howard racer that had rested there awaiting my return. My thoughts began to return to my homebuilding days and what might lie ahead."

And from Audrey....

"It was great to have Howard back safe and sound, but in the back of my mind I was concerned about the activities that would soon begin in our garage! We had other things that needed attending to first!"

Welcome home, Dad!

Once Paul was released from active duty in the Air Force, he was unemployed! Never one to lose sight of the value of a friendship, he quickly followed up on an earlier contact from his Army Guard days....

"Prior to going on active duty with the Air Force in Korea, I had been with the Army National Guard as a Maintenance Officer, Supply Officer, Operations Officer and pilot. When I asked Major Sarkow to

take over my position, I hadn't put any provisions into the agreement, such as upon my return I would transfer back to the Army Guard and into my original position. I was out of a job!

"I had become good friends with General Ralph Olson, our current State Adjutant General, having previously flown him around the state on numerous occasions in the L-17 Navion. During my tour in Korea he had written several times. I thought that was very nice, although probably a bit unusual for a man as busy as he! In his last letter he said that upon my return from Korea I should come see him. Within a week, Audrey and I drove to Madison.

"Upon entering General Olson's office, and after the normal greetings, handshakes and small talk, he asked if I was ready to go to work. It was a welcome surprise and I answered, 'right now.' He asked if I was interested in becoming the temporary Base and Wing Commander of the 128th Fighter Interceptor Wing in Milwaukee during its post-war buildup period. This, I must admit, was a bit of a shock, but I eagerly accepted. He told me to report to the base and start getting it organized for the return of the other Guardsmen who were being relieved from active duty.

"Here I was, a first lieutenant in command of a Wing consisting of two squadrons, the 176th Fighter Squadron in Madison and the 126th Fighter Squadron in Milwaukee. Colonel Levenson was still in Korea, as was Captain Dowd, but there were still many others left here with much higher rank than mine. However, I was the only rated pilot, which was a requirement of the command. During the drill periods when our 'weekend warriors' came to the base, I always felt a bit uneasy having 'bird' colonels (lieutenant colonels) report to me, a first lieutenant, standing in front of all the personnel lined up for roll call!"

At the same time, Paul was forming friendships among those who held a different focus on aviation....

"I had earlier met Bob Nolinske in the Guard and introduced him to the social activities at Hales Corners Airport. Those activities had con-

Audrey and Tommy with friends, Bob and Lois Nolinske

tributed greatly to bringing pilots and their families together. During the time I was in Korea, Bob and his wife, Lois, befriended Audrey, and they occasionally went out to dinner in the evenings. As a result, our friendship grew and would play an important part in the beginnings of EAA."

Paul's work in the Air Guard remained foremost, although being assigned to a unit without flying airplanes was not to his liking....

"My work at the Air National Guard base was very interesting. I employed a large number of people who supported those still on active duty in Korea. I also was tasked to get the base ready to receive the aircraft and personnel when they returned to our control. We especially needed Air Technicians, and I remember one in particular, a young second lieutenant named Killian Morkin. He became a good friend and supporter, later ending up a colonel and the commander of Volk Field.

"At the time, we had no aircraft as they were still in transition from the war. One day I received copies of orders notifying us that the 176th Fighter Squadron in Madison was to receive two 'H' model Mustangs, the latest version of the F-51. Liking Mustangs as much as I did, I wrote my current Group Commander (and CO prior to leaving for Korea), Colonel Oliver Ryerson, to request that both aircraft be transferred to my squadron in Milwaukee. Later we often talked and laughed about the matter. They delivered the Mustangs to me and I finally had airplanes under my immediate command—even if it was only two! More important, they were both available for me to fly!"

Paul's brief contribution to the Korean War effort had come to an end. He was home again, busily employed by the Wisconsin Air Guard and thinking about private aviation. In spite of Audrey's apprehension, their garage was destined to return to its previous state—including the junk pile! There was really only one piece of unfinished business....

The friends Paul had left in charge of the loosely structured homebuilder group were unable to keep it going during his absence. If anything was to become of the idea, it would be up to him. Of course we know he accepted the challenge and soon began to take charge, aided by Audrey and a few friends. Little did this small and dedicated group realize what an important part of aviation history they were about to write—nor did Paul or Audrey Poberezny understand what tests of their union lay ahead!

Chapter Twenty-Two

The noise at Milwaukee's Curtiss-Wright Airport was deafening and most in the crowd had covered their ears in a futile attempt to shut out the painful intrusion. But just as it reached unbearable levels, it subsided, and the people began talking excitedly, now free to use their arms and hands to make gestures and point at the sky. The object of their attention, and the source of the noise, was a group of biplanes bobbing and weaving in the distance, apparently involved in some type of formation flying.

Actually, it was a staged air race—an exciting addition to the second annual Milwaukee Air Pageant being held this sunny, September afternoon in 1952. The noise was coming from the Pratt & Whitney 450 horsepower radial engines that powered the war surplus PT-17 Stearman biplanes through the bumpy, late afternoon sky. The airplanes were now roaring down the back stretch in preparation for their final dash to the finish line. The clamor briefly shifted to a lower pitch as "G" loads built up during the few seconds it took the machines to complete their final turns. As they approached the crowd again, the cacophony once again rose to deafening proportions, each engine screaming out every last revolution. And the winner? The gray one—by half a length! While the others throttled back and pulled up for their landing approaches, the nose of the winning airplane slowly eased up and completed a victory roll.

One spectator stood out from all the rest. In part, it was the evening dress she was wearing; it was also her mink stole, her outrageous hat—and the fact that her eyes remained closed during the entire race! Helen Cromwell, better known as Dirty Helen, had come to watch one of the pilots in the race: her friend, Paul Poberezny—pilot of the winning entry. It was his first air race and first air show since his recent return from Korea.

After Paul was safely on the ground, Helen opened her eyes. She began telling Audrey and everyone else within earshot how exciting air racing was, but that she hated to watch Paul fly because he was her friend and she didn't want anything to happen to him. She then invited everyone to drop by her place that evening and celebrate Paul's "victory." What better way to start life after Korea!

"I had fun flying that 'race,' although we also had a lot of fun that night at Helen's place! The Cole Brothers and many of the other performers and participants were there. We talked about flying, the air show, and the fact that so many people seemed to want me involved again with the homebuilders group we started a year or so earlier. They felt there was a need for such an organization but that there was no one else who seemed willing to take charge. I told them I would have to think about it, knowing Audrey would be a large part of my decision. I also told them I was disappointed in their not keeping the group active while I had gone to Korea.

Audrey in her kitchen

"I suppose the seed of leadership was already planted because Audrey and I could only come to the conclusion that I should get involved and that she would be willing to help me. It was December 1952 when Audrey sat at the kitchen table to type two or three dozen postcards setting forth a January 26, 1953, meeting for what we thought would be a local Milwaukee airplane homebuilders club. Like our earlier meetings, it would be held at the Gran-Aire facilities at Curtiss-Wright Airport, courtesy of Mr. Bill Lotzer. Bill was a great supporter of our movement and is due much credit for having faith in

what we were trying to do for aviation. Later he was instrumental in forming the National Aviation Trades Association, which is still in existence today."

At the same time, Paul was busy preparing his Wisconsin Air Guard unit for its post-war role. In November, his temporary assignment as Base Commander reverted back to its rightful owner, Colonel Levenson, who had returned from a tour in Korea. Paul became Commanding Officer of the 128th Fighter Interceptor Group....

Paul ready to go in the F-51H

"Colonel Levenson returned as Wing Commander and I was appointed Group Commander, still a first lieutenant. I finally received a squadron of twenty-five F-51D Mustangs to replace the P-80s that had been taken to Korea. At the same time, orders came in to transfer our two F-51H models to the New Jersey Air Guard. Captain Howard Mattes and I delivered them, while Colonel Levenson followed in our newly acquired C-47, serial #43-48164. It was an airplane I would become very familiar with over the next many years while flying some 6,700 hours in it!"

1953 was a pivotal year for sport aviation because it was the year the soon-to-be-named Experimental Aircraft Association (EAA) passed through its embryonic stage. From now on it becomes increasingly difficult for us to separate Paul and Audrey from EAA; nevertheless, we will attempt to do

just that, for it is their story we are telling, not EAA's. With so much focus on the organization, it is easy to overlook the fact that for the next seventeen years Paul maintained his full-time position with the Wisconsin Air Guard. EAA was his volunteer work, as it was for Audrey! In addition, Paul constructed and flew several homebuilt airplanes, helped his wife raise a growing family, and even enjoyed a few social activities—all in a twenty-four hour day!

Neither of them had any idea what they were about to start. They were just two people with enough stamina and dedication to make whatever came before them, work. Audrey sums it up....

"Everyone keeps asking how I felt about starting the organization. I didn't feel anything because none of us knew at that time what it would become. To us it was just another flying club and we had no thoughts other than to help it get started. We didn't plan for it to gain worldwide recognition."

Young Tommy

Audrey continued being a full-time mother to young Tommy, who was well into his sixth year and experiencing public school for the first time. Babe pursued her career with the telephone company and filled in at home…a home that was about to undergo drastic changes!

January 26, 1953, was a cold, wintry day, certainly not ideal weather for venturing outside. In spite of the elements, more than thirty hardy souls made their way to the Gran-Aire facilities at Curtiss-Wright Airport that evening to participate in a historic event—the first meeting of what would become the Experimental Aircraft Association. After unanimously agreeing that an organization should be formed, they went on to discuss such items as its purpose, name and scope. A short slate of officers was elected. Not surprisingly, Paul became the first president (a position he would hold unbroken for the next thirty-six years). Carl Schultz was elected vice-president and Bob Nolinske, Paul's friend from the Air Guard, secretary-treasurer.

In typical Poberezny fashion, Paul had invited a representative from the CAA to speak: Mr. Tony Maugeri. Mr. Maugeri made a presentation on the government's position regarding experimental aircraft and then suggested what he felt a group of "significant size" might accomplish. By involving CAA from the start, Paul revealed his wisdom for political matters. The decision to work with, not against, the aviation governing body quickly blossomed into a mutual respect for the problems and solutions facing both "sides." Many times their relationship would produce satisfactory solutions from near-impossible situations....

Bob Nolinske, Paul and Carl Schultz

"Having worked in government for some time, I realized that any future success our organization might have, would be gained by working with the CAA, not against it. I was impressed with Tony Maugeri, he being from the 'old school' and full of common sense. Looking back, it is apparent that many of the fellows in the CAA at the time were like Tony. They too loved aviation and did whatever they could within the constraints of their positions to promote it. Today, for an increasing number within what is now called FAA, it is just another job!"

Tony Maugeri, who is now retired and living in Florida, writes....

> Before I met Paul that evening, I had very little knowledge of his aviation background. But as the evening progressed, I became aware that he and I shared many common elements in our goals, experiences and dreams. During the thirties, I obtained my A&E certificate and my private and limited commercial pilot licenses. I owned five airplanes and worked on and flew them and many others. Following wartime duties as a US Navy pilot, I joined the CAA as a Flight Standards Inspector in 1947.
>
> During that first meeting, a bond of friendship began to develop between Paul and me.

Tony Maugeri in 1953

Because of it, we were able to develop rules, inspections, flight tests and other programs—each spelling safety—for the building and flying of amateur built aircraft…rules that would be accepted by the CAB. After the CAB gave us a tentative 'OK,' Paul did an excellent job of monitoring and spreading the word that 'safety' was paramount for further development of the amateur building concept.

Although Paul and I have been separated by great distances for many years, he still calls me 'Compare,' which in Italian, means, 'close friendship.'

THE
EXPERIMENTER
FOR
AIRCRAFT BUILDERS

VOLUME I NUMBER 1 February, 1953

A NEW ORGANIZATION

This is the first issue of "THE EXPERIMENTER", a monthly publication to be sent out to every member of THE EXPERIMENTAL AIRCRAFT OWNERS AND PILOTS ASSOCIATION and interested agencies.
This association has been in the planning stages since November 1951. A number of meetings were held at Curtiss Wright Airport in Milwaukee over a period of a year. We found that enough interest was shown by people to form a non-profit organization to encourage the developement of any type of aircraft by individuals through experimentation and home building.
Our January 26th meeting at Curtiss Wright Airport gave us some very sound ideas and a very good representation. We were fortunate in having MR. ANTHONY [illegible], C.A.A. [illegible] INSPECTOR for this area, present. And we know with the help of individuals in positions such as his will make for a stronger organization. MR. [illegible] was called upon to give his ideas on such an organization which were very favorable and brought us up to date on procedures used by C.A.A. in issuing airworthiness certificates for experimental aircraft. I know that his talk enlightened and encouraged all of us. After MR. [illegible] completed his talk a vote was taken of all enthusiasts present to form an organization. It was unanimously voted in favor of starting an experimental aircraft association.
A move was made and the motion was seconded to elect PAUL POBEREZNY, Milwaukee as President; CARL SCHULTZ, Hales Corners, Wisconsin as Vice President and ROBERT [illegible], Milwaukee as Secretary & Treasurer.
The name of this organization was opened to discussion with the possibility of shortening it. It was agreed upon that a vote would be taken on a permanent name for the organization at the next meeting.
The newly elected officers are to prepare a constitution and by-laws for approval by members at the next meeting and also information concerning incorporation.
Figures of $3.00 and $5.00 membership fees was the topic of discussion and will be voted upon at the next meeting, February 23rd, at Curtiss Wright Airport, Milwaukee. It was suggested that either the first or third Monday of the month be designated a permanent meeting night. It will be voted on at the next meeting and will be published in the March issue of the EXPERIMENTER.
(continued - Page 2)

"MAYBE"

The feeling is running "high" that with a strong organization, enough pressure could be brought to bear in the right places that some sort of limited airworthiness certificate could be issued time proven experimental aircraft to enable the owner to carry passengers. It is a goal to work for.

"LOOKING AHEAD"

We have many good movies scheduled for future meetings. A 16 mm sound film titled "BIG RACE FOR LITTLE [illegible]" is being obtained from the GOODYEAR TIRE AND RUBBER CO. for showing at our next meeting, Feb. 23. It is a film covering some of the Goodyear Trophy races of the past few years. Word has it from some of the fellas that have seen this movie-"It's really terrific", so don't miss it.

"HELP"

O.K. FELLAS! IT'S UP TO YOU NOW. We have a fine organization started, but we still need more members. Tell all of your friends who are interested in experimenting about our new group. Bring them along to the next meeting, or if unable to attend, send their names and addresses to the editor of this publication. Remember, if we are to have a strong organization we will need a large membership of interested individuals.

NEXT MEETING!!
February 23, 1953 8:00 P.M.
Curtiss Wright Airport
Milwaukee, Wisconsin

EAA's first publication

Over the next few months, the group's organizational structure rapidly began to take shape. The name "Experimental Aircraft Association" was approved over the longer and somewhat plagiarized alternative, "Experimental Aircraft Owners and Pilots Association." After considerable discussion, annual dues were set at five dollars; Paul explains why....

"There were many who resisted the five dollar dues, thinking that three was more than sufficient. While saying five dollars was too much, these same people would spend five or even ten dollars at the bar buying drinks after the meeting. I convinced them that we must have a solid financial basis in order to survive...a thought that continues to this day."

Believing that good internal communication was critical, Paul created a newsletter—at least he *and Audrey* did! She transferred his scratchings into a readable format via their old typewriter and then mailed mimeographed copies to the members. In a few months, she switched to a stencil that Paul took to work, paying one of his technicians a dollar to run off copies on the Gestetner machine. Secretary-Treasurer Bob Nolinske, and his wife, Lois, sent out meeting notices and recorded the minutes.

It was decided to call the newsletter *The Experimenter*, and the first issue went out in February 1953. Eventually it was upgraded through the talents of Ray and Bernice Scholler and their small printing company, Times Publishing, in Random Lake, Wisconsin. The Schollers would become lifelong friends of the Pobereznys, and of sport aviation....

"In September 1953, I met Ray Scholler through a friend of mine, Harry Chaplin, who was then president of another Wisconsin aviation organization. Harry showed me a slick, eight-page publication called *Badger Airway Beacon* that Ray was producing for them. We were impressed by the quality and by October had our own slick publication, *The Experimenter.*

***Special friends,*
*Ray and Bernice Scholler***

"Ray and Bernice Scholler are two wonderful people who have been extremely important to the development of EAA from 1953 to the present. Their names come up over and over again throughout the history of the organization. They have been EAA volunteers since the first convention and today manage the Theater in the Woods. Ray has missed only two board meetings since 1953, overcoming fog, snow, ice, and whatever else might have stopped a lesser person.

"We not only developed a good working relationship with Ray and Bernice; we became great friends. Our families have grown up knowing each other and we maintain that same close relationship to this day. They are even helping us with this, our first book!"

Audrey adds....

"Ray and Bernice are two of our longest—and best—friends. I remember working with Bernice at the early fly-in conventions, driving those huge tractors and cutting grass. Ray would check in every now and then, wanting to know if we needed a break. One time we were cutting grass in the warbird area and finished before he came back. When he couldn't find us, he called the controllers in the airport tower and asked them where the tractors were working. They said we were in the transient aircraft parking area, and he soon found us...I thought that was pretty good thinking. Another time, we were cutting grass when Bernice's tractor caught fire! We have so many good memories of these fine people. EAA wouldn't be what it is today without Ray and Bernice Scholler."

Bernice at work on the EAA Convention site

Communications with his fellow officers and directors were not limited to the monthly meetings. Paul was in constant contact, passing on his beliefs and philosophies and making sure his feelings and recommendations regarding any new proposals were quite clear. It was a format he would use throughout his term of office. His philosophy was really quite simple: he expected his board to work as hard as he did. To this day, Paul feels that others who share the same interest should work seven days a week—he still can't understand those who don't!

Paul formed a committee of eleven persons to provide technical advice to the membership. He later expanded their duties to include overseeing the increasing number of plans that were being offered for sale. It was all in the interests of the movement, as he explains....

"There were some who thought the purpose of our technical committee was to redesign their airplanes, when really it was only to make the designer's plans more accurate, thereby ensuring the structural integrity of the airplane. By doing so, we hoped to avoid having problems with the government who might later on decide to shut the movement down because of too many unsafe practices."

Membership in EAA was open to anyone having an interest in the purpose of the organization, regardless of race or sex or anything else. Membership cards were introduced, and the constitution and bylaws were written and approved. Aviation films and/or guest speakers were scheduled after the business portion of the monthly meetings. Early speakers included Tony Magueri, Steve Wittman, Frank Tallman, Dr. F.A. Torrey, and Bob Bushby. A popular ending to the evening was aimed at a different pleasure—eating. Lois Nolinske writes, "Audrey and I decided to serve 'lunch' after the meetings. I would call in an order to a local butcher shop and it was delivered late afternoon. Audrey came over to our place to pick me up that night and we would prepare our gourmet delights and transport them to the meetings at around 10:00 P.M. Our most popular items were raw beef and onions. Everyone chipped in what they could afford to cover our expenses."

But as is often the case with donations, the amount collected generally fell short of the amount spent. When it did, the girls made up the deficit from their own pockets!

CAA Inspector, Tony Maugeri, was a frequent guest and EAA's first Honorary Member. He helped the group understand the peculiarities involved with changing the regulatory process within an increasingly watchful central government agency. By doing so, he instilled a belief that cooperation between government and its "customers" (the public), was the only way to go. In other words, he said they should "go along to get along!"

In recognition of his support of the organization, Bill Lotzer, president of Gran-Aire, became the second Honorary Member. Later that first year, Mr. Fred Miller of the Miller Brewing Company became the third recipient, also for his significant supporting role. Other aviation personalities were attracted to the group, Steve Wittman being the most famous early member. He added a high degree of professionalism because of his considerable expertise at designing, building and flying airplanes. When Steve Wittman talked about the need for safety in construction, everyone listened. It was another reason Paul asked him to be on the technical committee.

Steve expounded on the frequently tested theory that it is best to leave things alone when they're working—especially government regulations! He felt the current codes were actually quite liberal; that by challenging them, the group could bring about changes that were detrimental to the needs of the homebuilders. Too often this sage advice has been ignored by those who continue asking questions to which they really don't want answers!

Steve and his wife, Dorothy, quickly became friends with the Pobereznys. As their friendship grew, Paul began calling Steve, "Sylvester," a term nobody else could get away with; Steve, in return, referred to Paul as "Pablo." Eventually, they would work together on EAA and other projects, including the 1956 fly-in. Of course, Steve was forever pressing Paul to move the event to Oshkosh on a permanent basis.

New members continued to join the fledgling organization, primarily through word of mouth. But when *Flying* magazine published a letter to the editor in its April 1953 issue, national interest in the movement began in earnest. Written by Paul, the letter explained his newly revitalized homebuilt movement (Paul referred to it as the Experimental Aircraft Owners and Pilots Association because he wrote the letter before the name "EAA" was approved). He also encouraged anyone with an interest in homebuilt airplanes to contact him. The editor had added, "In view of the great number of readers who have expressed an interest in homemade airplanes, we're happy to report the name and address of a pilot who is backing the wish with action."

A logo was needed and the search for one led to a successful conclusion in California, from where George Collinge submitted three tasteful designs. One of them, the one on the right, was adopted and has become the internationally famous EAA symbol.

Paul continued filling a variety of positions in the Wisconsin Air National Guard, as the unit slowly returned to its authorized postwar strength. In March 1953 he was relieved as CO of the 126th Fighter Interceptor Group and appointed Aircraft Maintenance and Flight Test Officer. In July, he also became Flight Commander of the 126th Fighter Interceptor Squadron; August brought a well-deserved promotion to Captain.

As Flight Commander, Paul planned most of the squadron trips. This makes it easy for us to understand why his airplanes rarely followed the shortest distance between two points! Courtesy of the Wisconsin Air Guard, Paul had become EAA's flying ambassador! He visited members in a growing number of states: South Dakota, Indiana, Utah, Illinois (several times to visit Ned Kensinger's operation), and California (to talk with Ray Stits about starting the first EAA chapter). Current EAA Foundation Board Member, Jimmy Leeward (then a mere youngster) recalls watching a military C-47 pull up to the ramp at Ft. Wayne, Indiana. Rather than stop at the Guard facility, the airplane proceeded to the civilian ramp where it unloaded all sorts of parts, none of which appeared to have military ancestry. After putting a few items back on board, the airplane took off. Jimmy asked who it was; the answer came back, "Paul Poberezny!"

Paul qualified as both test pilot and instructor pilot in the C-47, T-6 and F-51, and was designated a Unit Instrument Flight Examiner. His non-flying duties included Ground Safety Officer, Assistant Adjutant, Personnel Officer and working member of the Air Guard aircraft accident investigation board. He even found time to put his creative genius to work, designing the familiar Minuteman shield that soon adorned the tail of *all* Air National Guard airplanes. Coincidentally, he wrote a comprehensive manual on the markings of ANG aircraft.

In mid summer 1953, Paul and his squadron mates attended their final field training camp in the P-51 Mustang, a two-week affair held annually at Camp Williams, now Volk Field. In August, his squadron swapped most of its Mustangs for F-86A Sabre jets. This precipitated a lengthy series of checkouts and proficiency flying in the new (to them) kerosene-burning speedster. Paul obviously had a full-time job with the Air Guard, so how did he balance this "paying" career with his volunteer EAA duties?

"As EAA began to attract more and more interest, it became increasingly difficult for me to keep up with all the correspondence and other activities. If it hadn't been for Audrey, I would not have been able to handle it. Fortunately I also had support within my Air Guard unit, as they believed what I was doing was a benefit to all in aviation."

1953 Wisconsin Air National Guard Summer Camp at Camp Williams (Paul is fifth from right)

Let us not forget there was a civilian side to Paul's life: his home, his family, and the building and flying of homebuilt aircraft. He sold his first airplane project, *Little Poop Deck*, to a flying club in Sturdevant, Wisconsin, no doubt providing the motivation to finish *Little Audrey*.

"Little Audrey" nearing completion

The airplane flew in late August—just in time to participate in the air race at the first EAA Fly-in. Of course "our" Audrey was thrilled about having airplanes occupy the entire two-stall garage all winter and spring....

"Activities on South 56th Street were definitely beginning to pick up. For the most part, they centered around the construction area—the garage! I certainly didn't appreciate having to keep our car outside all

winter, but there was no room in the garage with Paul's airplane and the one belonging to Bruce and Gil Pitt called 'Yellow Jacket.' Actually, there could have been others, as parts and pieces were constantly moving in and out of there. I managed to find time to sew the fabric for Paul's airplane and help with some of the others.

Paul and Tommy working on "Little Audrey" in the garage.

"Once each month, four or five of us would gather around our dining room table to address our less than sophisticated publication (with the photos stapled to it) and affix postage stamps. This function was later moved to the Nolinske basement."

1953 laid claim to the first "official" EAA fly-in. Wasting no time, the group had joined forces with the third annual Milwaukee Air Pageant, scheduled for September 12 & 13 at Curtiss-Wright Airport. Although insignificant by today's standards (twenty-two homebuilt aircraft), the turnout proved there was genuine interest in the movement. More important, it encouraged Paul to believe that future events would grow in stature and complexity. It also taught him a few valuable lessons....

"We were amateurs! I could be found scurrying all over the airport, parking airplanes, greeting pilots, running to the pay station, trying to find motel accommodations and, in some cases, helping to solve

and fix maintenance problems. I had also never given a speech in front of a very large group, and admit to being more than a little nervous before doing so.

"Our purpose for having the fly-in was to provide a service to those who came to the event. We didn't make commissions from any of the food vendors, so they had no reason to worry about how they left the facility after the event was over. As a result, when everyone else went back to work on Monday, I found myself surrounded by garbage at the airport. All alone I picked it up—the chicken bones, paper cups, napkins and other trash. It was then I established the high standards of cleanliness we have become known for at our annual fly-in convention. I also learned that many other things must be changed: availability of toilets, containers for garbage—and to set forth the spirit that nothing should be thrown on the ground! I reasoned that since aviation was known for its high standards, why not carry them through to our normal activities? From then on, cleanliness would be a part of any future fly-in or EAA event. There must never be another mess like this one! Even today, those who attend Oshkosh are often heard to say they cannot believe so many people can get together and yet leave the grounds so neat and clean."

Ned Kensinger, one of the early fly-in participants, wrote about his visit to the first fly-in....

> When we held the very first fly-in convention in Milwaukee there were only a few airplanes in attendance. I was there with "Tater-Chip" and Dick Owens with his Parakeet. However, since I was too big to get into my midget, I flew Dick's Parakeet and he flew the Chip. It was a combination we used every time we went to a race or air show where both airplanes were to be featured.
>
> Paul was delighted to see us. We were relieved to be there because we had flown in some pretty heavy weather to get there. Everyone in attendance had a wonderful time and rejoiced at the apparent success of our first get-together. As I recall, we were all treated royally by Fred Miller of Miller Brewing Company, who took us out to dinner one evening. I believe there were 140 members and guests at that first dinner.

"Tater Chip" (top picture) and "Little Audrey"

Leo Kohn

In the October *Experimenter*, Leo J. Kohn submitted an article about Paul's airplane, *Little Audrey*. In it, he mentioned the airplane's performance in the air race held during the fly-in: "Those who attended our fly-in at the Air Pageant, saw the triangular cross-country race which involved five of these small planes. We can't say that Paul placed in the first three; but on the other hand, he didn't have to push his ship since there was no one behind him!"

Paul was EAA's perpetual promoter, the absolute diplomat. George Hardie, another early member who contributed greatly to the organization's success, recalls meeting his friend again: "I ran into Paul at the 1953 fly-in and we renewed our old acquaintance. I asked him where he had been and he replied, 'Korea!' His response to what he was doing now was that he was building an airplane in his garage. I said, 'You're kidding!' To which he replied, 'No, come on over and see...' I was soon heavily involved in the EAA movement."

EAA was becoming a habit for a lot of people as new volunteers were attracted on a regular basis. One of them, Harry Zeisloft, exemplifies the spirit of EAA and its first family as he describes his initial encounter with

Audrey. He had asked, "What can I do to help?" He then adds, "The answer kept me busy for the rest of my life!" Similar exchanges would be repeated many thousands of times over the coming years. And Harry? He continues to be involved to this day, a long-serving member of the EAA Board of Directors.

But it wasn't always Guard or EAA business that occupied Paul's mind. He still dreamt about one day owning his own airplane factory....

"I recalled having an earlier conversation with Bob Skuldt while we were both on active duty in Madison. Bob was also the Airport Manager at Truax Field and had mentioned having seen an old airplane in a building downtown. In the early fall of 1953, I called to ask if he would take me to the place. He agreed, so I hopped into one of our F-51s and flew it to Madison. Soon we were at the Shoelkopf Machine Shop looking at the remains of the famous Corben Sport Plane Company. We listened to Mr. Shoelkopf tell of his experiences with O. G. Corben and how he (Shoelkopf) had put money into the corporation, while Mr. Corben did the promoting. He told about the extensive design work that included input from the aeronautical engineering classes at the university, and that Mr. Corben departed prior to the war, leaving him (Shoelkopf) holding the bag financially.

"The material had all been put in storage. When I saw it, my eyes opened wide! There were crates of wing ribs, a complete 2-place Corben Junior Ace with the fabric still in place, and miscellaneous fittings, jigs, fixtures and tubing. There also were two Model A Ford engines converted for use in the Super Ace and several 40 horsepower Salmson engines, a five-cylinder radial of French design. As if that wasn't enough, he took me into the office area and showed me all the drawings for each of the designs. I felt like a blind dog in a butcher shop! I asked if it was for sale. The answer was 'yes' and the amount was two hundred dollars. A handshake clinched the deal and I was off with some of the original drawings of the Super Ace and Baby Ace. We placed them between cardboard and then Bob took me back to Truax Field where we laid them on top of the machine

Paul in the F-51 with his precious cargo

guns in the wings. I hoped nothing would happen to my precious drawings on the way home!

"Along with Sergeants Steve Ratz and Mike Terlizzi and a pair of rented four-wheel farm wagons, we later returned to Madison and hauled the Corben Company back to Milwaukee. I felt quite proud to have my own airplane factory, although Audrey didn't exactly share my enthusiasm. In fact, she gave me a 'half turn' about spending our money on such things. I ended up selling some engines and the complete Junior Ace—which I should never have done!"

Mike Terlizzi

The EAA chapter program started from a request submitted by a young Californian named Ray Stits. Ray believed in the movement and wanted to start a chapter on the west coast. An amendment to the constitution allowing for the establishment of EAA chapters was approved and, on January 24, 1954, EAA Chapter #1 held its first official meeting in Riverside, California. Another hard-working proponent of the sport aviation movement had surfaced—its president, Ray Stits. Paul shares part of a conversation....

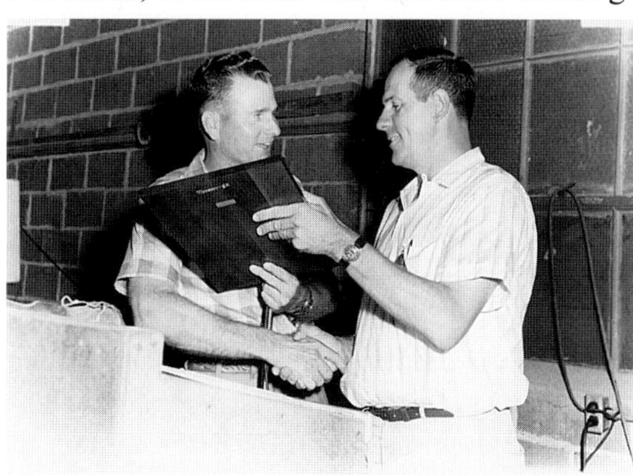
Ray Stits and Paul

"One time when I was talking with Ray about the future of the EAA, he told me it will grow into the largest and most active group of aviation enthusiasts, builders and fliers in the US within five years. How right he was—and how much he has helped us get there. Ray Stits has been one of our greatest supporters through the years."

Telephone calls continued to increase in record numbers, but not as much as the need for more room to house the rapidly expanding organization in the home on South 56th Street. Paul recalls a temporary solution....

"We decided to install an oil furnace and get rid of the coal bin in our home. I quickly claimed the area to make into a small EAA office, and with the help of Carl Walters and Bob Nolinske, cleaned out the remains and painted the walls. At the same time, the kitchen was remodeled, including new cabinets and a new kitchen set (table and chairs). We moved the old wooden set into the basement, along with one of the old kitchen cabinets and had our first EAA Headquarters! The original table, one chair, and the typewriter are on display in the Founder's Gallery and Mini-Museum in Oshkosh, along with samples of our early publications."

Paul, Carl Walters and Bob Nolinske in the coal bin office on 56th Street

---

National interest in the association increased dramatically after *Mechanix Illustrated* ran a feature article on homebuilt airplanes the following spring. It was a forecast of things to come, although the potential for rapid growth apparently caused Paul more than a little concern. He had earlier met with Detroit-based designer, builder, air racer and EAA member Neal Loving, and recapped their conversation in his December 1953 column in *The Experimenter*. Paul said,

"...and I might add that when an organization gets too big for its britches, it is on its way out—so let's make sure it doesn't happen to the EAA!"

Chapter Twenty-Three

1954

From now on, each year would be busier than the previous one. This pretty much holds true for any growing organization, and EAA was definitely in that category! Paul and Audrey put in a full day's work, and *then* tackled their EAA chores. What kept "super volunteers" like them going? It wasn't the salary: there was none. There weren't even any benefits, unless being on call twenty-four hours a day can be termed a "benefit." No, what kept them going was the praise of the members. People are quick to complain, but not always as quick to applaud. When they do, it means a lot. At times, it might have been the straw that kept the camel going.

The following excerpts came from recent letters sent by those who knew Paul and Audrey throughout the early years of EAA....

> *"From the very first I had the impression of a man who looked you in the eyes and had that determined look of leadership...with a smile! In Paul, we found a man we could—and would—follow and trust. A true homebuilder and a pilot who could fly any aircraft and do it better than any of us!"*
>
> —John R. Barcus, EAA #14

"Paul always reminded me of the Pied Piper; people were eager to follow him."
—Lois Nolinske

"No one else would have made it go! He (Paul) had that peculiar kind of a personality that overcame all the petty jealousies that would have destroyed the organization under most other men!"
— Arlie J. Nixon, EAA #68

"If I had to choose one word to describe Paul and my association with him, it would be 'gentleman'...the man is a true gentleman! ...I certainly hope that Audrey gets equal billing in this book; she has earned it. I have been in love with her since the first time I saw her! She is a truly beautiful person. If every man was blessed with a partner like her, it would be an almost perfect world."
—H. Earl Morgan, FAA retired

"Not only is Paul a great organizer, but also an honest and straight forward person. One of his statements has touched me and has become a factor in my life: do not offer criticism unless you can also offer a solution."
—Robert W. Bushby, EAA #26

"In all of the years I have dealt with Paul and EAA, I have never found him to be unreasonable nor the requests of EAA without foundation."
—Charlie Schuck, EAA #1060

"I'm sure Audrey will have a prominent place in any story about Paul—her skill and dedication made it possible for Paul to accomplish what he has."
—Roger G. White, EAA #41

"Paul has never changed, he has been a friend of our family and through all his success, he still knows who his friends are."
—Marion Cole, EAA #48

"Although I greatly appreciate the efforts of George Bogardus and others who played a part in obtaining the freedoms we have to design, build and fly our own airplanes, it was Paul Poberezny who took the ball and ran with it.

...I was very impressed by the amount of space devoted to EAA in their home and the obvious amount of paper work it took to

prepare for a fly-in and keep EAA running smoothly. All my early 'Experimenters' were hand addressed by Audrey; and after seeing all that paperwork, I realized that her responsibilities were extensive."

—Leon York, EAA # 57

"It has been interesting to watch Paul grow over the years from a leader of a small Homebuilt Aircraft Club to a seasoned and successful Diplomat, Business Executive, World Renowned Aviation Consultant and Promoter.

—Ray Stits, Charter President, EAA Chapter #1

"Even though I have told everyone for close to 50 years that you are the greatest pilot I have ever known (next to me), I will continue to do so."

—Cliff Bowers, former Operations Officer, 176th FIS

"The mark of a successful life is whether the world is a better place just because you have been there. This great family certainly qualifies."

—Ned Kensinger, Charter President, EAA Chapter #2

"As the Wright Brothers changed the course of the world from a bicycle shop, so has Paul Poberezny preserved that legacy from his garage. ...and co-star, Audrey, is no bit player in this scenario!"

—A. Scott Crossfield - first to exceed Mach 2

"As everyone recognizes now, Paul is a charismatic leader who can get most anyone to do anything for 'the Movement'! ...and all through this, all these years, is Audrey, Captain of the support group of Audrey, Tom and Bonnie, aided and abetted by Ray and Bernie."

— Harry C. Zeisloft, EAA #1402

No doubt, Paul was in the right place at the right time—and with the perfect partner! He continues describing his activities during 1954....

"Our monthly meetings continued at Curtiss-Wright Airport. As the word got out, more people throughout the country wanted to join us. This meant more mail and more telephone calls. Before long, there was little time for anything else but to work at the Guard, build airplanes and answer mail! Audrey did much of the correspondence and if it wasn't for her support, there would be no EAA as we know it today! Bob Nolinske and his wife handled the books, mailing and

other chores. We estimated we were all putting in about sixty hours a week (total) on EAA duties! Audrey quipped that I should put my bed either in the garage or the EAA office in the basement. I'm sure Lois felt the same about Bob.

"It was commonplace for the four of us to drive to Times Publishing in Random Lake and pick up the boxes of magazines that Ray had printed. We always enjoyed a good dinner in the small town, which at the time boasted a population of just under four hundred. We brought the magazines back to Bob and Lois's townhouse and put them downstairs. The following evening, or shortly thereafter, we held a mailing party where we would hand address, fold and stamp our slick publication. It was fun, but we soon found it took more than one mailbox on the corner to accept all the magazines we mailed out!"

Bob Burbick

In February, Mr. Robert (Bob) Burbick (CAA Branch Chief, General Aviation Maintenance, Washington, DC), was an invited guest at the monthly meeting. Bob had come to Milwaukee to learn more about this new organization and talk to its members about the regulations concerning amateur-built and experimental aircraft. In addition, he expanded on what he thought the amateur builder could mean to the future of aviation. He recalls having a talk with Paul later that evening:

> After the meeting I had my first chance to really get to know Paul and our friendship continues to this day. ...we sat in his car in front of my hotel and talked. I was convinced that here was the person who could carry the amateur-built program to a successful future. I was most impressed with his vision, aviation skills and understanding of the problems involved. We talked into the wee hours of the morning and I felt I could depend on him to keep me accurately informed of how we could carry out the objective of the amateur-built program. I advised that we, CAA, would consider he and the EAA to be the industry spokesman if he could expand his organization to reflect a nationwide consensus. Time has proven this decision was correct. I think his leadership is recognized worldwide, and without any doubt, EAA is the leader in all phases of sport aviation.

Paul describes how the first article in *Mechanix Illustrated* became instrumental in putting EAA on the map....

Paul Poberezny, EAA President, poses with the sport plane he rebuilt from a midget racer. It measures 18 ft. overall, has 140-mph top speed.

They Build 'Em and Fly 'Em

You say you'd like to fly your own plane, but can't afford it? Let the EAA help you build your own dream-ship.

By John L. Scherer

Photos courtesy Leo J. Kohn

TOO many private flyers have found, through the years, that in order to participate in their beloved sport, they must possess above-average financial means. Consequently, many have given up flying. Yet, if U. S. private aviation is to get out of the doldrums it is imperative that the average workingman be brought into the picture. This can be done only by making flying less costly.

Tackling the problem in a practical manner, a group of ambitious pilots and mechanics have formed the Experimental Aircraft Association with headquarters in Milwaukee, Wis. Encouraged by the government through liberalization of the Civil Air Regulations covering home-built aircraft, this group has undertaken the design and construction of their own flying machines, as well as the modification of stock aircraft in order to improve performance.

With the full realization that they can build and fly their own planes only so long as they are safe, these men have set up minimum standards which are above those set forth in Civil Air Regulations. They have appointed a technical committee to advise and assist members, enabling anyone with [*Continued on page* 82]

80 *Mechanix Illustrated*

"Early in 1954, I was contacted by John Scherer of *Mechanix Illustrated* and asked if I knew anyone who could write an article about the construction of a homebuilt airplane, including detailed drawings. The only two members who came to mind were Steve Wittman and Ray Stits. However, both were in the business of selling drawings, and to put them into a magazine certainly would not have been profitable for them. As I had imagined, their response was negative.

"Mr. Scherer was disappointed, but he still wanted to pursue the article. I realized this was a great opportunity for those of us who loved to build and fly our own airplanes as we could promote our interest on a national scale. Most people looked at private aviation as mainly transportation for the business executive, and the airplanes were priced accordingly! I began to wonder if we couldn't make aviation more competitive with other recreational pursuits, such as motorcycles, sport cars and speedboats, by showing the homebuilt movement as a reasonable alternative. I agreed to help with the article and use a much modified Corben Baby Ace as the project airplane.

"Mr. Scherer said the magazine would pay me $250, so Mike Terlizzi, Carl Walters and I went to work while another talented friend, Stan Dzik, made up the drawings for a new Baby Ace Model C. The airplane we built now hangs in the EAA Air Museum in Oshkosh. It was greatly responsible for the enthusiasm and the successful development of the Experimental Aircraft Association.

"None of us expected the response we got from that first article written by Mr. Scherer for the March 1954 edition. It was about the homebuilt movement and how it provided a less costly alternative to the expensive, factory-built airplanes. Within three days I received 126 letters—and that was before the magazine hit the newsstands in Milwaukee! The next day 43 more arrived, and so on. This response told me that those who made their living in aviation hadn't done much to encourage the average individual to fly or build an airplane for recreation or sport. Nor had the manufacturers done enough to bring flying to the average citizen. I saw a great future for anyone who could develop a kit-type airplane that was available in various stages so that the initial outlay didn't discourage the individual. One has only to look at the wide variety of kits on the market today to appreciate the amount of interest out there."

Following this introductory article, there were to be three more articles detailing the actual building process of the Baby Ace. They would be written by Paul next year—after he had finished and flown the aircraft. *Mechanix Illustrated* would publish them in their May, June and July 1955 issues.

The following short tribute entitled "Indebtedness," was taken from the March 1954, *Experimenter*:

> The success, thus far, of the EAA, is not all attributed to the long hours put in by the association officers, but also to the wives, Audrey Poberezny and Lois Nolinske, who have gone along with their husbands' ideas that private aviation can be brought back to life. You will remember they were at the first fly-in in Milwaukee last September to greet and register you, and they will be there again this coming August 7th and 8th.
>
> Audrey and Lois prepared a fine snack for members after the February 22 meeting in Milwaukee to help make the meeting more enjoyable. Recently Audrey sat behind her typewriter and typed 74 letters in one long evening. Both Lois and Audrey adjust their household chores to take care of association typing which, if (it) keeps on the increase, may prove too much for them. But we husbands and all the members of the association owe them both a great big, THANK YOU!

Paul has a long history of helping others with an interest in aviation. He demonstrated it early by providing assistance to a man who later became very well known for his aviation related work in the movie industry....

"About this time, I remember a gentleman coming up the drive to our house, knocking on the door and asking for me. He said his name was Frank Tallman and that he lived in Glenview, Illinois. He had heard about me and wanted to know if I would be interested in building up a WW I Spad fighter for him. He said he was an 'old airplane' buff and had a number of Spad parts. In fact, he had also bought out an entire collection on the east coast and was having some of the restoration work done at a technical school in Boston on a Sopwith Camel and others. Frank invited us to see his collection at his home. Soon Audrey and I, along with Bob and Lois Nolinske, were in Glenview looking at the wing and other parts of Frank's Spad, and all the other memorabilia he had on the walls of his basement.

"When his arrangement with the school didn't work out, Frank asked if I would restore his Camel. I had to tell him I was too busy to do either of his airplanes but suggested Ned Kensinger of Peoria might help. When this eventually came about, I offered the use of our Guard C-47 to transport the airplanes from Boston to Ned's place. Frank was in the Naval Reserves, which made him eligible to fly as my copilot.

"Off we went in the old reliable C-47 with Sgt. Waligorski as our Flight Engineer. After staying an extra day in Boston so Frank could clear up some legal problems he was having with the airplanes, we squeezed the Sopwith Camel, a Nieuport 28 and several LeRhone engines into the C-47. It was difficult to get up to the cockpit! We left Boston late in the evening, bound for Peoria. Due to tremendous headwinds, our ground speed was only about 85 miles an hour, so we had to land at Mansfield, Ohio, for fuel. Although the base was closed, I knew the Maintenance Officer...the airplane was soon serviced and we were on our way.

"During the flight from Boston to Mansfield, our right engine had briefly cut-out one time. It ran perfectly for the next hour and a half, so I didn't pay any more attention to it...until an hour out of Mansfield when it happened again, this time more than once. After I moved the mixture control to full rich, the engine seemed to run well, so we continued on to Peoria, landing at around 1:30 in the morning. Ned met us with a group of volunteers who unloaded the cargo and helped sweep the aircraft clean of pieces of fabric and old rotted wood.

"We took off for our next stop, Glenview, Illinois, where Frank was to get off. Arriving there at 4:30 A.M. that cold, dark morning, we left the engines running while Frank got out and Sgt. Waligorski climbed into the copilot seat for the short flight back to Milwaukee. Shortly after takeoff, the right engine began to backfire and run rough, finally quitting altogether. I feathered it and we finished the trip on one engine, landing at daybreak.

"Frank promised to attend one of our fly-ins with his Camel when it was completed, which he did the next year (1955). He was member #88, a loyal one who appreciated the early help he received from this small organization. He later moved to California and formed the Tallmantz Corporation along with Paul Mantz, doing movie and stunt flying. Paul was killed while making a film and Frank took over the business, later to lose his own life in an airplane crash during poor weather conditions east of Los Angeles. I was pleased to be able to assist him and feel that by doing so, I indirectly helped promote aviation through his success in films."

Tony Maugeri, Paul, and Ned Kensinger

Paul's friendship with Ned Kensinger paid unexpected dividends when Ned rounded up enough warm bodies to create EAA Chapter #2 in Peoria, Illinois. Ever the supporter, CAA's Tony Maugeri was on hand with Paul that April 15, 1954, evening to present Ned and his group of thirty-six with their charter…and a good talk on the homebuilt movement.

It gets easier to forget Paul's full-time job with the Wisconsin Guard although, admittedly, more and more of his trips took on the appearance of camouflaged EAA missions. From his June 1954 column in *The Experimenter* he writes: **"I have done a lot of traveling this past month and talked to a great many EAA members. I had an**

opportunity to fly a C-47 out to California and while there had the chance to attend the Riverside Chapter's first dance, which was a great success. I talked to many of the members, such as Chapter President Ray Stits, Ed Scheff, Lester Cole and many others. Fellows, it really was a pleasure and I enjoyed your hospitality. I also just completed a ferry trip to Oakland, California...took our National Guard T-33 out there for overhaul."

Plans were well under way for the second EAA Fly-in, now moved up to the first week in August. However, Paul and Audrey had something else going on at that time....

"It was in July of 1954 that our daughter, Bonnie Lou Poberezny, was born. Tommy was now almost eight and already had attended fly-ins; he knew what it was like to be surrounded by airplanes. Bonnie arrived only two weeks before our second fly-in. Even so, Audrey could still be found in the small, two-wheel trailer supplied by Leo and Jim Geib of West Bend, where she and Lois registered members. Again, it was Gramma Ruesch who came to the rescue and minded our new arrival at home."

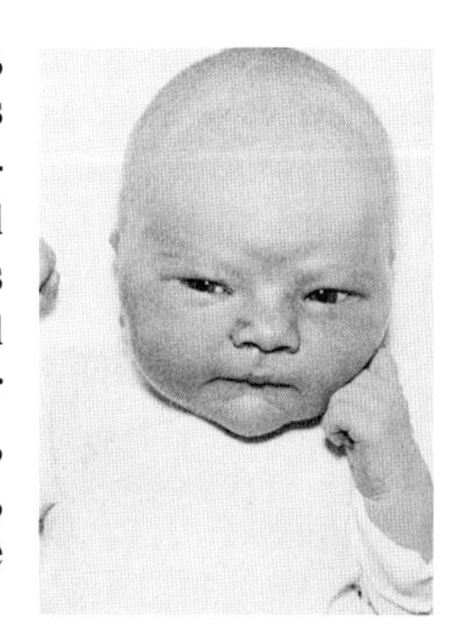

"We were busy getting ready for the 1954 Fly-in when, on July 13th, an eight pound, seven ounce baby girl we named 'Bonnie' arrived. Paul was so kind as to offer to bring my typewriter to the hospital—so we wouldn't fall behind in our correspondence! One of the nurses overheard him make this touching offer and politely told him that it would not be allowed—but he always tried! I worked at the fly-in, as I was able to leave our small baby at home with my mom. It was exciting to have more airplanes and more members attend this year's event...and we signed up several new members too!"

Audrey and Lois at work at the 1954 Fly-in

So now there were four—five if you count Grandma Ruesch, who was the cornerstone of this family! Had baby Bonnie known her future would involve helping her parents deal with the steadily increasing tide of letters, she may have asked for a change in venue!

As expected, the second annual EAA Fly-in was more successful than the first. The lessons Paul learned the previous year were not forgotten....

"I assigned various chairmen to the 1954 Fly-in, including Leo Kohn as awards chairman; a hangar committee consisting of Paul Ollenberg and Ken Heidger; George Gruenberger for lodging; David Frantz along with Don O'Leary and Jim Peplinski in charge of aircraft welcoming and parking; and myself, Steve Wittman, George Hardie and Bob Nolinske as the program committee. Of course we knew we could count on Audrey and Lois, and they were greatly assisted by Mary Kohn and Phyllis Kemp. Poor Audrey had barely returned from her short, two-week maternity leave after delivering our daughter!

"Our two friends and supporters from the CAA, Tony Maugeri and Bob Burbick, volunteered to judge the awards for outstanding design and workmanship. Other dignitaries who made presentations, included Mr. T. K. Jordan, Wisconsin State Aeronautics Commissioner, Wiley Wright, Director of the General Aviation Section (CAA), Carl Clifford, Deputy Director, and from the Aeronautical University in Chicago, Mr. Al Stott. Miller Beer's Chief Pilot, Joe Laird, assisted with the dinner arrangements and supplied their beautiful hangar at General Mitchell Field—plus all the beer we could drink! We charged $1.50 for each ticket to cover the cost of the food. Of course, the list of volunteers that help make an event like this successful could fill its own book.

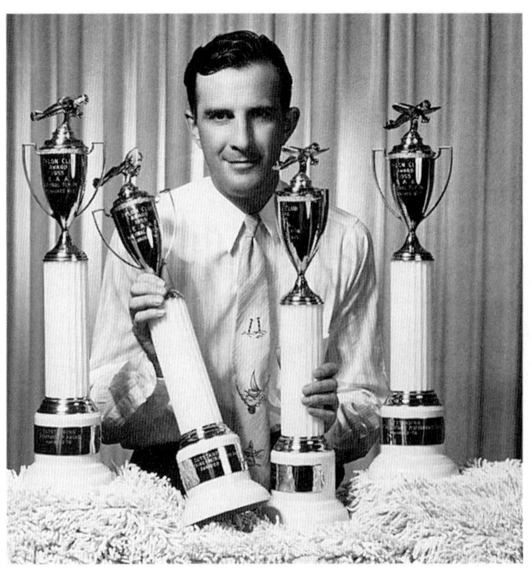
Nick Rezich with the trophies he donated

"EAA had its first award winners; each received beautiful trophies donated by Nick Rezich. Ray Nelson and Jack MacRae tied for the Greatest Distance Award (they came from the same airport in New York). My good friend Neal Loving easily took the Most Outstanding Design Award with his *Loving's Love* racer, and Richard Schroeder

received the Workmanship Award for his beautiful, all-metal home-built, *Air-Mate.* I was honored to win an Achievement Award.

"This was our first national convention and election of officers. We delayed the elections scheduled for earlier in the year so that all members could vote at the business meeting that Sunday morning. I was re-elected president and Bob Nolinske, secretary-treasurer. Leo Kohn, another hard working volunteer, became our new vice-president.

Little Tommy in "Little Audrey" at the 1954 Fly-in

"There was a sportsplane air race held in which I participated (and won) in *Little Audrey*. All EAA members could enter, provided they held the proper pilot qualifications. The air show again featured the popular Cole Brothers, along with some other acts. The local press was invited and the major flying magazines had representatives on hand to report the event. Even television was contacted and tentative arrangements were made with NBC for its Camel News Show coverage.

"EAA supported and encouraged participation in the Air Pageant's 'Teen-Hi Airlift' program that gave local kids a free ride in an airplane. Saturday morning was reserved for teenagers and Sunday for kids under twelve. Although it wasn't called a 'Young Eagles' program, the idea was the same; everyone realized that getting youth involved in aviation was the key to its long-term survival. Several Milwaukee businessmen had donated their time and money to stimulate interest in these kids and flew over 1500 of them during the first two years of the project. As I have said many times before, there is really nothing much new in aviation!

"Although we didn't have a separate category for them, one could say our first warbirds came to the second fly-in. Jim Geib from West Bend, Wisconsin, flew his Eastern FM-2 Wildcat, and Robert H. Davis from Bloomington, Illinois, brought a rare Grumman G-32A. Both airplanes attracted considerable attention.

"The fly-in was a huge success with over two hundred members in attendance. Our membership had grown almost tenfold in less than a year, having been at 73 in September of 1953 and now over 700 after the fly-in. Even more pleasing to me was that our renewal rate was almost 100 percent, and that we had over $1700 in the treasury with which to promote aviation."

Air Guard summer encampment. This year it was held between July 31 and August 14—right through the EAA Fly-in! Here's how Paul overcame that obstacle....

"I completed my annual two-week encampment with our Air National Guard Squadron in Alpena, Michigan. It was scheduled during the period of the EAA Fly-in, so I attended camp until Friday and then flew a T-33 back to Milwaukee for the weekend. After the fly-in, I returned to the camp on Monday morning.

"We were training in the F-86 Sabres that year and I enjoyed the opportunity to improve my flying of that wonderful aircraft. The

F-86 formation - Howie Mattes in the lead, with Paul on his left wing

North American demonstration pilot was there, a man named Bob Hoover; he made the Sabre do things it wasn't supposed to do! It reminded us of Bob Love's earlier demonstration in the F-89. I also remember getting into a bit of trouble when I later took off and performed a similar routine in another Sabre—and wore the tires down to the cords!"

The following stories came from the 1991 book, *History of the Wisconsin National Guard*:

> …in 1954, our Summer Camp was at Alpena, Michigan, with the Milwaukee unit. The troops went on buses—some of them so old they had chain drive! With only a few breakdowns, they arrived in Alpena. The objective for Summer Camp was to fly as much as possible—at least enough to beat Milwaukee! That was always our objective but we weren't always successful.
>
> We didn't have enough airplanes so we had been loaned some from the Air Force—they were not as well maintained as ours. The high spot of the encampment was the day Bob Hoover came in to put on a demonstration flight for us. He asked for the worst airplane we had—it was one from the Air Force—and proceeded to do all kinds of magic with it, including a downwind take-off out of a short field landing. It was hard on the brakes but it was a great show.

> Summer Camps were not all flying. The medics, who should have known about the effects of alcohol on the human body, threw a party one year but they 'needled' the beer. They added alcohol and some of the pilots who thought beer didn't have much effect on them had difficulty handling it. One got too close to the source and passed out. The medics considerately called an ambulance, took him to the infirmary, put a full length leg cast on him and let him sleep it off. When he woke, he could not remember what happened, and worse, couldn't think what to tell his wife!

Paul adds…

"While I was glad to be able to attend both events, I returned home to a stack of letters over a foot high, not including the ones Audrey had already answered! It took me another two days to answer them—and then it was time to get *The Experimenter* out! I needed thirty-six hour days!"

As a result of all this mail, Paul's homebuilding efforts slipped to a lower priority, as did his non-military flying. There just wasn't enough time! A clip-wing (what else?) Heath Parasol was relegated to the rafters in his hangar, never to be finished. The only project underway was the Baby Ace, and it had to be completed to honor the magazine commitment. Regarding "who" did all the work around the house…well, the truth can now be told by Audrey....

Working in the coal bin!

Audrey adding the final touches… after painting the garage

"I was amazed at how small our mailbox seemed to become each week as the mail increased. I also remember being so excited about EAA taking in $37.50 in one day! Quite a windfall, I thought at the time!

"At first I could process the mail while Bonnie took her nap, but that soon changed and I had to spend longer hours working in the evenings. Tommy was a big help entertaining his sister and reading the newspaper to me while I fed her. He ran errands for me and took care of many little chores around the house so I wouldn't have to run up and down the stairs as often. He would take the clothes line down (we didn't have a dryer), but I could never convince him to take the diapers off the line!"

Paul and Audrey were each putting in at least forty hours a week on EAA duties. The mail load was staggering, the membership kept increasing, and their home was becoming a national landmark!

"With EAA in our daily routine, there was never a dull moment around the house. Whoever had heard of the organization and happened to be passing through Milwaukee would stop in. It was always a pleasure to meet the fellows, some nights parking as many as fourteen cars up and down the street. I'm sure the constant traffic was a bit upsetting to Audrey and her mother—and I always wondered what the neighbors were thinking!

Tommy entertaining his new sister

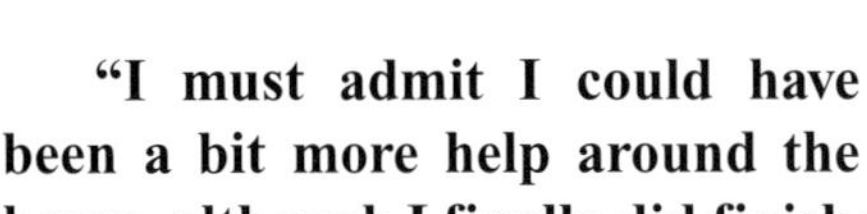

"I must admit I could have been a bit more help around the house, although I finally did finish painting the storm windows! It was either that or keep tripping over them! Audrey would place them so I couldn't miss them when I got home from work.

Audrey leaves a subtle message for Howard - STORM WINDOWS!

"I had lots of help with the Baby Ace Model C from Mike Terlizzi, Dave and Ben Frantz, Bruce Pitt, Newt Stansfield and Carl Walters. We were making good progress, as were a growing number of other builders. At last count there were now nine homebuilt aircraft being built in Milwaukee, with another five in the planning stages!"

Baby Ace Model C under construction

Some stories can only come from a military environment....

"There was to be a National Air Guard cross-country race scheduled from Los Angeles to a destination on the east coast. As we still had our F-86 Sabres, we felt we had a pretty good chance to win; soon a pair of Sabres were bound for California. Before I knew it, there was a call saying our jets were down on a road near Las Vegas, New Mexico, and that one was damaged. They had flown into some big thunderstorms and, with only ADF for navigation, were soon lost and low on fuel. They ran out of options and landed on a remote stretch of highway, rather than eject and lose the airplanes. While landing, one of the jets hit a power line that sheared off half its vertical stabilizer and rudder; the other wasn't damaged. I immediately assembled a crew and headed out.

"I landed the C-47 at an old emergency strip that had a runway but no buildings. When we checked into the hotel, we asked where the pilots were. The answer was that they were across the street in the bar! Sure enough, there they were, the local 'heroes,' still in their flying and 'G' suits, drinking beer and talking to the locals.

"I made arrangements with the unit at Kirtland AFB to trade for an F-86 aft section, which they sent along with a fuel truck, power unit, and some tools. Working alongside the road, we had the airplanes ready in two days. The police then blocked off the highway and the guys strapped in and took off. It was an odd feeling to watch them disappear down the hill and then reappear on the other side during their

takeoff runs. They both got airborne but failed to meet at their rendezvous, so they made their way back home individually... never making it to the air race!"

"Another Saturday evening, Audrey and I were going out for dinner when the telephone rang. It was Base Ops telling me that four of our F-86s were heading back to Milwaukee, low on fuel. Six of them had originally been scrambled to chase a B-36 'target' and had returned to Madison with 'bingo' fuel. While they were gone, a snowstorm had moved into the area and only two were able to land. The other four tried to make it back to Milwaukee but ran out of fuel. Two pilots were killed. It was a tragic event that showed the risk of operating jet aircraft in an unfriendly environment."

"I was assigned to take an F-86 down to the depot at Kelly AFB in Texas and asked Audrey to pack me a lunch. I got there around noon and pulled out my black metal lunch bucket. The flight line crews couldn't believe that a jet pilot was sitting on the wing of his jet, eating his lunch as if he was just another factory worker."

Paul flying "old 8164" while being "bounced" by fellow squadron mates in F-86 Sabres

Paul was awarded the Senior Pilot Wing (#6) in August (wing #7, the Command Pilot Wing, would come in 1959.) In the fall, just as he was getting up to speed in the Sabre (and appointed test pilot in August), the unit began switching back to the ill-fated F-89 Scorpion. Paul was also a designated test pilot for the T-33, and in December added Base Flying Safety Officer to his list of "extra" duties. He managed to squeeze in trips to Texas, Illinois, Massachusetts, California, Michigan, Georgia and Utah, to name a few. He also visited CAA headquarters in Washington for the first of innumerable visits he would make over the next several decades, proving once again he was the ideal person to represent the movement. (He went to lobby for a separate category for homebuilt airplanes but was told that until there were more of them on the register, it wouldn't be practical.)

1954 was quite a year for the "local airplane club." EAA membership was well over 900 and people were joining from all over the United States and several foreign countries. The monthly meetings in Milwaukee were drawing at least 100 members, more than half coming from further than 100 miles away. The never-ending influx of letters that required an answer averaged out at well over fifty per day—day in and day out!

Each month *The Experimenter* was being mailed to more than two thousand addresses that included EAA members, subscription-only customers, and a growing complimentary list of CAA and other recipients around the country. This was a brilliant marketing ploy, for it got the message out to a much larger clientele in a shorter time period.

There were other milestones this year. Steve Wittman became the first person to have a homebuilt airplane approved by the CAA to carry non-paying passengers. Foster Hannaford, Jr. acquired liability and property damage insurance (at reasonable cost) for EAA members and their experimental aircraft. The CAA committed to work in conjunction with EAA, and a strong working partnership had begun in earnest. Even the Canadian equivalent of the CAA showed an interest in EAA's amateur-built aircraft movement and had asked to be kept informed!

Ray Stits started the first EAA chapter in California; now there were seven up and running, with another thirteen in the works. *Experimenter* advertising revenues were up. Publicity coups ranged from the magazine article in *Mechanix Illustrated* (Leo Kohn), to others in *Time* (Paul), *Air Progress* (Burton Kemp) and *Flying* magazines (Leo Kohn). There was local coverage in newspapers (Leo Kohn) and on TV (Nick Rezich). Celebrity Arthur Godfrey acknowledged Paul's letter in a return note of his own. The word was getting out!

But the strain was beginning to show; Paul was looking for some relief from the long days with little or no home life....

"The 'full-time' volunteer job at EAA left us very little time for ourselves—if any—and we sometimes began to wonder why we subjected ourselves to such a task. But when we received letters complimenting our efforts to restore an interest in private aviation, it gave us renewed effort to keep going. So much of my gratitude is owed to Audrey and the many others who spent so much of their time assisting our aims. Looking back, I don't know how—or why—they continued to do so."

Finally. in his December column, Paul caught up on some old business—a mere six months after the event occurred, **"I, in my maze of letters, forgot to mention in our August issue of *The Experimenter* that we had a new addition to our family last July—a fine baby girl. So, for a week and a half, Lois Nolinske carried the full burden of EAA secretarial work."**

The year ended on a sad note....

"Three of our earliest members and best supporters lost their lives in a tragic airplane crash on December 17, 1954. It was a foggy night with low ceilings and they were taking off from General Mitchell Field in a converted Lockheed Ventura bound for Canada. Joe Laird (member #7) was the pilot; his brother Paul (member #8) was copilot. On board was the President of Miller Brewing Company, Fred Miller (member #150) and his son, Fred, Jr. The crankshaft on the right engine failed just as they were passing the north end of the runway. The airplane crashed and burned, and all lives were lost. EAA suffered a great loss with the untimely death of these men who had done so much for our organization and for so many others in the area."

"Where should I dump her, mom?

Chapter Twenty-Four

1955

The calendar provided no rest for our tireless couple as EAA continued to impose its increasing demands on those who gave so much of their time to keep it operating. True, the larger the membership, the more that can be accomplished. But it still takes someone with that innate ability to keep all the cogs greased—including their own! For EAA, it was Paul Poberezny. For Paul, it was Audrey!

The Baby Ace is ready for final inspection

The much-modified Baby Ace was finished and ready for its pre-flight inspection. Milwaukee CAA Inspector, Tony Maugeri, recalls doing the honors: "When Paul finished building his first homebuilt, the Baby Ace, he called me to perform the final inspection prior to his first flight. I went to the hangar and there was a good looking airplane with an eager pilot ready to go! The airplane appeared to be ready for flight—until I checked the controls. Something didn't appear to be right…the aileron controls were reversed! I don't think Paul flew that day!"

"I had taken it out to Mitchell Field in Milwaukee and assembled it. Our local CAA Agent, Tony Maugeri, ran the inspection. No sooner had he moved the stick when he came forth with this remark, 'Poop Deck, what's this—you push the stick to the left and the left aileron comes *down*?' In other words, the controls were reversed—after at least twenty-five people had moved the stick to see how they worked!

"Carl Walters, Chuck Cornwall (another CAA Agent), Tony and I got our heads together and in no time had it straightened out. Next there was the paperwork, then the test flights. The first two tests were taxi runs; on the third, I lifted off about ten feet to check for wing and tail heaviness. After adjusting the right wing strut and resetting the idle adjustment, I was ready to go. I opened the throttle and was in the air within 125 feet, but soon noticed that I had to keep forward stick pressure in order to keep the airplane flying level. As I increased speed, the pressure also increased, so I kept it throttled back and cruised at about 75 mph. The ailerons felt a bit stiff and slow to respond, but it was a real pleasure to sit up there and cruise along in a product of my own. I didn't even notice it was the middle of winter!

Test Flight

"Later we made an adjustment to the stabilizer and installed a metal fairing over the gap between the rear spar and the aileron. After that, the airplane flew very well. It indicated 30 mph as it touched down for landing, 95-100 at cruise...and it would get out of a pickle patch!

"It was the beginning of what would soon be a large number of Baby Ace homebuilt aircraft providing their builders with the joy of flight—at a much lower cost than anything offered by the manufacturers of light airplanes!"

The kid from Ghost Alley who always wanted to have a real airplane factory had "done good!"

Stan Dzik and Tony Maugeri congratulate Paul on a successful test flight

1955 was another busy year in the Air Guard. After shedding his temporary assignments, Paul was free to concentrate on his primary duties as Unit Aircraft Maintenance Officer and Test Pilot for an increasing number of different airplanes. In January he checked out in the B-25 (actually a TB-25K), and in March, qualified as a B-25 Instructor Pilot. Next, it was time to reacquaint himself with the F-89 Scorpion that had replaced the legendary Sabre the previous fall. With its advanced fire control systems, rear seat Radar Officer, twin jet engines and much heavier gross weights, the Scorpion took some getting used to. In addition, its low engine intakes were an open invitation to FOD (foreign object damage); the smallest pebble could ruin an engine in a heartbeat. It was normal practice for

squadron personnel to walk the ramp and runway areas prior to commencing flying operations each day, picking up garbage that could destroy an engine and possibly the entire airplane and crew. FOD remained a significant problem and would cause a number of engines to be destroyed.

Even without FOD-induced damage, the early model Scorpions incurred an abnormally high percentage of engine problems. Until improvements were made, the airplane offered plenty of challenges to its pilots. There wasn't a great need to practice single engine procedures—they got to do it for real on a regular basis! And Paul got more than his fair share....

"As F-89 maintenance test pilot, I enjoyed the challenge of the job; but there were also many times when I was scared. I experienced more forced landings at Mitchell Field than anyone else, which was saying a lot in that airplane. Sitting there, getting ready for takeoff, recording all the engine readings, and wearing an oxygen mask in temperatures that ranged from ice-cold to boiling hot...was like being in a dentist's chair before he starts drilling! But once you released the brakes, you became occupied and didn't have time to think of anything else except the aircraft and the mission.

F-89 Maintenance Test Pilot - Paul Poberezny

"One winter day, I was taking off on a routine test flight in a Scorpion. The runways were icy and slippery, which meant there would be poor braking action. If I had to return and land shortly after take-off, I wanted to have less fuel on board. Less fuel meant lower approach and landing speeds and a better chance at getting the aircraft stopped. So before I took off, I lengthened my afterburner run-up period—much to the chagrin of the nearby FBO! I ran each engine in burner for about four or five minutes while I slowly wrote down the instrument readings. That decision probably saved the airplane—if not me!

"I was alone, as I didn't need a Radar Operator for this particular test, and had just gotten airborne when the airplane began to feel 'funny'—like it wasn't really accelerating! A quick glance at the tachometers showed the right one winding down! I thought to myself, this can't be happening to me—not right after takeoff in full after-burner! I knew I had to dump fuel fast if I was to remain in the air, so I reached down and pushed the dump valve switch, jettisoning about 1600 gallons of jet fuel. That was when the tower called to ask if I had a problem. I told them to stand-by. They came back telling me I was trailing a lot of 'something' behind the airplane and again asked if I had a problem. I told them, 'Don't bother me! I've got enough problems!' The first thing you do in an emergency is fly the airplane and I was doing just that, trying to get set up for a return to the base. Talking on the radio was the last thing on my mind!

"After everything was under control, I told the tower I had 'lost' an engine and was returning to land, and for them to get the fire trucks out. I always called for them; they were my extra insurance policy! A lot of guys think, aw, don't worry about them. But what if they needed help and it arrived a few precious seconds too late? Besides, it's good practice for the rescue crews too!

"I kept thinking: OK, you've got a one-engine airplane...big deal! Just don't come in too high, and don't get behind the power curve. You keep talking to yourself, going over the procedures, and telling yourself to take it easy. Then all of a sudden, it's over! You taxi off the runway and shut down in the chocks...the dentist's chair wasn't too bad after all!"

Throughout 1955, J-35-A35 engine failures became more numerous. One of Paul's fellow squadron pilots, Howie Mattes, experienced a double engine flame-out! That caused a service-wide grounding of the F-89 until more reliable power plants could be installed. However, they were in service for the summer encampment, the third airplane and the third location in as many years. (In 1953 it was F-51s at Volk Field, in 1954, F-86s in Michigan—now it was back home for the F-89C Scorpion.) This meant lots of practice for both ground and air crews, as the airplane had introduced a higher degree of complexity into the operation. At least the F-89 was going to be around for a number of years (once its mechanical problems were sorted out), which would add to the long-term stability of the unit.

Because of his extensive experience as a military test pilot (and his earlier trysts as a barnstorming youth), Paul was constantly being asked to per-

form test flights of homebuilt airplanes. Since the same basic principles apply, he was also very good at it....

"Some people question the courage it takes to get into and fly a homebuilt airplane, one that someone else has built in their back yard or garage. I tell them that with my experience, I have a pretty good idea what an airplane will do *before* I get into it. I also make sure I have a long enough runway. If the taxi test feels good, I get airborne and remain in ground effect until I can feel a proper response from the controls. Then I climb a bit higher to again convince myself that all the controls are working properly and that the weight and balance feels fine. During this time, which is really quite brief, I am prepared to immediately put it down on the runway if anything isn't to my liking. Only after passing this critical stage will I leave the airport area and begin to explore the remainder of the aircraft's performance envelope at higher altitudes.

"One airplane I flew out in Torrance, California, was a mid wing race plane called the *Terrill Special.* It was a fast little sucker—a real handful! I had just taken off and the speed had quickly built up to 220 mph as I climbed away from the runway. All of a sudden there was an explosion! It took me a few seconds to realize the canopy had come off! I slowed down and decided to 'feel' the airplane at different speeds before returning to land. Its normal approach speed was around 85 mph, which was quite fast for the type. I discovered that I should carry an *extra* 10 mph more to make up for the turbulence caused by the missing canopy: 95 or 100 mph would do! As luck would have it, when I got back to the airport, the wind direction had changed and I was now facing a crosswind. I had a problem seeing over the nose, but I finally wrestled it down...I don't mind telling you it was a difficult airplane to fly.

"At the same airport, I flew a biplane in which a fellow had installed a much larger engine. As soon as I took off I could feel the airplane shudder. Looking back, I saw the entire tail shaking. Apparently the engine was too big and its vibrations were traveling through the airframe. I pulled the throttle back, eased it around and landed. I told them it needed more bracing for the horizontal stabilizer before anyone should fly it again.

"After being so close to it for many years, you can often just walk around an airplane and pick out things that should be different. Some days it's best not to fly at all! You learn to leave your ego at home and trust your senses."

Paul and Audrey's affair with EAA continued at a home-wrecking pace. Early that year, *Experimenter* circulation exceeded 2500. As a result, more letters poured in from the membership. Paul tells of answering them in unusual places, such as at 12,000 feet in the Air Guard C-47 while enroute to another destination, or in a hotel room halfway across the country waiting for the weather to improve. His travels led him to more states and more visits with EAA members as he pursued his guard duties. His diary began to read like a country and western song: Ohio, Michigan, Texas, Missouri, Indiana, New Mexico, Pennsylvania, Wyoming, Oklahoma, California, Kansas, Utah and DeeCee! There is nothing like a personal visit from El Presidente to fire up the troops, and Paul was certainly out there giving it his best.

After two more visits to Washington this year, his face was becoming a familiar sight in the halls at CAA headquarters. Each time, Branch Chief Bob Burbick offered a different challenge. *"What constitutes an amateur-built airplane?"* And later, *"How far can a kit manufacturer go?"* Questions that would someday require answers.

Back in February, Paul announced his Board of Directors: Stanley Dzik, David Frantz, Leo Geib, George Gruenberger, Bob Nolinske and Newton Stansfield. (Did these men know what they were getting into?) The board was introduced to the membership at the first annual mid winter meeting held later that month at Curtiss-Wright airport. Expectations were that as many as four or five hundred members would show up for this inaugural affair, but the weather decided otherwise! Attendance barely reached 125 due to a totally miserable winter day—sleet, ice and all the other things that cause northerners to retire in the south. However, the concept was sound and it gave the membership an opportunity to voice their opinions more than once a year, although they were always welcome to attend any of the regular monthly meetings.

The CAA was directed by their political bosses to reverse the startling decline in student pilot, mechanic and other aviation applications that had followed the post-war surge. AIM, or Aviation Incentive Movement, was the name of the program handed to the Washington bureaucrats who dutifully began to promote it through their field offices. The timing couldn't have been better! EAA and its membership appeared as the only real hope for reversing this downward trend.

Apparently the members agreed too; many of them sent letters to *The Experimenter* supporting this thought. C. W. Lasher of Hialeah, Florida,

wrote: "I say, give the responsibility and the privileges to the people who want it and who have worked for it by demonstrating an active interest and desire for it—the homebuilders. …we need a few more men like Wittman, Poberezny, Stits and Dzik who have a realistic and down-to-earth understanding and can separate the necessary from the unnecessary." Edward Miller from Kent State, Utah, stated: "You have done in the short time you've been in existence, more than all the aircraft manufacturers put together could ever do toward the furtherance of private aviation. I think the explanation is fairly simple: the EAA has no 'gimmick.' You're not out to get rich quick, but only to give people like me a chance to get into the air where we otherwise would just have to sit and watch the other fellow fly."

Apparently Paul was on the right track. He also knew that until private aviation captured the interest of the younger generations, it would remain in a precarious position regarding its ability to survive. Each year the task would become more difficult, as aviation pulled further away from mainstream special interest activities.

The Experimenter was fast becoming the "bible" of the homebuilder crowd and by the spring of 1955 had grown to sixteen pages. Information about members and their projects was solicited and published. Notices appeared from a growing number of EAA chapters and members, now hosting more and more aviation events throughout the country. Individuals and companies in the business of selling plans and supplies purchased more advertising space, taking advantage of the increasing circulation that had, by year's end, surpassed the 3,500 mark.

Feature-length articles were written on a variety of subjects, including a two-issue spread on homebuilt helicopters by Igor Bensen. There were several articles on gliding and an extensive report on the all-wood and tailless "Plank" glider (an example is currently on display at EAA's Pioneer Airport). Paul wrote an article on the Milwaukee Light Plane Club of the 1930's, while Ray Stits asked for (and received) financial assistance for the hurting aerobatic pilot, Lester Cole. (Lester had suffered back injuries in an airplane accident and was financially drained by the high cost of healing.)

EAA's first Technical Advisor, Stanley Dzik, christened a detailed series of articles in the September issue; in December, George Hardie and Jack McRae teamed up to inaugurate a series on the history of homebuilt designs. EAA was incorporated as a non-profit organization in the State of Wisconsin. It also hired its first employee, a part-time clerk-typist by the name of Mike Everson who wisely kept his day job with the Milwaukee Air Guard. No doubt Paul and his small band of hard-working friends were putting together a complex and exciting organization!

National interest in EAA rose to new heights when Paul's articles detailing the building of his Baby Ace appeared in the May, June and July issues of *Mechanix Illustrated.* Admittedly not a writer, Paul (and Audrey) spent many long hours struggling with the content, knowing this exposure would mean so much to the movement. He was absolutely on target. The articles generated inquiries, not only from other interested homebuilders, but from a variety of organizations, politicians and bureaucrats. The scope and intensity of the response helped establish EAA as the leader of private aviation in the minds of CAA personnel. That, coupled with Paul's resolve to play the role of mediator rather than wild-eyed reactionary, served him and the organization well. Had he not been so inclined, the final outcome of EAA's relationship with CAA might have been completely different. A quote from one of his columns in *The Experimenter* sums up his conciliatory attitude, **"Occasionally an incident is brought to my attention regarding a misunderstanding. But there are always two sides to a story and it is hard to decide who is right, with only one."**

The 1955 EAA Fly-in began with hopes of hosting up to a hundred home-built airplanes. Actually, over two hundred showed up, except that most of them were general aviation airplanes bringing their pilots in for a look at this new thing called EAA. Poor flying weather once again haunted the Milwaukee area during much of the weekend, keeping the number of experimental airplanes down to a few more than thirty...still, a fifty percent improvement over last year!

Stanley Dzik was EAA's first "official" Convention Chairman. This was another smart move on Paul's part for it allowed him to oversee the entire operation, rather than get bogged down in one or two areas as he had in the past. With the freedom to roam, Paul could better judge the overall quality of the event. Besides, Stan did a whale of a job! He had the schedule of events ready by June and got everyone pumped up over what they felt was going to be a real barn-burner. Since their contact with Miller Beer

was gone, Keith Kummer brought a new sponsor on board: the Joseph Schlitz Brewing Company. They supplied the registration trailer and assisted in other areas.

Stan Dzik - one of EAA's first Directors, first Technical Advisor, and first "official" Convention Chairman!

1955 marked the first three-day fly-in, agreed to since most members arrived on Friday anyway. Milwaukee's largest and finest downtown hotel, the Schroeder, was selected as convention headquarters and bus transportation was arranged between it and the airport. The annual EAA business meeting was held Friday afternoon in the hotel; the same three officers were re-elected, indicating either blind faith in their leadership abilities or an aversion to doing the work themselves! Movies were shown that evening.

Non-aviation events were also planned on Saturday for those with interests other than airplanes, including morning and afternoon tours of the Schlitz brewery, and shopping (nice combination!). Saturday evening was reserved for the annual awards dinner and dance—and you can guess on what hot, muggy weekend the hotel air conditioner decided to fail!

A summary of the evening activities was printed in the August 1955 *Experimenter*:

> Then came the big banquet and ball in the evening. Again no air conditioner! Still, we had about 180 people seated and all seemed to enjoy the evening. Mr. Wiley Wright (CAA, Washington, DC) gave a fine talk about the CAA which should have enlightened many of us. Then came the time to award the trophies.
>
> …Steve Wittman received so many awards that Wiley Wright went and got a huge serving tray for Steve to collect them on. Paul Poberezny received a real 'Do It Yourself' award from Nick Rezich and it proved one of the lighter moments of the evening.

> It consisted of a ruler, saw, hammer, screwdriver, airplane and paint brush, all mounted at crazy angles to each other. To say the least, it was very original.

EAA's first "stand-alone" fly-in was a success, if only because everyone who attended had a good time. At least one member from every state in the union signed in, including Frank Tallman who, as he had promised, brought his restored WW I Sopwith Camel. An estimated five to ten thousand spectators took advantage of free admission to view the homebuilt airplanes and learn about the organization and its people. That kind of exposure can pay dividends later on.

Steve Wittman and the many trophies he won at the 1955 fly-in

Audrey's dividend came in the form of spending the following Saturday evening banging out *Experimenter* articles on the typewriter so the magazine could get out on time. Paul wrote in his column, **"Not many wives will prefer a typewriter to an evening out—especially a Saturday night. We sure owe her (Audrey) a lot, fellows, for without her cooperation...no EAA!"**

Some things never change—although maybe it was the best offer she got that night!

Later that fall the EAA board approved a long-standing request by Steve Wittman to hold the 1956 Fly-in at Oshkosh. In return, and to help provide additional exposure for the event, they asked Steve to schedule some record attempts and other aviation activities along with the fly-in. The newly formed Antique Airplane Association, headed then as it is today by Robert Taylor, also asked to be included in the program. Their request was

quickly approved...apparently antiquers and homebuilders share many of the same family genes. It would all prove to be an interesting combination.

Over the years, Paul and Audrey have met people from a wide variety of backgrounds, most of them joined by the same love for aviation. In a few cases, this shared emotion served to overcome social and physical barriers that normally would have stood between those who "have" and "have not." One such relationship involved a gentleman by the name of Lambert....

"Stafford 'Casey' Lambert of St. Louis, Missouri, was a well-known pilot with many years behind the stick. Before the war, he flew with Charles Lindbergh in the Army Air Corps reserve squadron at Lambert Field in St. Louis, so named after Casey's uncle. During the war he served in the Navy as a pilot, although it was in the armaments division, a subject in which he was keenly interested.

"Casey was one of our early members and shared the desire to build his own airplane. He called me after reading my article in *Mechanix Illustrated*, saying he had decided to build a Baby Ace on floats with a Continental C-85 engine, complete with starter and generator. He asked if I would help him build it, but I told him I could only provide guidance; there wasn't enough time for my own projects, let alone anyone else's. He said he would appreciate any assistance I could give, and that he would find someone else to help him."

Audrey intercedes....

"One day, these two men came to our house, ordered a lot of supplies and materials, and then left, saying a truck would be down soon to pick it all up. One of them, Cal Lathom, looked quite nice; the other, the one who was doing all the ordering, was very poorly dressed. I asked Howard, 'Who is this guy anyway?' He didn't really know either. My suspicions as to whether this man could afford all that he was ordering were growing. After they left, I asked Howard to call Ed Knaup at Mitchell Field where they had parked their airplane, and inquire about him. Ed said, 'Give him your house!'...and then told us about his family history. Mr. Lambert, or 'Casey' as we would soon get to know him, was part of the Lambert Pharmaceutical family. His mother came from the Anheuser-Busch (beer) family, and Casey himself owned an engineering firm in St. Louis. He obviously had plenty of money and could afford to buy all the parts if he wanted!"

Paul continues....

"Casey started the Baby Ace project at his summer home in

Minocqua, Wisconsin. At his request, one Sunday afternoon I flew up in *Little Audrey* to look over the parts he had laid out in his shop. I landed at what was then a little grass strip with one hangar, known as Woodruff Airport. Casey was waiting there in his Rolls-Royce with a number of house guests and plenty of cold champagne—I was overcome by the reception.

"We returned to his place and he showed me around. There was a main house that had several bedrooms, a kitchen, dining area, and a living room with a fireplace. Scattered around the grounds were a number of smaller guest houses. Casey's living quarters were located above a large combination hangar and boathouse on the lake. Inside were pictures of the many airplanes he had flown, including a Lockheed Sirius he bailed out of when its wing came off! There was a beautiful Aeronca K on floats in the hangar, as well as several speedboats.

"When he took me into his shop, all I could say was, 'What a hobby shop!' It was very well-equipped—even better than those used by many of the light plane companies of the day! I helped him and Cal Lathom lay out the fuselage sides, and returned to Milwaukee the next day.

"During the Baby Ace building process, I made a number of trips to Minocqua; most of the time, Audrey came with me. Later, Ray and Bernice Scholler joined us, and then Art and June Kilps...we always had a good time. I once took Audrey for a ride in the float equipped Aeronca K, which was in excellent condition, still having its original fabric! It was one of many amphibian airplanes Casey owned.

Audrey, Cal Lathom and Casey Lambert

"When Casey's Baby Ace on floats was completed, I was asked to perform the test flights. Without a doubt, the aircraft possessed the finest workmanship I had seen up to that time. Cliff DuCharme and his staff at Ace Airplane Company were responsible for much of the finish work, as Casey had taken it there when it was about half finished. The airplane flew very well, cruising at 100 mph with the floats. Its takeoff run on the water was about 400 feet, and it had excellent stall and glide characteristics."

"Casey later crashed his Baby Ace, hitting some power lines while making an approach to land on the lake. The airplane was badly damaged but he was OK. We built a second one, and that airplane is in the EAA Air Museum. Casey was a man of many interests, with the ability to support them all: guns, photography, boats—even race cars. I recall one race car in which he installed a Merlin engine. Sometimes he'd have a tow-truck follow him because the car was so long he could not always find a place to turn it around; the tow-truck was used to lift it up and point it homeward."

Audrey finishes the story....

"We became regular guests at Casey's summer home in Minocqua and spent many fun times in his company. We also visited him at his homes in Florida and the Virgin Islands. He was a big man, handsome...and a bachelor. He always had good-looking women after him—and even some who weren't! Although he wore old clothes during the day (certainly nothing that would tell you his financial status) he insisted on proper dress for everyone at dinner. Whenever we visited him, we always made sure we had the appropriate clothes to wear.

Paul and Audrey's unplanned stop

"One time, as Howard and I were passing overhead in an airplane, we called him on the aircraft radio (Casey always kept one turned on). He asked us to land and visit with him, which we did. He met us at the airport and soon invited us to stay the night. We said we had to get back to Milwaukee but he insisted, so we told him we didn't have any dress clothes. No matter, he said, and called the house to let his other guests know that casual dress was acceptable for tonight only! We stayed.

"One year we were invited to a New Year's Eve party at Minocqua. As you can imagine, it was quite an affair. At midnight, he rolled out this cannon that he restored with whitewall tires and lots of brass, and fired it into the lake! The noise was so loud it surely woke up everyone within miles of the place...it even knocked over a sofa on the porch!

Audrey with Casey's New Year's Eve cannon

Casey Lambert

"We visited Casey on many occasions over the next twenty years and enjoyed each one of them. I think he was a lonely man who appreciated having someone like Howard to talk airplanes with. At some of the dinners, he would ignore his well-known guests to talk with Howard. He always sent presents to Bonnie and Tommy; one Christmas it was a portable phonograph. He was a very generous man, but if he ever thought you were taking advantage of him, you were 'out.' Casey passed away on October 3, 1975...Tommy's birthday."

The Corben Aircraft Company underwent a few changes of its own in 1955. Paul knew it would not be good for him—or EAA—if the membership felt he was profiting from his position as president. The solution he came up with was to turn his airplane company over to Cliff DuCharme. Cliff operated a fleet of twenty-five Stearman crop-duster aircraft and was one of the larger retail suppliers of Stearman parts and equipment. He was a good choice to take over the reins of the struggling operation. For a while Paul remained involved, although at a much lower level. Later he withdrew completely, preferring to concentrate on EAA, the Air Guard, and his family...probably in that order!

Another story involved Paul and Audrey, Bob and Lois, and a trip to Grand Haven, Michigan. The occasion was an air show sponsored by the Junior Chamber of Commerce (forerunner to the Jaycees). A special invitation had been issued to EAA and Paul was only too happy to accommodate. He would fly *Little Audrey* while Bob Nolinske brought up the rear in the Baby Ace. Because both airplanes were single-seaters, the wives would have to go via Capitol Airlines; the "catch" was that they must agree to bring along a "climb" prop for *Little Audrey*! Don't you know that made for quite a scene at the airport check-in counter…people tripping over the propeller while agents asked, "What's the matter girls, don't you trust the propellers on our airplanes?" When Paul met the airplane at the other end, he noticed the pilot staring out the window. Paul asked what was the matter. The pilot said he just wanted to see who was going to claim that propeller!

Soon after this trip *Little Audrey* went to a new home. Paul sold his little modified racer to Joe Yutz in Pottsville, Pennsylvania; now he was a "pure" homebuilder, having only the Baby Ace in his stable. But that too would change—as we should have known!

During the year, Captain Poberezny added several more accomplishments to his Air Guard portfolio, including a Beechcraft C-45 checkout and a B-25 Instrument Flight Examiner rating. The latter was in addition to his previously held F-89, T-33, C-47 and T-6 examiner ratings, and his test pilot and instructor pilot duties. But highly qualified as he was, Paul was still human. After one agonizingly long return trip from California in the C-45, he almost made a perfect three-point landing—on the props and tail wheel! But the "gear warning horn" woke him up in time to lower the landing gear, thus saving his pride for another day. When it comes to landing "gear-up," they say there's, "them that has, and them that will." Paul's "will" would come later.

In December, he was appointed Telephone Control Officer, which gave him the ability to authorize local and long distance phone calls. Whether or not this was a Christmas present from the Air Guard, we'll never know. Nor will we know if EAA profited from the arrangement. Loose lips sink ships!

Before leaving the military side of Paul's life, we should note that he was not "all work and no play." He managed to have *some* fun in the air, as a letter from Arlie J. Mucks, Jr. of Madison, Wisconsin, explains:

> On another day, we took off in this old "gooney bird" and flew around Milwaukee. When we got to 10,000 feet Paul said, "we don't need two engines," so we feathered one. After awhile, Paul said, "we should glide for awhile," so he shut off the sec-

ond engine. Here we were, two birdmen acting like a glider. It was really quiet. After we sailed around and reached about 5,000 feet, Poop Deck pushed the feather buttons, the engines started up (thank god), and we zipped back to the airport. This actually told me Poop Deck was fearless.

The relationship between EAA (Paul) and the CAA was growing stronger. Paul consistently preached the need for EAA members to operate within the confines of current CAA guidelines, rules and regulations. His focus was now aimed squarely at the homebuilt movement, although he realized there would probably be a backlash of differing opinion coming from those who chose to modify existing designs of standard category aircraft. He also knew that his organization must create its own track record before it would be afforded any credibility. Only by showing a sustained ability to produce and operate homebuilt airplanes in a safe and responsible manner would they be able to influence the regulatory world in which they operated. Paul stated his platform in an *Experimenter* column, **"Tony (Maugeri) said that the EAA is to be congratulated for bringing back the friendliness to private aviation which had been missing for a long time, and that the CAA is willing to cooperate 100% with our association. It should be our goal to encourage experimentation through new designs, rather than clipping the wings on standard category aircraft and adding higher horsepower engines."**

Paul's column in the December *Experimenter* expressed his growing frustration at receiving criticism from those who failed to grasp the "big picture." This quirk affects many aviation (and other) groups where the membership is more interested in its own problems than those of the movement as a whole. Paul reminded EAA members of their responsibilities, **"...you fellows who are not as close to the many problems we have at Headquarters, probably don't realize there are those in many places in aviation and other strategic places who do not recognize the value of our undertakings and who would just as soon see amateur-built aircraft stricken from the books. So when you build or fly, remember that you as an individual, through carelessness in construction or operation, can be a deciding factor in the eyes of the public as to whether we shall be able to continue with our aims or that they should be relinquished."**

Our new home, with EAA's offices housed in the basement…
9711 West Forest Park Drive, Hales Corners, Wisconsin

Chapter Twenty-Five

1956-58

The next three years brought Paul and Audrey more of the same, albeit in larger doses. There was more work with the Air Guard (the income), and more work with EAA (the challenge). Neither would bring drastic changes to their lifestyle, other than to overload an already chaotic schedule. So instead they added a new challenge of their own....

"The volume of work continued to grow. I was working two jobs, building airplanes, flying both military and civilian planes, maintaining combat readiness, and traveling a great deal with the military throughout the country. Audrey kept busy dealing with our two children and EAA. (Thank goodness for her mom!) In spite of all this, in the spring of 1956 we decided to build a new home. I can't quite recall why, except that we had outgrown the one on South 56th Street—especially the small area we used as the EAA office! I guess we were just young and thought we could handle anything that came our way. Anyway, we decided to proceed with our plan.

"On Sundays, we would drive around the various neighborhoods looking at different styles of houses, trying to get an idea of what kind of home to build. The next step was to find an attractive location with a bus stop that was convenient for Gramma, preferably in the Hales Corners area, a suburb on the southwest side of Milwaukee.

"I flew the Air Guard B-25 around the city and found an area called Forest Park Manor that was owned by a Mr. Froemming. Forest Park Drive became our choice, as it was mostly lined with beautiful trees in a country-like setting. We purchased a beautiful lot and soon began building our new home…all the while keeping in mind the basement for EAA Headquarters!"

Audrey continues....

"By March, our new house was under construction by our friend and builder, Fred Rogers. Part of the down payment was the money Howard received from his article in Mechanix Illustrated; another was the Baby Ace Paul built for the Mechanix Illustrated article. He didn't want to see it go, but we couldn't afford both it and the new house, so Fred Rogers had himself a good airplane. We also did whatever we could ourselves to keep costs down. Howard was spending several nights a week at Ace Aircraft in West Bend. On those nights, as soon as Mom got home from work, I headed out to the house and painted until dark. Today I wonder where all that energy came from—we certainly never had a moment to sit and do nothing!

"Along with all our other chores, we had to plan our move. It occurred on July 12, 1956, one day before Bonnie's second birthday. The basement was designed to house the EAA operation. It was set up as an office with desks, a mailing table, a table for the Board of Directors meetings, magazine racks, and a place for my washer and dryer. There was another small area where I could hang clothes in the winter. We installed a larger mailbox for the ever-increasing amount of mail, although I was already well-known at the Hales Corners Post Office as our new address was published before the house was finished. Mom moved in with us and sold her house on South 56th Street. We left behind a lot of memories, but we were looking forward to many more in our beautiful new home."

Audrey and Val Brugger at work in the basement

The two Poberezny children were growing up—the toddler with no hair, and the "wannabe" teenager. Paul and Audrey could not have coped without Babe's support; she added a much needed stabilizing influence and a degree of normality to the family's hectic lifestyle. For Audrey, having to balance children, household chores, EAA and everything else, meant she was constantly living on the edge. It is a tribute to her vitality and inner strength that she was able to keep up with all the demands during this difficult period.

To illustrate the diverse yet similar frustrations the couple experienced, a story involving one of Paul's cross-country Guard trips comes to mind. His airplane (C-47) had developed engine trouble over Iowa, enroute from Ogden, Utah, back to Milwaukee. After flying on one engine for about an hour, a significant weather front appeared in his path. Paul wisely decided not to challenge it and landed at Moline, Illinois, for an engine change. At the same time, Audrey was having engine problems of her own—with the family lawnmower! She'd been wrestling with it all afternoon, trying to beat the same storm that forced Paul to turn back. (***"I also had to do laundry, cut grass, rake leaves, paint, shovel snow, look after the kids…!"***) The machine finally quit altogether, leaving her with a half-cut lawn and a full head of steam. As Paul found out, her attitude toward engine failures was not favorable. Instead of receiving the expected gush of sympathy when he called to let her know of his troubles, he received, **"quite a blast!"**

Another story takes us back to the Korean War period, again to show this feisty lady's determination (and ability) to cope. The bathtub faucet had begun to drip badly. Not wishing to spend money on a plumber, Audrey

took it apart herself—even though she had never done so before. All the parts were carefully placed into a box in the exact order they came off. With little Tommy in tow, she went to the hardware store to ask what was wrong. The men in the store found it amusing but eventually pointed out the need for a new washer. New part in hand, Audrey carefully took her box of goodies home and put everything back together, piece by piece. Not surprisingly, it worked!

Tommy

"Tommy always brought home straight-A's, so when I went to a parent-teacher night I expected to hear praises about his progress. One time I was fooled. I went into Mr. Ross' class and was told that Tommy had become a problem student. I was shocked as I hadn't heard this before, so I asked Mr. Ross to explain. He said that Tommy always finished his work before the rest of the class, which was good, but then he would start bothering the other children. I suggested to him that Tommy was bored and needed something else to do; that he (Mr. Ross) should give him extra assignments. As soon as he did, the problem disappeared.

"Tommy's interest in sports really began to develop during this period. Unlike his father, he became very good at basketball and baseball. The first time Howard saw Tommy score a basket at a school game, he yelled out 'Look, he made a hole-in-one!' Bonnie and I were so embarrassed that we moved to a seat far away from him!

"Tommy more than made up for his physical size with determination and leadership and was generally made captain of whatever team he was on. He also was a very good student and took his homework seriously. He was a good kid."

Tom Poberezny has gone on to enjoy a spectacular career in aviation. Indoctrinated into the EAA way of life at an early age, he succeeded his father as President and CEO in 1989. Since then, he has provided stable and decisive leadership during a period that has seen significant growth and expansion. An accomplished aerobatic and air show pilot, he also spent a record twenty-five years flying with the Eagles formation demonstration team. Tom lives in Milwaukee with his wife, Sharon, and teenage daughter, Lesley. Here is his recall of life as young lad in those early, pre-teen years....

> Growing up in the Poberezny home in the 1950s meant that there was always an airplane project in the garage, people visiting constantly and EAA meetings every month in our basement. Between school, friends, sports and all the things that are important to someone in their pre-teen years, I had no idea what impact this activity would have on the future of aviation.
>
> I thought every kid experienced the smell of welding torches and dope being applied to fabric and that having an airplane in your garage was commonplace. Dad was totally dedicated to flight and his enthusiasm rubbed off on everybody else. He was the focal point. Everyone wanted to know what he was doing and learn more about his vision for the club that he had started a few years earlier…EAA. "Hangar flying" in the family garage was a "pastime" for many while they helped with the latest airplane project.
>
> Through all this Mom was a steady influence. She welcomed all the people who visited or called at all hours of the day or night. There were daily trips to the airport and numerous projects and letters to answer. Dad was traveling a lot because of his full-time military commitment, therefore, my mother quietly and efficiently got everything done.
>
> My grandmother was a tremendous influence on both Mom and Dad. She would take care of my sister and myself, provide support for my mother and understood the passion my father had for airplanes. Little did I realize this passion would be transformed into a leadership role in aviation that would last for decades and become an important part of aviation history.

Bonnie

"After two years living up to the nickname her father had given her at an early age, 'Bonehead' Bonnie finally began to grow hair. As she grew older, it became more difficult to convince Tommy to entertain her because she often interfered when his friends visited him. She just want-

ed to be part of his grown-up world. When he ignored her, she would dress herself in his cowboy outfit: jacket, hat, boots and a toy gun. As she hadn't yet learned right from left, she often had his boots on the wrong feet. Apparently her little feet were small enough to fit in either one because her smile certainly showed no signs of hurting feet!

"Bonnie always enjoyed being with Mom and me. At an early age, she was already volunteering to stuff envelopes for EAA, and did so for many years. But the tables sure have turned—now I volunteer to help Bonnie!"

From the day she was born, Bonnie was surrounded by EAA and became involved at a very early age. She continues to this day, both as a valuable employee and a volunteer, and is currently tasked with multiple roles: Executive Assistant to her father and brother, Events Manager, Docent Coordinator, and Chairman of Guest Relations during Convention. Bonnie lives in Oshkosh with her teenage daughter, Audra.

Before leaving the Poberezny children, we should mention that Paul was able to spend *some* quality time with his offspring. An excerpt from his February 1957 Homebuilder's Corner proves it, **"Take today, for example—Sunday—I decided to take my 2 1/2 year old daughter for a ride before dinner so as to give the wife some trouble-free time to prepare the noon meal. Naturally, there is only one place to take a 2 1/2 year old girl, and that is to the airport...."**

Naturally!

For the remainder of the decade, the Milwaukee Air Guard held on to their F-89, T-33, C-47, B-25, C-45 and T-6 aircraft while Paul continued in his dual roles as maintenance officer and test pilot. In 1957 he received a new title: Flight Test Maintenance Officer (same duties, fewer words). He overcame more challenges in the air, landing the B-25 at Waukesha Airport in 1956 with a runaway prop (and making the local newspapers) and suffering through three F-89 engine changes at Cheyenne, Wyoming, in 1957. In March 1958, he received the ten-year Air Guard service medal with ribbon.

Wisconsin ANG B-25

Norm Poberezny (second from right) assists with another F-89 engine change

His squadron continued its all-weather, Air Defense role with the F-89. (In 1962 the unit would switch to a refueling role and be issued KC-97F tankers.) Paul continued to attract some of the more popular extra duties: Base Security Officer, Wing Flying Standardization Board member, Base Motor Pool Officer and Motor Vehicle Accident Investigating Officer. As if that wasn't enough fun, he was put in charge of the Personal Equipment Account, including supervising all Personal Equipment Technicians. In 1956, he was made project officer for the annual gunnery meet—no doubt a reward for being a good Telephone Control Officer the year before!

As improvements to the F-89 were introduced, the squadron received each subsequent model, culminating in 1960 with the F-89J that sported a pair of nuclear tipped, Genie air-to-air missiles. The most exciting version was probably the preceding F-89D that was in inventory during the 1958 and 1959 summer camps at Volk Field. With a total of one hundred and four, 2.75 inch rockets in its oversize wingtip pods, this machine could really let

loose with serious firepower. The excitement increased dramatically while flying ninety-degree intercepts to the "targets" and firing all those rockets at close range! Pity the poor T-33 target-tow pilots who could only hope for accurate shooting!

"There are many stories I could tell relative to my experience in flying with the Air National Guard, and quite a few resulted from flying the F-89. We had all models of it over the period of time we used them. Our biggest problems were engine reliability, which we mentioned earlier, and hydraulic failures. One time I was up on a test flight and everything had gone well. I still had plenty of fuel left, so I decided to go over to Rockford for some practice approaches. On what was to be my last approach before returning home, the hydraulic pump failed and the landing gear wouldn't retract. As I didn't have sufficient fuel to make it back to Milwaukee at low altitude with my gear hanging down, and I couldn't land at Rockford because the runway was closed for repairs; my only option was to head for Madison and hope the fuel gauges were reading low. They read 'empty' as I made my approach to land at Truax. Shortly after touch-down, one of the engines flamed out due to fuel starvation…then the other one. I ended up being towed to the ramp and flown home in their C-47."

Little Bonnie welcomes Daddy home

"Because our F-89s were on alert, we often had some interesting scrambles. In order to keep jet fuel from venting onto the asphalt and causing damage to the surface, buckets were hung under the fuel vents. Sometimes the ground crews would forget to remove them in their haste to launch the airplane. As the aircraft was taking off, the tower would call out, 'There's an 80-knot bucket on the runway!' (Or whatever speed they thought it had departed the airplane.) One time a bucket managed to stay on long enough to fall into the back yard of a nearby home. I'm sure it caused the owner to wonder how such an item could

possibly be part of a modern jet fighter! But we didn't have to address that problem very often because they usually fell off on airport property."

"Another time, my CO and Flight Leader, Colonel Levenson and I ferried a couple of older F-89s from Milwaukee to the 'boneyard' in Tucson. As we taxied down the mile of highway leading to the storage yard, EAA member Bill Rousch spotted the Wisconsin ANG decal on our aircraft. It wasn't long before he was at Base Operations and we were deeply involved in a discussion on homebuilts. Colonel Levenson could only shake his head and ask, 'Poop Deck! Does this happen wherever you go?' Bill later took me out to watch salvage operations on the B-29s and B-36s. It was a homebuilder's paradise: pulleys, fittings, safety belts, turnbuckles and so much more, all going to the smelter!"

The Baby Ace perched on the wing of a F-89 - with Paul are Stan Gronowski, the Northrop F-89 Technical Representative, and Colonel Levenson

Paul eventually flew one particular F-89 on its last flight. Because of his efforts, the airplane was rescued from the salvage yard to become part of the EAA collection.

In January 1957, Paul received the very first Billy Mitchell Award. This prestigious honor was to be issued annually by the State Air Force Association to the person with the most outstanding contributions in the promotion of flying. It was created and given in honor of aviation pioneer, General William "Billy" Mitchell, for whom the Milwaukee squadron, and later the airport, was named.

General Mitchell's sister, Mrs. Martin Fladoes, presented the plaque to Paul, describing him as "a tireless worker in the development of experimental aircraft," and that he "...was instrumental in forming the Experimental Aircraft Association with the objective of aiding flying enthusiasts who were interested in flying their own airplanes." She closed with, "Nothing could have pleased my brother more than having this squadron named in his honor, and he would have been happy to know that a person of such high caliber as Paul Poberezny received this plaque."

It appears that Paul and the Experimental Aircraft Association were seen as one.

The famous *Mechanix Illustrated* Baby Ace was gone. How could Paul sell this labor of love? Because he needed the money for his new house with the new garage that could now be filled with a new airplane project! The latest tenant was a single-place, low wing sport plane of his own design, the "Pober Sport." By October, Paul, his brother Norm, and a few volunteers had it on the gear, although it wouldn't fly for three more years. Audrey noted, ***"...the first thing a fellow gets excited about when building an airplane is 'getting it on the gear!'"***

In a 1958 *Experimenter* column, Paul recalls a typical winter night during the building process: **"Dave Frantz came over one winter night to help. After about three hours in the garage he said, 'You know, a fella has to be nuts to be out here working on an airplane like this.' I asked him what he meant, as lots of fellows were doing this sort of thing in garages all over the country. He said, 'Yes, but not with the temperature at 15° above zero!' I thought, Audrey, Audrey, can you spare me a few dollars for some heat? This time I promise not to buy tubing instead!"**

Paul later wrote that he and Norm were, **"...out in the refrigerator (garage) working away. We have to work fast to keep warm and I hope my wife Audrey notes that we need a heater. So far, she has ignored the fact completely!"**

The Pober Sport under construction

Note: In 1966, EAA received the *Mechanix Illustrated* Baby Ace as a donation from Ray and Bernice Scholler. Today it hangs in the EAA Air Museum, surrounded by a partial recreation of Paul's first garage on South 56th Street. The "Pober Sport" was donated in 1970 by Kenneth Bride and George Walrath, and is on display in the museum along with *Little Audrey*. The latter was located and donated in 1991 through the combined efforts of W. H. "Bill" Turner and EAA Chapter #1, whose members restored, test flew and delivered the airplane. Only Paul's first project, the clip-wing Taylorcraft *Little Poop Deck*, is lost to the future, having been destroyed in a fire caused by a careless welder's spark.

By early 1957, Paul was no longer involved with Ace Aircraft; he frowned on those who joined EAA purely for personal gain and did not want to be similarly accused. One would think that after all the free labor he and Audrey donated over the years, this would not be a worry. Not only was their time given, but many supplies, utilities, and other day-to-day expenses were paid out of their own pockets so that EAA could maintain a positive cash flow early on.

Steve and Dorothy Wittman welcome EAA to Oshkosh

The 1956 EAA Fly-in was held in Oshkosh—the first time it moved away from Milwaukee. Rather than being the only attraction, as was the case in 1955, EAA shared the spotlight with the Antique Airplane Association, the new Canadian Ultra Light Aircraft Association, and a locally produced air show that included air racing and other events. Added to the above was the "traditional" two days of bad weather! It was all a bit much and caused more than a few temper tantrums to be displayed along with the airplanes.

Access to members' airplanes was difficult, at times impossible. Crowd control was poor and the CAA almost shut things down on several occasions. Paul explained the problem as having "too many chiefs…!" Audrey and Lois were exposed to their first taste of "unhappy campers," when they were scolded by a few misguided members for woes beyond their—or EAA's—control. And then there was the food shortage at the Friday evening affair.

Audrey and Lois shared their fly-in duties

It wasn't all bad. Approximately 50,000 (?) people attended the three-day event, including over 500 EAA members. Experimental and antique airplanes totaled 51, and were joined by nearly 300 general aviation machines. Midget class air races were held on Saturday and Sunday, with Steve Wittman edging out Bill Falck in the hotly contested finale. Howie Mattes showed up as promised with a Wisconsin Air Guard F-89—in spite of the short runway! And a fine array of forum speakers played to full houses during the day and evening programs. Several national magazines covered the event, later writing articles that caused the Poberezny mailbox to shrink one more time.

The familiar faces of the fly-ins -
Julie Schmid, Verna DuCharme, Bernice Scholler, Lois Nolinske and Audrey

It was decided that future EAA Fly-ins would be held as a singular attraction. If EAA wanted a national fly-in, then its membership should accept full responsibility for putting it all together. Because most of the "hands-on" volunteers lived in the area, the event returned to Milwaukee for the next two years.

Bonnie joins her parents at the fly-in

The 1957 and 1958 fly-ins came and went, each an improvement over the previous one. Both were held at the old Curtiss-Wright airport in Milwaukee (the airport was renamed "Timmerman Field" a few weeks prior to the 1958 event!). Jim Custin was chairman in 1957, George Hardie in 1958. The number of experimental aircraft in attendance now exceeded sixty, and record numbers of EAA members flocked to each annual pilgrimage.

One of the more interesting fly-in stories involved a "roadable" airplane built by Leland Bryan from Milford, Michigan. The Autoplane II, as he called it, was licensed as a car *and* an airplane in Leland's home state. He had driven it in Michigan and several other states with no problems, other

than attracting considerable interest. Now that the machine was in Milwaukee, it was decided to drive it downtown for an interview with the *Journal* Aviation Editor, William J. Normyle. When the police heard about this contraption with a whirring propeller motoring through their fair city, they tracked it down at the Journal building and "grounded" it. Apparently the chief felt it was unsafe because the propeller might come off.

Leland Bryan's "roadable" airplane

The Experimenter's talented advertising manager, Wes Schmid (who is still active today and serves as EAA Secretary), had provided a one-way escort. But Wes didn't have a hitch on his vehicle, so he drove Leland back to the airport to get his tow car. Such are the trials of an aviation pioneer in a conservative, northern city, although the resulting front page story in the Sunday paper picturing Leland, his auto-plane, and one of Milwaukee's finest, surely helped attendance figures!

The Milwaukee Police didn't care much for the Autoplane, as witnessed by Wes Schmid, George Hardie and Leland Bryan

Bob Nolinske, Harry Zeisloft and Paul on stage

The question of why no commercial aircraft were participating at EAA fly-ins was answered in Paul's September 1957 *Experimenter* column: **"At this year's fly-in, which as many of you know attracts thousands of people from all over the US and Canada, no effort has been made to invite commercial aircraft manufacturers to attend and display their shiny, expensive, single and twin-engine planes. 'Why?' many of you ask. Well, after five years of begging them to come, and them making us feel it would be such a privilege to have them, it's enough to discourage anyone. So, after many letters passing the buck, or hearing 'we are too busy,' we have done the next best thing—we forgot them! And the future? At the prices of these machines? Maybe EAA efforts, our members, or the design contest will be the answer for the average guy. I hope so. If I thought otherwise, I would not have burned the midnight oil for the past five years trying to foster this movement."**

Audrey verifies this curious lack of interest by stating that she too was upset. She knows the manufacturers were invited because she mailed the letters! Later on when they did show up, they had to pay. Audrey quipped, ***"Maybe we should have told them it was going to cost them money all along, instead of offering it for free!"***

It was decided to look at another site for the 1959 EAA Fly-in, as the event had outgrown Timmerman Field. Chet Wellman suggested Rockford, Illinois, so Paul and some others paid a visit to the airport. Everyone was very impressed by how well the grounds and facilities were maintained; Paul said it was kept like a golf course. When Airport Manager Bob Selfridge offered to help and included a building for their use, the decision became an easy one. Chet Wellman was appointed event chairman and the site was approved.

Many of Paul's other "pet" programs began to increase in stature. The airplane building program implemented by EAAer Robert Blacker at Chicago's St. Rita's High School was now well into its second project, having completed and presented their Baby Ace at the 1957 fly-in. The new

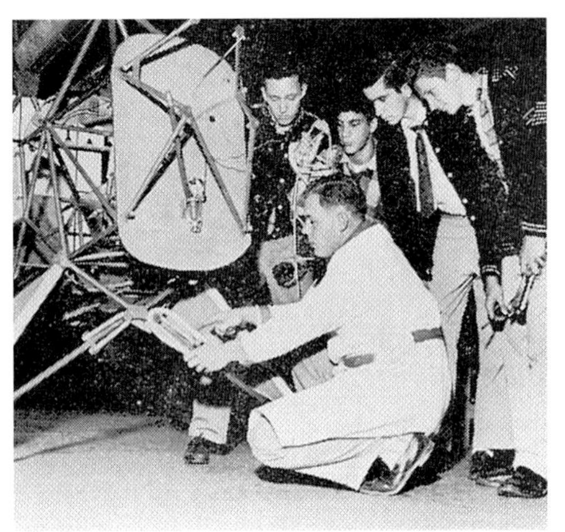

Bob Blacker and his students

airplane was being constructed from recently developed EAA Biplane plans, another of Paul's ideas that had come to fruition. In 1958, Bob deservedly captured the coveted *Mechanix Illustrated* trophy for Outstanding Achievement. Later on, his fledgling program would evolve into EAA's successful, Project Schoolflight.

The EAA chapter program was enjoying a rapidly expanding role and Paul often commented on its purpose in *The Experimenter*: **"EAA chapters can be very educational, beneficial, and a lot of fun. They provide an outlet for those with a common interest in aircraft design and construction; they give one an overall appreciation of the many problems that are encountered while building an aircraft; and they provide increased knowledge on the subject of aviation. The chapters must be built into a strong 'voice of the homebuilder'—a representative appointed to be the official spokesman on matters pertaining to the welfare of the local group and to coordinate with National Headquarters on matters pertaining to the welfare of the amateur aircraft movement and EAA."**

By the end of 1958 there were nearly fifty EAA chapters scattered throughout the US and several foreign countries, proving that the spirit of flight can overcome a multitude of barriers. The Canadian Ultra Light Aircraft Association was founded by Keith Hopkinson, a long-time aviation supporter and EAA award winning builder of Canada's first approved homebuilt, a Stits Playboy. The relationship forged the way for similar efforts in Australia, Germany, Switzerland and South Africa. Europeans, especially the British and French, were considered leaders in the homebuilding field at the time and

Audrey updates the Chapter Map

freely shared information and visits with their American counterparts.

Membership numbers had almost reached five thousand, with no end in sight. In order to prevent the members from having an identity crisis, a growing line of EAA merchandise was offered. Paul remains partial to those original dark blue jackets with the white stripe and EAA logo, noting that the single design provided wearers with instant recognition anywhere in the country. Even today, in a styling climate that changes with the seasons, there might still be room for such uniformity.

The first EAA Scholarship fund began its fundraising campaign in 1956. Soon after, the ambitious EAA Design Competition was born. Its goal was to encourage the design of a practical homebuilt airplane that was "simple and inexpensive to build, safe and easy to fly, and capable of being towed home to the garage for storing." It was one of Paul's favorite programs, for he felt that only by having a more practical airplane would the movement ever develop broad market appeal. There had been several attempts at producing such a design, including a few dual-purpose auto-planes, but so far nothing seemed to have worked. Sport aviation, as with all popular sport and recreational interests, must be affordable and readily attainable if it was to become widespread.

Paul explains the EAA Design Competition to an interested member

Part of "The Experimenter" editorial staff burning the midnight oil to meet publication deadline (left to right): Wes Schmid, George Hardie, Bob Nolinske, Bernice Scholler, Audrey and Paul.

The EAA magazine *The Experimenter,* underwent a name change. Briefly it became *"The Experimenter and Sport Aviation"* and then *"Sport Aviation and the Experimenter."* Distribution remained the same: free to EAA members and by paid subscription to non-members. Today, that one magazine has evolved into multiple offerings covering everything from ultralights to warbirds. Audrey recalls that first name change....

"I realize that Ray Stits was a very busy man, and that he and his wife, Edith, put in many long hours at their business. But can you believe it took Ray almost two years before he noticed the name had changed on our magazine?"

Audrey fills orders for back issues

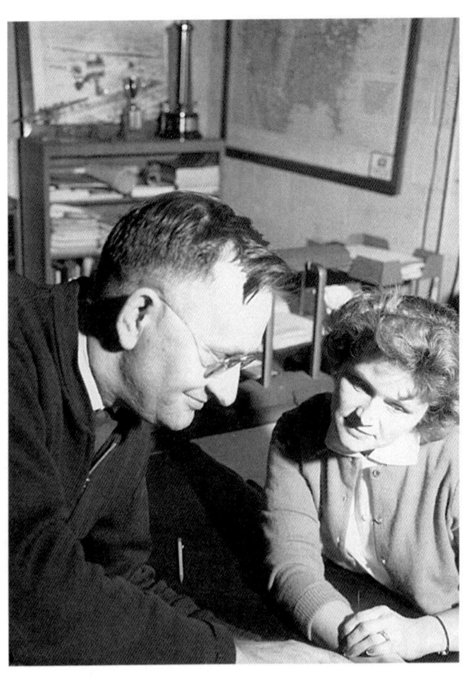

George Hardie assists in answering an inquiry from a member

In a year-end letter to his board, Paul said the growth of the organization called for a fully active board and that the demand on their time was only going to increase. After outlining his priorities, which included membership drives, headquarters building and air museum funds, design contest funding, chapter programs, and government relations, he made a prophetic observation....

"In reviewing the history of EAA, I believe you all will agree that this organization has grown to such proportions that we have what could be called, 'having a tiger by the tail!' ...and we don't dare let go!"

After completing a flight in the F-89 Scorpion, Paul is greeted by two contestants in the Gas Model Contest sponsored by the Billy Mitchell Chapter of the Air Force Association and the Experimental Aircraft Association.

Chapter Twenty-Six

Paul

This chapter includes a collection of Paul's thoughts and writings taken from the years leading up to 1958, the time where we chose to pause in the telling of his and Audrey's story. They provide increased insight into his personality and outlook during those formative years. Notably, much of his philosophy remains valid to this day.

Paul is a unique individual: complicated, yet simplistic. And he has two basic motivating forces: airplanes and people. Driven by a passion for aviation, he is also blessed with a *com*passion for people. When we made it known some years ago that this book might be written, the many encouraging letters we received shared one common theme: Paul's love for people. Chapter Twenty-Three depicts a few examples; there were many more. People have been as much a part of Paul's life as have airplanes. To find out more, let us return once again to the 1950s....

To rally human beings around a common cause requires leadership. Many are those who say Paul is a great leader, and they do so with proper justification. A "leader" is defined as one who leads, which infers that others must follow...**"One must have vision, not only to the future of aviation, but vision to see what our fellow humans can and will do to overcome present day problems with a minimum of restriction. Though the cry, 'Get out of my way!' may be somewhat selfish to particular special interest groups, it usually works out best for the majority."**

Do we say that today's CEO or production manager is a "leader"? Or just a "boss"? There is a difference—if nothing else, in the time factor…"**…those who accept the responsibility to lead and guide are expected to do this on a 24-hour basis. I know this is true in my case where the phone will ring 24 hours a day and people stop in at all hours. It is their schedule that matters, not yours. They may expect you to answer for other peoples' actions or change the philosophy of the association. They even challenge my personal status. People often read many interpretations into the 26 letters of the alphabet to suit their own needs, views and outlooks."**

It has been said we are in danger of losing our source of great leaders. They came from a generation that held moral values and family traditions in high esteem…at least they did in public. Instilled with a strong work ethic and a built-in sense of duty, they also retained the capacity for compassion and understanding of those truly less fortunate. They commanded genuine respect and loyalty, based in large part on their personal qualities and standards—qualities that seem far less important today.... **"I have never limited my views as to who could be a member of EAA and who could not. I felt that all progress would be accomplished by human beings: flesh, blood and bone. A person might just be an enthusiast today, but tomorrow could become a homebuilder, 'antiquer' or contribute in some other part of our world. To exclude any talent would not be in the best interest of aviation."**

Being a leader means having compassion for your fellow human beings, and Paul has demonstrated this quality over and over again....**"I have always adhered to the policy of giving personal attention to each letter I receive and have written answers to thousands of them. Many times I was told to throw some of them away, saying they don't mean anything—especially if the person wasn't a member. But I believe that if someone takes pen in hand to put thoughts on a piece of paper, it is a great challenge for that person and certainly deserves an answer. Though it often became quite hectic to keep this philosophy going, I have continued it over the years.**

"We held monthly Board meetings in the basement of our home. A great deal of progress was made by holding them that often, though I would have preferred them to be more frequent. They were a big help toward developing ideas and philosophies for the organization and I give credit to all those fine officers that drove many miles each month and spent so much of their time in support of my dream, the EAA. The majority were quite dedicated; very few were not."

Dedication and perseverance are two characteristics that must be on any leader's standard-equipment list. No options allowed here: lead by example....**"During many of my travels around the country on military business, I would stop at civilian airports and discuss civilian aviation with people. If I stayed all night, I would try to get together a group and form a chapter. If there was already a chapter there, I would arrange to meet with some of its members. At other times I would visit with one or two members in the area."**

In order to earn credibility while leading from one's personality, rather than a pocketbook, there must be an unshakable belief in the mission....**"EAA is an all-encompassing sport aviation organization and from it great things are happening. The revived interest in sport flying does not mean the airplanes have offered much that is new. What they have offered is self-education to many, many thousands of human beings who can now read blueprints, work with hand and mind doing welding, woodworking, fabric and engine work and become familiar with all the problems associated with aviation. Our country is much richer for this."**

Leaders must have an agenda that others can relate to....**"As for the future of amateur aircraft construction here in the United States, I would say it looks very good. I believe such things as a very good safety record, high workmanship standards, and a willingness to cooperate has brought amateur-built aircraft into recognition. Our biggest problem is what can we do to insure that the highest possible standards of maintenance and construction are always met."**

Leaders often "cut to the quick"....**"One of my pet peeves is the fellow who stands up, and for the sake of making a speech, goes about telling what is wrong with aviation; that we should do this or do that...and then does nothing about it!**

"No doubt many of you have endured criticism by one or two individuals in your group who are 'professionals'—or at least they think they are! Well, don't feel too bad about it as I have never seen so many 'professionals' as I have in aviation! It seems that a great many are those who have merely successfully ascended and returned to good old mother earth without damaging their aircraft or themselves, and that alone makes them 'experts' on the subject."

A leader must have vision....**"You have all at one time or another heard it mentioned about how we need youth in aviation—get the young people flying! Why do you think they are not attracted to aviation? Is it because it is lacking in glory? Or is it too common, expensive, inconvenient, lacking utility, and filled with too many regulations?**

"Let's say we have a young fellow who figures he would like to do a little flying. First, with dual instruction going for an average of $12 per hour, he will need a job (1958 figure—today it is more like $40-60, but it produces the same ratios). When he finds one, he'll put in eight or nine hours of hard work for one hour's pleasure at the airport! Already this doesn't add up and, if he isn't overly enthused with flying machines, he's off to the used car lot with Mom or Pop. I don't have the solution, but I do know that if we can put more 'sport' and 'utility' into light planes, we should attract greater participation. I am inclined to think that maybe we in EAA will be the group to do this, don't you?"

Take risks....**"For the past almost six years, EAA Headquarters has occupied a good share of the basement of my home as well as Bob Nolinske's. We have also invaded the homes of George Hardie and Wes Schmid. In the near future, serious thought must be given to the establishment of a permanent office and the hiring of an executive secretary and clerk-typist to handle the increasing load of mail, the personal visits by members...and to better develop and serve the organization."**

And sometimes show a little frustration....**"I have found that heading EAA is no easy task. Views on aviation are many and varied; as are the people. To please them all is most challenging. To serve them in the manner they want to be served—to give them the full and undivided personal attention they feel they have purchased for the price of a membership—is not easy!"**

If the person is to be a leader in aviation, he or she must appreciate airplanes....**"The next best thing to aircraft ownership is to have one that you can keep at home. After all, ninety-nine percent of the time it's tied to Mother Earth! An airplane shouldn't belong to the birds, the thieves, or the elements. It should be at home in the garage where it can be taken care of; a family project that can be polished and loved. The car should be left outside—not the airplane."**

And *truly* love them (later quote)....**"Sometimes when I walk through our Air Museum, I have the feeling that it would be so nice just to put your bed in among all those airplanes and go to sleep at night with them. They are so much a part of me."**

The Poberezny Family

Chapter Twenty-Seven

Paul and Audrey

It is never wise to create a lasting impression from one brief sampling of time; like a snapshot, it is rarely indicative of the complete picture. Throughout this volume we have seen a mixture of writings, thoughts, and comments by Paul and Audrey Poberezny. Hopefully, we have presented an accurate impression of "who" they were at this point in their lives. It is safe to say "they" because even though Paul may have penned most of the philosophical thoughts, it was Audrey who edited and typed the final product. Her influence, as always, is hidden from the main stream.

What kind of people were they? Indeed, what drove them to maintain such a furious pace? Who would tackle something that had no ending and returned little reward other than an ever-increasing workload? How many couples would bring an organization into their lives and into their home…and then live with it twenty-four hours a day for almost seventeen years—without compensation?

For Audrey, it was not only the joy of sharing her husband's enthusiasm, but also because she could operate in a diverse environment that included EAA, her children, her mother, and her home. That streak of independence we earlier coined "quiet determination," proved to be an ideal asset for such a complicated lifestyle. She remained a steady base from which Paul could operate freely—he didn't have to worry about the home front as long as Audrey was there....

"You know, with Audrey, things have to be just right, which meant when it got to grass cutting and all the other things...well, she would just get it done. Of course, the fact was that I was also doing a great amount of flying."

Flying...Airplanes...People—these and other lesser ingredients make up the soul that is Paul Poberezny. On his own, and with Audrey providing constant support, he rose from poverty and rejection to a position of leadership and responsibility. Although his formal education is lacking in diplomas, the knowledge he possesses exceeds anything available in a classroom. His forte is the "people-skills" he accumulated over the years: negotiating, motivating, understanding, focusing, helping—and how he put them all to work.

Looking back, it becomes obvious that something had to suffer. When most of your waking hours are taken up with work, in this case with Air Guard or EAA duties, there is precious little time remaining for family functions. Paul admits he sometimes shortchanged his family obligations in order to keep up with his outside interests. Since his Guard duties also took him away from home, it can't all be blamed on EAA.

It bothered him that so many of the others had difficulty seeing things as he did, although it must be understood that Paul has a peculiar inner drive. He puts the organization ahead of almost everything else in his life. He lives and breathes, thinks and plans aviation twenty-four hours a day, seven days a week; and it bothers him when others fail to keep up. He is driven: a taskmaster. Yet he never asks for more than what he himself gives. This devotion, which some term an obsession, is not shared by most people. Sacrificing part of the present for a better future is not how they choose to operate.

Great persons make individual sacrifices, otherwise they aren't properly focused—and there is certainly no doubt about Paul's focus! But had he not been interested in airplanes, or had his Ancient History teacher been less interested in his students, there is no telling where Paul would be today. Possibly he would have developed another interest and pursued it with similar fervor. But for those of us in aviation, we are thankful that it was the flying "bug" that infected him. We would not be enjoying flight to the same degree today, were it not so. Which leads us to EAA....

Growth means growing pains—especially in a volunteer-based organization. Members can be quick to demand and slow to contribute; the "few" generally keep things going for the many. After almost six years in the driver's seat, there were times when Paul became discouraged and distraught—sometimes to the point of questioning his direction and motivation. He believed so strongly in the movement, yet he also realized how much of his and Audrey's lives were being sacrificed for it. Did the membership appreciate what their organization was doing for them? Was he leading them in the right direction? Questions for which there were few honest answers, except time.

Paul has always bared all—at least "all" regarding his flying experiences! Many a time he would candidly expose his own shortcomings in the hopes of justifying his stance for a more professional organization and the need for a proven track record. A good reputation is not made overnight, but it can be ruined in seconds!

There was so much work to be done by his small core of volunteers—no matter how dedicated they claimed to be. And it kept increasing, month after month. How long could he expect their dedication to last? Could he carry on alone if they were to abandon him?

In spite of all this uncertainty, Paul forged ahead, accepting any and all challenges that promoted his vision. Again, the main reason he could do so was Audrey. When you have someone of her capacity behind you, faithfully providing a support system that is both solid and unwavering, then you can afford to take risks. Even so, it was a case of all or nothing. Had Paul burned out, EAA was a "goner." The dilemma remained...and it begged a solution. The solution turned out to be both Paul and Audrey!

Leaving an ongoing story without a definite ending can be awkward, and yet this is as good a place as any to do it. Besides, we look at this as a pause, not an end. We pause at a time of growth, where there was hope, excitement, and anticipation of a future without limitations. The Poberezny family, including the unflappable Babe, was healthy, and had somehow adapted to this bizarre lifestyle. EAA was on solid financial ground; there was increasing talk of establishing a permanent office, hiring a staff...even building a museum! The strains of becoming a large organization had not yet materialized, nor had the insidious political infighting and turbulence that frequently mars a pathway to success. More important, Paul and Audrey had shown the world they could handle the pressure and the responsibility. In any case, their die was now firmly cast. For the rest of their lives, EAA would be the center of their existence...their Shangri-la!

And this is only the beginning…

Chapter Twenty-Eight

Until Next Time....

We are now in the closing days of 1996. EAA has grown to over 165,000 members, and more than half a million people have belonged at one time or another over the past forty-four years. There are almost nine hundred chapters worldwide, accounting for about a third of the total membership. EAA has over two hundred employees housed in a modern, attractive headquarters complex in Oshkosh, its permanent home since 1983. The adjoining museum is world class and features an operating airport that relives the Golden Age left behind decades ago. Paul's imaginary bed would look very much out of place on the shiny floors of the main museum building. But if he could get away with it, he would be among some of the finest examples of aviation artifacts on display anywhere in the world. The annual EAA Fly-in Convention draws in excess of 850,000 people and more than 12,000 airplanes during its seven day run. It enjoys a permanent site in Oshkosh, designed and maintained solely for that purpose. All this—and more— started in a basement on South 56th Street in Milwaukee.

Over the years, many wonderful people who played major roles in Paul and Audrey's early lives have left us. Aviation took some; the Lord has them all. Perhaps the biggest loss for Audrey, beside her father, was losing her mother to a sudden heart attack in 1968. Babe was there right to the end. She lived and worked and played side-by-side with her daughter, son-in-law and grandchildren, helping keep the family together during those chaotic years when everything seemed to be happening at once. After she left, the void was never filled. The irony is that a similar cause took both Audrey's parents; the consolation is that they are together again—a team. Just like they started out.

Paul has been retired since 1989, although he remains active as Founder and Chairman of the Board. Since then, he and Audrey restored a nearby

nineteenth century farmhouse and are living comfortably in it. Their cozy home is immaculate, and the grounds, which are considerable, are always well groomed. Not surprisingly, they do most of the work themselves, assisted by a pair of matching John Deere tractors, Audrey's machine features an automatic transmission, power steering and cruise control—a lavish display of Yuletide affection from her practical-minded husband a few years ago.

Overhead, on good flying days, those same biplanes that captured Paul's imagination as a young lad still cause him to run out of his shop at seventy-five years of age to watch and wave at the volunteer Pioneer Airport pilots circling overhead…except that he no longer climbs up on the roof! Paul still flies the Mustang, Corsair, B-17, Ford Tri-Motor, Travel Air, Cuby, and a variety of homebuilts. And anything else with wings. His hangar contains pristine examples from Beechcraft, Piper…and Harley-Davidson—his own, not his brother's. There are at least half a dozen projects underway, from a trio of Junior Aces to a PT-23, Fokker Tri-plane and a mid wing design still in the developing stages. He stays involved in the daily operation of the organization, making his rounds and feeling the pulse of those who work and volunteer. While his body may show the inevitable signs of age, his mind continues to come forth with ideas and plans.

Audrey still prefers to operate in the background, yet she willingly accompanies Paul through an endless schedule of EAA and chapter functions. She enjoys spending time with her two teenage granddaughters, Audra and Lesley. Paul, she figures, can have a little leeway now and then.

During a recent sewing session with Bonnie's daughter, Audra, Audrey's ever-present EAA radio interrupted their discussion when someone transmitted, "The Robin is down!" Having just watched her grandpa fly overhead in EAA's newly restored Curtiss Robin—the same one that disappointed him as an airport brat sixty-one years ago—Audra urged "Nana" to do something, her voice now edged with panic. Nana looked up from her work and replied with a hint of complacency, "Another forced landing…if he can do it in a B-25, he can do it in a Robin. Besides, if he couldn't handle it, he wouldn't have flown. Don't worry…he'll be just fine!"

At that moment, the radio sputtered again, "Diamond One! Red One! We're down in the campground and everything is fine!" The tenseness immediately left the faces of the two women as the ensuing relief caused smiles to reappear. They looked at each other but said nothing. It wasn't necessary: they had already communicated. It was the sewing machine that broke the silence....

Paul and Audrey - 1996

About Co-author, Bonnie Poberezny

Born just 18 months after EAA began, Bonnie Poberezny and EAA grew up practically side by side. Her volunteer efforts began when she was old enough to stuff envelopes and they continue to this day. She has served in a volunteer leadership capacity for over 25 years in a variety of Convention areas including Membership, Finance and Merchandising. In 1970, she became the first Secretary to the newly formed International Aerobatic Club and played an active role in the 1980 World Aerobatic Championships held in Oshkosh. Today she is Chairman of Guest Relations during the Convention, having recently switched roles with her mother, Audrey, who formerly held the position and now volunteers with her daughter.

As a member of the EAA staff from 1972 to 1982, Bonnie filled a variety of roles that included Advertising Manager, Executive Secretary to the EAA Divisions, and Office Manager. A move to Texas in 1982 provided an opportunity to expand her volunteers efforts to other areas; she taught computer literacy on the elementary school level and received national recognition for her volunteer efforts on behalf of education.

Bonnie returned to the EAA staff in 1993 and currently holds several titles: Events Manager, Docent Coordinator and Executive Assistant to the President (brother, Tom) and Chairman of the Board (father, Paul). As might be suspected, she is no stranger to airplanes, having assisted on a number of homebuilt airplanes and soloing in a Citabria on her 16th birthday. She also shares her father's interest in motorcycles, having recently owned a two-wheel "cruiser" model.

About Co-author, Chuck Parnall

Charles "Chuck" Parnall has an extensive aviation background in both civilian and military environments. He served ten years in the Royal Canadian Air Force, earning his pilot wings in June 1968 and being selected as a flight instructor on CT-114 (Tutor) jet trainers. In 1972, he began an exchange tour with the USAF flying T-38 Talons with the 560th Flying Training Squadron at Randolph AFB, Texas. The tour included a year with the famous Operation Homecoming Flight that was tasked to upgrade former Vietnam POWs to flying status. It was his most memorable flying experience to date. His last military duty was as Staff Officer Academic Training for Canadian Forces Training Command in Winnipeg, Manitoba.

Upon leaving the military, he moved to Texas and entered into private business, soon becoming a US citizen. Later he purchased, restored, and flew a DeHavilland Vampire jet trainer. This led to a position with the nation's only flying jet museum, Jim Robinson's Combat Jets Flying Museum in Houston, eventually becoming its president. Coincidentally, he managed the corporate flight department that included a Gulfstream G-II and an Aerospatiale helicopter. At the same time, he and Jim Robinson started the Classic Jet Aircraft Association; a year later Chuck became its president and served in that capacity for over five years. In 1992, he became EAA's Director of Flight Operations, a position he held until June 1996.

Chuck has written a wide variety of articles and short stories for magazines, periodicals, and newsletters, beginning as a columnist for a Canadian drag-racing tabloid in the mid-sixties. He produced the jet association monthly newsletter for over six years and has contributed to EAA's Warbird and Sport Aviation magazines, among others. He has known Paul and Audrey since 1986 and worked with Paul on several aviation projects. They both share a love of riding motorcycles from the famous American manufacturer, Harley-Davidson.

In addition to the Vampire jet, Chuck has owned Cessna 175, 172RG, 170A and Piper Pacer aircraft. He holds a US pilot license (commercial, single and multiengine land with instrument rating), a Canadian commercial and a US Letter of Authorization (LOA) for both Vampire and T-33 jet aircraft.

MILITARY PILOT WINGS
1942 AWARDED TO 1959
PAUL H. POBEREZNY
GLIDER PILOT
SERVICE PILOT
PILOT
LIAISON PILOT
ARMY AVIATOR
SENIOR PILOT
COMMAND PILOT